COLLAPSING
C A R E E R S

COLLAPSING CAREERS

How the Workplace
Short-changes Mothers

Joanna Grigg

First published in 2007 by Vision Paperbacks,
a division of Satin Publications Ltd
101 Southwark Street
London SE1 0JF
UK
info@visionpaperbacks.co.uk
www.visionpaperbacks.co.uk
Publisher: Sheena Dewan

A catalogue record for this book is available from
the British Library.

ISBN: 978-1-905745-09-8

2 4 6 8 10 9 7 5 3 1

Cover and text design by ok?design
Printed and bound in the UK by
Mackays of Chatham Ltd, Chatham, Kent

This book is for Libby

CONTENTS

ACKNOWLEDGEMENTS

Many people have supported me through the research and writing of this book: my research assistant Sophie Tanner has been enormously helpful in collecting most of the profiles of the people who speak through this book, as well as reading, editing and giving something of herself to the project. My agent Charlotte Howard, those at Vision, especially Charlotte Cole, Louise Coe and Kate Pollard have all made important contributions. My family have been fantastic as always; special mention to Tom, Nick and Wills. Friends and colleagues have tolerated my moods and distractions. Peter has supported me in his inimitable way. And above all, a mention to the people who've talked to us: book research is all very well but it's in conversations that the 'feel' of a subject comes through and, with no prospect of reward, many people have given their time generously. I thank you all.

Introduction

At a time when work and all that it entails is finally being debated (and by that I mean that the high-fliers are starting to take it seriously rather than just us losers), I reflect on my own working life — two decades of juggling a family with work — and feel sorry for the young mums I see pushing children to nursery school at 7.00 am.

I still work hard now: I get up at 6.00 am, exercise, sort out the teenagers (by height order, breakfast choice, those in or out of bed), shout goodbyes, zoom into the office at 7.45, work a full day, come home to look after the family then collapse into bed, hopefully by 10.00 pm. I think how lucky I am that I've had 20 minutes' thinking time in the car by the end of the day and that I've been able to:

a) sit, chat and laugh with colleagues;
b) think about my work and career and how to move it on;
c) spend quality time with my family;

because I know that most of those 7.00 am mothers don't have this.

For years I worked as hard as they did. Though I had been employed as a sales manager for many years, it was impossible to

1

juggle this career with being the main carer of three small children. Instead, I had to sacrifice my career and became an adult education tutor because that was the only professional work flexible enough for me to be able to do. I never sat down (I lay down between 9.00 pm and 5.00 am, with up to five interruptions during that time) and rarely stopped at all, spending much of my earnings on childcare and madly juggling favours and neglect when the children were ill, stroppy or when yet another emotional or practical disaster struck. The 7.00 am-ers have all this – and probably more, because things aren't, as you'd expect, getting better: they're getting worse.

Every year 30,000 women in the UK are sacked, made redundant or leave their jobs due to pregnancy discrimination.[1] This happens all around the world; comparative figures aren't available though this example shows how commonplace – and scary – it is. A pregnant childcare worker in Australia chose to end one working day at 6.00 pm even though she was only contracted to work until 3.00 pm. This happened during a Christmas party and she had already told her employer that she need to leave 'early' – she was sacked for this despite working three hours more than she was contracted for.[2] She won her case in the Australian courts and was awarded compensation, but there are thousands of women there, and around the globe, who never get to court and are forced simply to accept their treatment. Many, many more women are, like me, forced to give up their jobs because there is no halfway arrangement in place to allow flexible working. Later, many go into low-paid, unskilled yet flexible work because their former employers won't take the risk of adapting the workplace to allow them back. Some take a complete career break and later find they can't get back into their career, or any reasonably paid work, at all. Their skills are lost forever, to themselves and to the economy.

For some unknowable, ridiculous, perhaps even stupid, reason, I carried on fighting to do my low-paid, no-benefits, demanding work. Some of my friends gave up work and threw themselves to the mercy of their partners for their security (later, some came to regret this). Others stuck with their careers and barely saw their kids or partners (with consequent emotional disasters). One gave up altogether.

Conservatives (small 'c') jump on this: that's why women need to stay at home to look after the family. It makes sense . . . sort of. Liberals (small 'l') tell us we can have it all . . . which we can, or might be able to one day . . . when governments, employers and society make the changes to facilitate it. In the meantime we still have to live it and the economy still has to suffer.

This book is the story of women 'living it' in the modern developed world: trying to have fulfilling family lives as well as rewarding and lucrative careers with consequent lifestyle accoutrements. It looks at why, in today's society we still can't have both without paying a price so huge, many wonder whether it's all worth it. The book discusses what's going to happen next, in the context of governments, economies, life experience, common sense and the scores of women who have talked with me about their experiences of having both a family and a career. It's called *Collapsing Careers* but could equally be called 'Collapsing Sanities', 'Collapsing Relationships', 'Collapsing Economies' or 'Collapsing Societies'.

Having a career and a family has gone beyond a 'choice' thing for many women. Economics suggest that it's getting beyond a 'choice' thing for many governments. Front pages carry research confirming that the workplace needs the women who currently fall away from their skilled work. This only spells one thing: disaster. In a world where equalities are only put on agendas when governments are forced into corners, might this be a positive stage in women's social development? Imagine a scenario where women truly are equal: that is, where we have the financial clout and political power to be heard and have babies at the same time. It looks like governments are finally being forced into considering to enable this. But history tells us that governments are notoriously slippery. So what, then, can we be doing to ensure the best way forward for ourselves, our daughters and our sons?

1

How Jobs Happened

As a nation, a continent, a developed world – as well as in the world in general – wherever you look men are still more equal than women. The accident of biology that gave us the joy and privilege of bearing children continues its grip as, however hard we try, we're still seen as passive, less competent and tied to the home as soon as – and often before – we have children.

Laine, the mother of young twins, puts it like this:

> Having children takes a woman right out of the loop no matter
> how independent or successful she was before childbirth.
> Childbirth is what separates us from men; it takes us home in a
> biological sense and it's hard not to feel maligned, even patron-
> ised. Society tells us that 'What you are doing is so valuable', so
> why doesn't it feel like it is?

The Equal Opportunities Commission in the UK tells us that the difference in pay between what women will earn in a lifetime and what men will earn (£330,000/US$660,000) is enough to put down deposits on 19 houses, go on 525 extra trips or have 15 new cars.[1] Personally, I'll go for the 10,500 extra nights out with friends (seeing as it includes dinner and drinks).

This isn't hard to fix. We just need to change a few attitudes to ensure that women who choose to have children are sufficiently supported in their parenting to be able to contribute equally in the workplace. But are we changing as a society? Will we? And how, exactly, have we got to a point where women are equally competent in the workplace and asked to take equal responsibility in society, yet are still treated unequally? Literally little or no thought has been given to adjusting the workplace and associated social factors to allow for this. It sounds crazy that we've allowed it to happen – it's not as though overnight women started saying: 'I think I'll go out to work now.' Women have been an essential part of the workforce for as long as there's been work and a labour shortage, as this condensed history shows.

How the 'developed world' developed jobs for women

Allowing for where you live in the world and that national economies have developed at different rates and with different emphases over the past couple of hundred years, there has essentially been a change in the structure of the economies of the 'developed world' (or 'more economically developed' countries) from land-based (agrarian farming, with workers mainly out in the countryside working on the land) to industrialised (workers predominantly in towns in factories or an equivalent). The 'less economically developed' world is so-called so in part because it hasn't yet gone this way and its economies are still primarily land-based.

In feudal times (the 10th to 13th centuries) upper-class women took part in the Crusades and government with consequent high social, political and economic status. They were even allowed to participate in having and administering feuds. Less was documented about the ordinary working woman during this time than about these tiny upper classes. Most women were working in what we might now think of as a traditional way: on the family's smallholding, gathering food, raising a family and taking care of all the domestic duties. Overall, they performed a huge range of activities that slotted in with the family's and community's structures and needs. With an extended family on hand to watch the children and no obstacles to run them down, women were 'freer' to work in other ways: the divide between domesticity and work wasn't there in the same way as it is today.

When industrialisation struck, such as during the UK's Industrial Revolution in the 19th century, it brought huge benefits for our economies: we were able to make items for home use and export, and in exporting, we made enough profit to plough back into our ventures at home and overseas. We became rich nations, not so much through our earlier imperialist ploy (conquering other countries, enslaving their peoples and stealing their resources and produce, as typified by the earlier 'commercial age'), but increasingly through our own efforts underpinned by growing populations and increasingly skilled (or differently, and increasingly diversely, skilled) labour forces. This brought women (and children) into the paid labour force in large numbers.

Industrialisation happened at different speeds and to different extents around the world. Finland, for example, remained agrarian for longer than its Scandinavian neighbours (its economy had only just caught up through high expansion by the end of the 1980s before being torn apart again by a major depression in the 1990s). Finnish farm workers and their families worked together until relatively recently, regardless of whether they were male or female, with the extended family providing childcare and work levels set by seasonal demands. Gender wasn't much of an issue.

Once rural people (and that meant almost all of us) came to town the whole make-up of society changed, with some family members left behind in the countryside and others local or long distances away in other industrialised areas. In this set-up it became normal – and then ideal – for newly enlarged groups of middle-class families to contain one male paid worker with a stay-at-home wife/mother. Working class women worked outside the home until they had children. Then, if it was economically feasible, they too stayed at home to look after the children. And we can understand why. If you're in a present-day nuclear family without the support of nearby extended family (or even with this support), once you have your first baby you wonder how you're ever going to get dressed and out to the shops by mid-afternoon, let alone how you're going to go back to work. With an increasing number of children in your family, the likelihood of going back to paid work diminishes, not only because children are so demanding in terms of time but also because of the economic factor – the more children you have, the more expensive they are to have them looked after. Back then, with no real support available for many families, the obvious thing (if you could afford to) was to stay at home with the kids. In an age when women weren't a standard part of the workforce at any senior level, or considered equally skilled, this seemed to make sense to most people.

The First then Second World Wars brought employment changes for women. Between these, in the 1920s, the world slumped into recession and unemployment soared. With too few jobs, many women were pushed aside to allow men their 'rightful' place. But at that time women mostly did work that men didn't do, such as clothing and textile manufacturing, food preparation, typing and clerical work, teaching and nursing. So more women were still allowed to enter the workforce (around 15 per cent of the US workforce was female by 1939, compared with 9 per cent in 1920[2]). The Second World War (1939–45) made a huge difference in the US in much the same way as the First World War did in the UK in 1914–18: with men away, women were brought in to do the jobs men had vacated. However, these higher-paid, skilled jobs were whisked away from women as soon as the men came back from war.

Economic expansion did mean that employers now needed women, so gradually women's participation in the workforce increased. When women started working outside the home during the First World War and through the depression, some employers, even back then, offered childcare to enable female workers to contribute. Without legislation to stop it, what we'd understand today as workplace discrimination was standard: employers recruited women for some roles and men for others and didn't think twice about this stereotyping. Because women weren't thought to be such important contributors to the family income, these particular roles and types of job came to carry lower pay.

Accompanying the huge influx of women into the workplace over the past century has been a long and gradual decline in the number of men in work. In 1890 in the US, for instance, every 100 US households had 167 working males, but by 1980 that number had decreased to 78 per 100.[3] With women working, together with the decline of child and youth labour and the gradual increase of retirement for men (and women), men slowly came to contribute less to households. By 1980, approximately 58 per cent of US households also included a working woman.

Women have always worked but the type of work has changed: as described above, working for payment is a relatively new concept for us. And as well as factory-based and similar work associated with industrialisation, it also took the form of home working by the mothers and daughters of families (but not the fathers and sons). Taking in lodgers became more commonplace as people moved around to find work. Families' reliance on the mother's earnings grew steadily from those days, and married women became gradually more likely to be in full-time employment than in part-time work or staying at home. As, over the past 50 years more and more women have opted for training and work outside the home, this has meant that the proportion of women in the workplace has increased dramatically in all developed nations, leaving us with the current situation where women now form a considerable proportion of the labour force. This happened from the 1960s onwards in the US and most of Western Europe.

Sue from Devon in the UK describes how it felt to be a young woman at the end of the 1960s:

> My father always said, 'Girls don't need to go to university because they don't need good jobs; girls are just there to get married and have children.' So right from day one I didn't really think about having a career. I half-heartedly applied to a university to do a teaching degree but Dad said it was a waste of time. And from that point on I just gave up.

She goes on to describe the ambivalent mood of the time:

> If I look at the friends I had in the 1960s . . . my best friend went into teaching. It was sort of 50/50; there were women in my day who wanted a career, it's just the emphasis wasn't on it.

Another woman of the same age, Shenagh, a senior civil servant working in New Zealand, decided to take the career route:

> I left full-time education when I was 25 after [gaining] a degree and a professional qualification (I started work as a social worker), and then went back to university to do my masters degree. I then started a social work job in inner-city Manchester and stayed part-time while I had my first two children.

Options were finally arriving for women: to be at home with the children, to go out to a career or to create a mix of the two.

Finances often dictated which we chose, as they do now. But then it felt like a liberation, the beginning of real choice at last.

From chattels to chairs: birthing chairs to boardroom chairs

Labour force participation rates have now reached an all-time high: in 1997 a little over 60 per cent of US women over the age of 20 were in paid work.[4] We've adjusted to this, so it's easy to forget that women didn't even exist in legal terms (except as items owned by our fathers or husbands) until relatively recently. It's been less than a century since women gained the right to vote in the majority of the developed world (Australia in 1901, Norway in 1913, England in 1918, and the US in 1920 [5]). But it's taken a painfully long time to progress from being recognised legally to taking anything approximating an equal part in society. It's almost as though, once we had the vote and were allowed to go to university and get divorced, we sat back thinking that the world would become equal. In retrospect it's not hard to see why it didn't. Something we now take for granted was still missing: adequate contraception (and then later, changes to the law on abortion). Women who wanted a 'normal' life involving marriage would usually go on to have a number of children. The only way to delay this and build a career first was to delay marriage. Unmarried women who had sex were likely to have children. With no ready provision for childcare and with society's prevailing attitudes meaning that mothers were expected to stay at home and unmarried mothers were looked down upon, women were faced with a choice: aim for a career in a highly prejudiced workplace and give up thoughts of having a family, or toe the line and give in graciously.

Easy, effective contraception (the pill and an increasing awareness of fertility which gave 'natural' family planning more success) from the 1960s onwards brought a wave of radical women echoing the Suffragettes who'd campaigned for the vote.

Active, brash and in-your-face, these 1960s feminists made plenty of noise and told the world that it was irrelevant what sex we were. This time they could prove it by making their own choices about fertility and deciding individually whether or not to take on the workplace handicap of having a family. They brought about the beginnings of huge change, though this is taking a long while to filter through: there are still many people (women as well as men) who consider that women shouldn't be in the workforce. But the norm has changed and, on paper, we're allowed to make our own choices. Once it had been more-or-less accepted, from the 1960s onwards, that women could work, young girls grew up expecting equality and for the whole world to open up to us.

Natasha Carpenter is 23, single, has no children and works in media in London, England. From her experience so far she assumes that, of course, women participate equally in the workplace. She then looks one step further at how women behave in order to compete with men:

> The first wave feminism brought about equal rights, to a certain extent, in the workplace. The second wave of feminism cemented that. But then there was a kind of third wave feminist movement where women adopted more laddish behaviour in order to prove themselves equal amongst their male peers in the workplace, and society in general. And that's backfiring somewhat now. The 90s saw a massive rise in lad culture amongst women, fuelled by the media and fashion. But now things seem to be becoming more geared to feminine behaviour, all the strong women who've worked really hard are seen to be bullish and men seem to look for more submissive qualities in women in the workplace now.

We've come to the point where we take our workplace presence for granted and are working through different strategies to maximise our presence. Yet still, and this is common through interviews with many of the pre-motherhood women who are quoted in this book, the emphasis is on what men are looking for, what men want and how men see it. So much has changed . . . yet so little. The thought that perhaps we've gone too far and that women have abandoned femininity in order to get to the top is appealing to some and appalling to others.

Here's a conversation I had with a man I bumped into on a lovely walk around rural Gloucestershire, England. Geoff is in his fifties:

> Young women today seem to be taking on the worst of the gender split with laddish behaviour. They're loud, brash, behaving like men and achieving like men and not using the positive feminine traits. Young men, in turn, seem to be feeling emasculated: what is their role now?

Geoff is talking about women in every arena not just work. The very, very fast evolution of the workplace (however sluggish it may seem when battling with old-fashioned prejudices) allows us to behave like this if we choose . . . until we have children. That's when women who have been brought up to expect equality start to see how society and social policies are still rooted in the middle of the last century. We pay lip service to equality but don't facilitate it. Hence today's dilemmas, inequalities and waste.

And at the same time we have globalisation. This started by selling goods to countries that were easily accessible by boat and train, to those accessible by plane, and now that's changed to those accessible by any means at all. And as the means have changed so have our markets and the goods we sell. We're now able instantly to sell a software package to someone in a remote hut on the other side of the world if the technology's in place. This is good news for trade – but not necessarily for our trade; with much of our infrastructure still deeply rooted in industrialisation and in 'making things' in an old-fashioned sense, and with our high standard of living meaning that our salaries are (whatever it seems by the end of the month) relatively high, much production has moved overseas to factories in the less developed world where people are paid less. Wage costs are more or less equal across the developed world, yet in the developing nations they are roughly one-fifth of ours. Initially, these overseas production centres use fewer skilled workers but, increasingly, these other nations produce well-skilled workforces to compete with our own but still at a lower cost. Asia is producing twice as many engineers as Europe and four times as many as the US. So we're losing much of what we tend to think of as 'industry' – large factories producing goods to go onto trucks and into shops.

There's still some old-fashioned industry struggling on, and some doing well because its nature requires a skilled workforce that simply isn't available anywhere else in the world, such as makers of traditional furniture, for instance – or for other stay-at-home factors: perhaps the owners have a commitment to their local region and won't outsource overseas (though this is becoming increasingly rare as competition increases). Perhaps it's a new, small operation that might one day move away but at present is working well here. Whatever the reasons, we still have old-fashioned industry but not enough to keep us all in work and not enough to assure our futures as developed nations. Luckily, there are plenty of new and ongoing work strands. Many of us in developed countries have a strong innovative streak leading to a thriving 'ideas' industry. We're good at information technology, at emerging communications technologies and at other new industries or that we think of as less 'mainstream'. In fact, we're good at all sorts of things, though many are suited to small organisations with relatively small earnings (small- and medium-sized enterprises that, in sufficient quantity, and if they survive, do just fine for themselves and the economy). Western economies are generally sound, it's thought, because of our economic diversity and the depth of our 'knowledge economy'. There are pitfalls though — we're good at the information and communications technologies but we're not necessarily any better than many nations with equally well-educated workforces but lower wages (India comes to mind as a country where UK companies in search of a new piece of software can have it developed at a fraction of the cost). We have lots of good ideas yet many people feel that the support and resources aren't available to allow these ideas to be developed or to allow the development to be translated into workable businesses that benefit the economy. Our universities are full of innovators yet many universities aren't, traditionally, oriented at industry or a practical application of those ideas. Small innovators and inventors often complain that no one will take them seriously or help them develop ideas that later become successful enterprises in other countries. So there's good news and a booming economy, which commentators see no sign of slowing, yet in many ways we're still trailing in areas such as infrastructure, education — and attitudes.

Paul Adams, Vice President of engineering firm Pratt and Witney, sees that three forces have driven the world economically over the past 25 years: globalisation, new technology, and an increase in productivity.[6] We've been working hard. We've also cleverly thought through production processes and applied new technologies to increase our productivity enormously. This has been essential in order to compete in the global marketplace. We can feel the relative pressure within the workplace with the advent of 'presenteeism' (always being at our desks) from the 1980s onwards and performance-related pay reaching every workplace sector. As well as this communications revolution we're experiencing a revolution in information (commentators sometimes refer to this stage of our development as the 'Information Age') as well as profound political and economic change. As an example, although China has remained politically closed, it has opened up economically as a strong competitor. Projections show how China will soon be the richest nation in the world, followed by the US, India and Brazil. As this happens, it's not only the centres of production that change but also markets: with China's gross domestic product (a measure of its earnings) increasing at twice the rate of that of the US (8 per cent compared to 4 per cent), its demand for goods and services increases. This brings opportunity as well as the more commonly perceived competition.

The rise of the service economy

While traditional industry has been declining, the service and 'invisibles' sectors has been expanding. These include areas such as the finance markets, tourism, information and communications technology and other activities that don't involve visible goods. It includes commercial cleaning and the sex industry, childcare and eldercare. It involves work at all levels and is highly split in terms of sex. Almost all care work is done by women, as is most work in the insurance industry at clerical and administrative level, as well as most work in catering. These are low-paid, often 'second salary' jobs. Some are highly skilled (I've been astounded at the level of skill and experience demonstrated by some of the women caring for my children and, latterly, for my mother) yet most of these workers are being paid the minimum wage or only slightly more. This applies across the developed world: in Germany, for instance, 80 per cent of women are concentrated into 25 of the 376 trades requiring apprenticeships.[7] It's one of the most fundamental problems we face now in terms of gender equality: the service sector is growing, with increasing numbers of jobs filled by women on low wages. This perpetuates and increases the imbalance in pay between the sexes and increases the likelihood of higher male unemployment. Women such as Evelyn Murphy, the author of *Getting Even: Why women don't get paid like men – and what to do about it* may indeed want to get even, but most of us would be happy to be equal.[8] If we develop societies where men have increasingly little place in the workforce, will Geoff's perceived 'emasculation' of men increase, with repercussions for the nature and stability of society?

So we'll be nations of shopkeepers, nurses, nannies and cooks. And as the economy has moved towards the service industry and increased employment of women, much employment has become 'flexible' – part-time, short-term and often with no guarantee of future employment. It's not to say that women's increased participation in the workforce has made all this happen, just that as we've been allowed into the workplace, the pockets held open to us have been low paid, often without job security. We haven't caused it: we've been some of the casualties of it.

How we're adapting

Governments understand what's happening (or, at least, they understand whichever version of events best suits them) and gear policies accordingly. In the UK, for instance, the past two decades have seen institutions of higher education move closer together. Vocational higher educational institutions (HEIs) used to be known as polytechnics, but now have the 'university' tag and are considered at the same level. These new universities are more likely to be geared towards idea generation for industry than analysing rediscovered Shakespearean manuscripts. Smaller, more skills-specialised HEIs will soon be gaining the 'university' tag. Government-funded services for entrepreneurs have become more mainstream, and so on. Many people would say that these moves don't go far enough (the UK investment in research at universities, for instance, falls behind other developed nations) but at least it's a move in the right direction.

Yet it's generally understood that we simply can't compete in many disciplines or industries within a global marketplace. There are too many nations that undercut us and sometimes also provide a better product. As developed nations we insist on a high standard of living but we don't consider that, as a nation, we might not be able to afford it. (Do our dressing tables contain bottles of lotions that cost up to £50/US$100, for instance? Do we take it for granted that we'll buy coffee and lunch every day? Do we drive a car for each member of the family and go on several foreign trips a year?) It's okay right now but unless we beef up our economy in areas that will earn, and maintain, a large enough and sufficiently skilled workforce to run them, how long can it go on? Governments around the world are aiming to increase participation rates in higher education and looking at extending our working lives through postponing retirement ages. This should provide an ongoing skilled and experienced workforce that will help to maintain our high standard of living. It should also give us plenty of bargaining power, even though we're women. But does it?

There's a global redistribution of work, prosperity and power taking place, but this isn't benefiting most women any more than it's benefiting the poor and otherwise excluded. Just as before, women continue to struggle for any real level of social justice, security and the power to make decisions. The researcher C Wichterich suggests that perhaps in the future, some of us will carry on fighting for equality and rights within the system we have, while others will look for alternatives to the system and different strategies to achieve equality.[9] Wichterich goes on to say that 'dual strategies – both inside and outside, from the top and from below, local and global, gradual and visionary – will be necessary to gain strength in civil society'. Only then, says this women-centred commentator, will there be real power-sharing incorporating forceful opposition to the current state of being as globalisation continues to develop.

Moles in high places

A friend of mine sits on committees in England that review where the country is right now, where it's going and why, and then considers strategies to recommend to the government. My mole tells me some of the things the committees have debated that should be perfectly obvious to us and are key to our children's careers, even if it's too late for our own. As globalisation continues, there won't be much work left in the developed world that could not have been outsourced. Everything that can possibly be done in another, cheaper, nation will be. Could your work be done by someone in India or, more likely, China? Unless it demands person-to-person contact with clients, bosses or colleagues, the answer is 'yes'. If this contact can be made by telephone, email or any yet-to-be-developed means of communication, then your job won't exist here. This means that major tranches of work that we see as standard, such as accountancy, insurance and many roles within other industries, will simply cease to be part of the developed world's careers options. So, who's left? Hairdressers will do fine, as will caterers, plumbers, drivers and mechanics. Salespeople of a certain kind will do okay, and so will the accountants who need to be in the thick of things: some finance directors will exist locally though the accounts work itself may be emailed to the Philippines. Advisers who go in to help small businesses will be fine, too. Entrepreneurs will start new enterprises though they may later outsource a proportion of the work. Doctors and nurses will be in high demand. Gardeners, lawyers . . . on it goes. But what about our jobs and what do we tell our children? In this deceptively unstable era of work, researchers and commentators are working to predict the future of work and more of these predictions can be found in Chapter 8.

As the service industry, so highly populated by female workers, has many of the jobs that are staying, it's likely that things are set to get much better for women. Yet the level of this work in terms of salary and kudos is often low, as is job security. For a woman supporting a family this can be catastrophic and means that it's barely worth the fight of going out to work. Some find it impossible to manage without a social support infrastructure and find themselves living in poverty. As Wichterich says, young, flexible women who can move, who can work different hours and retrain easily are doing fine; mothers often aren't.[10] Some women find their way onto 'the vibrating springboard of the new knowledge, finance and technology markets that eventually hurl a select few upwards.' Most, however, don't.

Researchers Nuria Chinchilla and Consuela Leon describe the three major events to have taken place in the last hundred years which have affected the status of women:

1. The right to vote with its consequent legal autonomy with respect to civil rights;
2. Greater equality in access to education;
3. The massive entry of women in the job market.[11]

The first two of these are set in stone: no government is going to take the vote away from women, and no mainstream educational establishments are going to turn girls and women away (indeed, women are now participating and achieving more in higher education than men). In each of these, it's up to us how we perform. We can choose whether or not to vote. We can choose who we vote for (and Chapter 3 may make you consider this from a different angle). We (mostly) can engage in good education up to our late teens, often into our early twenties and then through our lives, allowing us into the world on an equal footing with men. And we can continue to participate massively as single women in the workforce. This, though, is where equality is turned on its head.

Laine cares full-time for her one-year-old twins and explains how, when she was pregnant, things had felt okay:

I worked [as a set dresser] on a few commercials while pregnant and it was interesting: so many men would come up to me and want to talk about their children. I was treated with care and respect and, believe me, unless you are the director, this is rare on set. That all goes out the window once you give birth. It is so hard not to slip into traditional patterns and roles as husband and wife when kids are born; the husband 'escapes into his work', the wife 'nags all the time', 'nothing the husband does is ever good enough', the wife is 'always complaining'.

I feel in the middle of an identity crisis; the change of status . . . priority, etc has left me feeling lost and insane. I see myself as out of the loop. In many ways I feel like a loser, like mother-hood is my last stop . . .

At the beginning of this book Laine asked why, if what we are doing as mothers is so valuable, it doesn't feel so. This chapter has given an overview of the way women's rights and participation at work have changed over time. The next chapter takes a micro-scope to the same issues and looks directly at our workplace. We battle with it daily, either in the thick of it or from the outside in our roles as new mothers. It's familiar and yet we only see a small part of it. Seeing the broader picture might not help women like Laine feel any less confused from her current vantage point but it might help us feel less alone.

2

WELCOME TO WORK

Picture yourself (or your sister or daughter) at school or university and then progressing on to work. For the motivated, this stage of their early career is exciting and full. Young women shine with promise. The natural optimism and idealism of youth is coupled with a workplace alive with possibilities. You have your whole working life ahead of you, partnership perhaps, children too, maybe. And up until now (assuming that you have the privilege and good health that a large proportion of our young people enjoy), everything's gone your way. If you've come into work at age 21 you have at least 10 or 15 years to build a career-base before needing to think about a family. There are problems and pitfalls, of course: not many of these career paths will turn out as expected but most of them will have a strong element of positive achievement and reward. You've enjoyed legal equality and equal access to education. And as Chapter 1 concluded, there's another step towards equality that women are making: equal participation at work. Enjoy the 10 to 15 years and then make a choice: are you going to participate in the workforce and compete on a par or are you going to disable your career by having children?

The place where equality goes wrong

Looking at how work has already changed and is continuing to change and where working mothers fit in helps to ground our thinking about our own lives and careers and how we can juggle these with raising families. There have been several monumental changes within the workplace over recent decades, shifts that we don't always notice in day-to-day. One of these is the slow change away from the idea of a 'job for life' with its nine-to-five and steady journey through one career with only one employer. It seems ridiculous and stultifying to us now that we might have had the patronage of (or looking at it from a different angle, been patronised by) one employer for our whole working lives, but that's how it used to be. Before we had geographical, social and career mobility we made our choice (or, more probably, someone else made our choice) in our teens and that was it. This can be summed up with a term that's bandied about to mean all sorts of different things: flexibility. The next couple of pages examine what it really means.

Work has become more flexible from both an employer's and employee's point of view. Flexibility from the employer's point of view gives enormous gains to an organisation: why employ a worker all day, every day, when the work might only be available two days a week, or might be seasonal or might be unpredictable? Far better to employ people when needed and only pay them for the time spent at work. The ultimate example is the 'zero-hours' contracts used by some fast-food retailers where, if there are no customers, workers effectively clock off. But they need to be ready to work again as soon as a customer appears so, in reality, they're simply sitting unpaid in the back room. This flexible approach works for some employers using some types of worker, but others have found to their cost that it's not always such a good move. Where people with certain skills are in demand from a number of employers, and because we want the job security of a permanent contract, many workers shun employers who only issue flexible contracts. Fast-food retailers have until recently had enough willing workers to call on but as the predicted worker shortage arrives, even these 'bad employers' are forced to make changes.

It's not only the hours we work each week that can be flexible. Another trend has been for employers to issue short-term rather than permanent employment contracts; in that way there are no long-term employees to become sick and take months off work, or grow old and need expensive pensions. These moves have contributed to the end of the 'job for life' and a new approach to careers. A career is now often defined as a series of jobs, not necessarily related to each other, rather than one long, slowly building specialised area of work.

As skills shortages grow and organisations see that they need to do more to attract and keep skilled workers, employers now offer a range of working options which give us more flexibility. These include family-friendly policies such as term-time working, reduced hours to fit with the school day, perks such as workplace nurseries and so on. There's another type of flexibility too. We don't need 'careers for life' any more than employers offer 'jobs for life'. We might train in one type of work but later decide we don't like it, or jobs might dry up, so we retrain into something else. These days, we build up a group of abilities, or transferable skills, to take with us from one job or one career to the next. Some base-level jobs require only these transferable skills, which might include being good with people or numbers. Employers will now often accept that new workers don't need specific experience if they can show a good range of skills, can be trained and are keen. We now have more choice of options that weren't available a few decades ago. We need this choice as many of the old careers and disciplines disappear and new ones emerge. New transferable skills are being demanded. 'Creativity' would rarely have been seen in a job advertisement 30 years ago but now it's a plus if you can take any given situation and move it on in a creative way. It's part of a range of skills tied in with entrepreneurism and the attitude that comes with it, one of the skills itself being known as 'flexibility'. This brings self-employment within the reach of far more people, including mothers, as we'll see later. There's also a shortage of workers with specific, developed skills in certain areas and industries. So on the one hand there's scope to move around in terms of career, though when we do we may end up being paid less if we're effectively 'starting again', and on the other, if we've developed the right skills – in industries that aren't being relocated around the globe – we're in a seller's market.

Flexibility

The term 'flexibility' can also be used to describe the way that organisations come and go, though the term 'stability' – or a lack of this – is perhaps more appropriate. Small organisations come and go faster than large ones. Multinationals are relocating around the globe, leaving the developed nations with many thousands of small- and medium-sized enterprises. The majority of these don't work out, in their first conceptions at least. The more our economy heads in this direction, the less stable it is for workers (both the entrepreneurs and their employees). Flexible and creative thinkers will be fine – we can retrain and find something else. But for people who aren't able to do this for any reason (varying from intrinsic personality or education through to disability or having the constraints of running a family at the same time), this lack of stability is unsettling. Even where organisations themselves are stable, they may not give the type of job security that we want. If they only offer short-term contracts it might make it impossible to get a loan to buy a home, for instance, and they won't provide ongoing training. Employers have transferred their risks onto us.

As well as work being more flexible (for good and bad) and less stable, it's become more intense. We must work continuously or, at least, that's how it can seem. We need to be seen at our desks (or equivalent) for as long as possible because being a good worker entails long hours, however many we've been contracted for. This increasing work intensity and presenteeism has resulted from gradual shifts: the economic need for organisations to be more productive (described in the previous chapter) and therefore to expect more from their workers, a shift towards the removal of less productive workers (and thereby scaring the ones who are left, as well as giving them more work) and the move away from organisations 'employing' people, to short-term contracts and self-employment with consequent increasing competition within the workplace. Work seems tougher nowadays. We certainly work long hours, although a look at the figures of working hours across Europe is encouraging: the average Frenchman or woman works 18 hours a week compared to 16.5 for the average Italian. In the UK the average is 21.5, whereas in the US the average is 25.[1] But when we remember that these figures include all workers, including those with part-time jobs, the picture changes. Looking at full-time workers, the average hours worked in Europe is 40.3 hours a week. In the Netherlands the average is 38.8 hours but in the UK it's 43.5 hours. Workers in France and Germany work 38.9 hours and 39.6 hours per week, respectively.[2] These levels have been falling. Back in the time of the Industrial Revolution men worked at least 55 hours a week but this has been decreasing since (with a UK plateau in the Thatcherite years of the 1980s). The latest, relatively low, figures are thought to be due to the European Working Time Directive. So why does it feel as though we're all working so hard? Is it because we're being more productive? Yes and no – although workers in France and Germany work less hours than in the UK, they're still around 20 per cent more productive that we are in the UK. We feel as though we're working so hard for two main reasons: one is that new technology never lets us go. There were good reasons to daydream as we walked along that corridor to deliver an important message to a colleague, in that we were allowing thoughts to percolate down and new, creative ones to emerge, but we've stopped doing it and now we email that colleague instead. We keep our eyes down and our fingers tapping. We have our mobile phones on all the time. Sometimes it seems that we are entirely work-driven. But it's also partly to do with the fact that women are now doing the same as men: not only is it possible for every social conversation to be about work, because we're all participating in the workplace and that's our common denominator in social time as well as work time, but because there's no one at home to handle the domestic side of things, there really is more work around in total. You feel as though you never stop working? Even if the hours you work aren't reflected in the national averages above, it could well be true because you're working an additional ten hours a week at home.

'Please have more children'[3]

This entreaty by the Sri Lankan Prime Minister was aimed at fuelling the country's army for its civil war but could equally be the battle-cry of many a Western leader who sees a chasm appearing in the supply of the young workforce. In the developed world we've increasingly 'voted with our contraceptives' and decided not to have children. If we've had a family we might have chosen only one or two children instead of three or more, as we may have a few decades back. Or, we've decided, for good financial, career and social reasons, to wait and then discovered we're too old to conceive. Given that it takes a fertility rate of 2.1 (which is the number of children that an average woman will have in her lifetime) to balance the size of the population[4] and that the UK's fertility rate is 1.73,[5] the number of young people being born and then coming into work is becoming too low. Us oldies retire and take our skills with us, costing the state a fortune in medical and social care but we don't have enough grandchildren coming into work and paying their taxes to sustain us or to boost the economy. With inward migration and a falling death rate, the lower fertility rate hasn't yet caused a crisis in most countries. There's a furore in the British tabloid press at the moment about Eastern Europeans coming to steal our jobs.

As mother and civil servant Anne Eriksson puts it:

> [Friends and I] were having a conversation on how difficult it has become for 16 year olds to get Saturday jobs because of Eastern European migrants . . . I suppose in theory there're plenty of opportunities for British workers to go and work elsewhere, although most of us don't speak another language so we haven't positioned ourselves very well.

But perhaps it's a good thing they're here to support our economy, and that we don't speak Polish and, generally, don't go to work in Poland or things would be far worse.

So these two major changes – flexibility and population size – are creating a massive change for everybody in the workplace. There are, though, other issues of particular interest to women.

The pay gap

A 2003 survey of US earnings by the General Accounting Office found that, after discounting other variables, there was a definite earning difference between men and women.[6] This holds true across the developed world. What was interesting about this particular overview survey was that its individual studies showed the difference between male and female earnings varying between 2.5 per cent and 47.5 per cent, depending how it was measured, though it was always women earning the lower figure. Old news. Perhaps more interestingly, the survey put a figure of

2.5 per cent as the cost to women's earnings of each child and an increase in men's earnings for each child of 2.1 per cent. These findings were accompanied by figures showing that married men earn over 8 per cent more than never-married men, though the equivalent figures for women showed no difference. So although it's not easy to explain how being a father in itself can increase your earning power, when taken with the support given within a home from the woman to the man, this makes sense.

When the UK Equal Pay Act came into force in 1976 the pay gap in the UK was 29 per cent. This figure has almost halved today. But at the rate it's now moving, it'll be another 80 years before we achieve equal pay.[7] The government is trying to address this with new initiatives to improve the quality of the part-time work available, and putting flexible working high on its priority list.[8] It understands how, with 57 per cent of UK women working in jobs beneath their skills and qualifications, if the barriers to women entering 'traditionally male' work areas were removed, the UK's gross domestic product would rise by 2 per cent, equivalent to £23 billion/US$46 billion a year.[9] To look more deeply into these sexual occupational divides, economics researchers Judy Rich and Peter A Riach sent two bogus applications for more than 400 jobs in four different professions to recruiters to see what effect sex had on getting a job interview.[10] They discovered what many women already know: sexism is embedded in the recruitment process. Each of the fictitious applicants had equal experience, qualifications and age profiles but of each pair, one had a man's name and the other a woman's. The researchers found that women were only half as likely to be asked for an interview for an engineering job compared with men, but that men were nearly four times less likely than women to get an interview for a secretarial post. Surprisingly, men also fared worse in accountancy, where 30 per cent of the workforce is female, and for computer analyst jobs.[11] 'Men's work' is traditionally thought to include engineering, physics, the judiciary, law and health service administration, while 'women's work' includes library work, nursing, teaching (especially in primary levels), caring, cleaning and so on, says a report from the International Labour Office.[12] This 'horizontal occupational segregation' is exacerbated by a vertical version, where men are more likely to hold senior posts (and therefore be paid more). There is a smattering of good news: in some new areas, such as the information and communications technology sectors and accountancy (as the Rich and Riach survey showed), as well as traditionally male areas such as the judiciary, women are making recent career gains. The disparities that do exist result from generations of perceptions about a woman's role. Even within one profession there may be stark differences in the earnings of different specialisms, and it's interesting to see how these coincide with the relative flexibility of the role. Where there's an amount of flexibility (in that the worker isn't required to make long trips that would involve staying away but can instead work a relatively standard day, for example), and where there are other workers on hand to take over their work should they be called away, earnings are lower. An example from the US is within the medical profession, where general practice (primary care, or family practice) is more accommodating than surgery. Surgeons may be called out in the middle of the night for emergencies, and also need to see one patient through an entire medical process without being able to transfer that patient easily to a colleague's care. As such, surgeons are paid more than general practition-ers.[13]

British women suffer the largest pay gap of all European countries: 17 per cent for full-time staff and 38 per cent for part-time.[14] A British report from the Women and Work Commission explains how women are more likely to be in lower-paid jobs to begin with and then, on returning to work, we find ourselves even further down the career ladder.[15] But we have ourselves to blame –

girls are more likely to choose badly paid careers (such as caring) over high earning sectors such as the professions or science and engineering, or to aim at careers where it's unrealistic to succeed in a highly paid role such as the entertainment industry (in one US study one-third of girls in middle school said they were aiming to be entertainers).[16] This is despite girls outperforming boys at school, university, postgraduate and much professional study. In much of Europe women routinely do 'male' work that many women in the UK barely consider suitable, with the exception of a few pioneering female examples. Then, after starting in lower-paid sectors, UK women are less likely to ask for the pay rises we deserve in a male-dominated workplace (managers are more likely to be men, even in female-dominated sectors). Even if it's a sector with good pay, we're likely to be offered a lower salary following a job interview, says Professor Marilyn Davidson. 'This is related psychologically to women being "worth" less than men'.[17]

Tanya, a recruitment consultant and mother of two young sons, sees this in her workplace:

> On the whole, men are more forceful when it comes to demand-ing salaries and benefits. Men tend to think more about the 'here and now', ie 'if I give an ultimatum and it's knocked back I will deal with that when it happens', whereas women are more likely to think about the consequences, ie 'I could lose my job, and may not be able to find another one', etc.

After an initial poor start we're then less likely to ask for, or nego-tiate, as good a pay rise as men. 'There is a psychological barrier,' says Davidson. 'Men ask for perks, while women ask for satisfac-tion. It's a socialisation thing – men are still regarded as breadwinners. It's the fault of organisations. If they did pay audits to ensure equality of pay, this would help narrow the gap.' So perhaps it's not all our fault. Careers advice directs girls into traditionally female occupations; once we apply for work we are offered less, and then societal preconceptions and brainwashing mean that we don't push for higher pay.

Yet this is all before we have children. The Women and Work Commission report goes on to show that it's mostly the arrival of children, and the allowances made by women for this, that secures the pay disparity. Mothers returning part-time to their old job quickly fall behind male colleagues, and women taking a new part-time job do even worse: 'You've only got to spend a couple of years part-time and that scars your career for many, many years because it takes you so long to catch up,' says Margaret Prosser, Chair of the Women at Work Commission.[18] And the problem isn't solely attributable to individuals' prejudices. Though rooted in sexist attitudes and history, the problem is partly because there aren't enough high-level part-time jobs available or the support to allow parents to work full-time. So UK women take lower-paid, part-time work and consequently earn 59p an hour for every pound a full-time man gets.[19]

Laine, the mother of twins mentioned previously, sees it from her own experience:

> Men still earn more than women because men make work their life, they prioritise work, they judge themselves by the work they do; companies know that men will put them first, often even before their own families. Women know better.

The report from the United States General Accounting Office - summarises the overall reasons for the pay gap.[20] The main factor, it claims, is working patterns: women have fewer years of experience, work fewer hours in each year, are less likely to work full-time and when they do take a break, are more likely to leave the labour force for longer periods. This is because women have additional respon- sibilities as well as their paid work and need time away from paid work in order to fulfil them. Other areas such as sector, occupation, race, marital status and type of work contract also have an impact; some of these factors affect men and women differently but there's no evidence to explain why this is. And finally, the report states, women are more likely to take up any universal offers of part-time working than men, which fits with our need to do so because of home responsibilities, rather than fight for the right well-paid job. There's a case for saying that because women are less experienced due to our absences from the workplace we should receive less salary, but when this is accounted for within the research there's still a large pay gap. And anyway, a proportion of the women who are ostensibly working part-time are in fact working as many hours as their full-time counterparts but catching up on work at home during evenings and weekends. Employers accept that the broader parenting skills transfer to the workplace. Yet many women are prepared, some are even happy, to exchange the potential of higher earnings for a more flexible working life or, as above, any old part-time work that fits in with the family.

Who wants the money anyway?

At the end of a long day at work, then more to do at home, I sometimes feel that none of this matters. I really don't care that men run my organisation (I don't want to, thanks), or that they earn more than me (I've got enough; we can afford a warm, dry, happy home and decent food and trips). But I'm forgetting that when my children were small I was almost completely reliant on my husband to provide for me and our children at the standard of living we were used to. There wasn't a lot of spare cash (eating out was a real treat) but we had a home that, once we'd slowly rebuilt and decorated, would be lovely, and most importantly was large enough for small footballers to practise dribbling down the hallway. But if my husband had stopped supporting us we'd have moved into something much smaller and our lives would have felt very different. However much I'd wanted to, though, I couldn't have gone out and earned what he was earning because I'd dropped out of a mainstream career when I had my children. It was my choice, rather than hand the children to a nanny and be absent from home for 12 hours a day (there was no part-time or suitable local work available). Yet whatever the reasons, at that stage I couldn't have provided adequately for my family. People might say that I shouldn't have needed to, yet it's still the position that many mothers find themselves in. It's one of the reasons that this does matter: for as long as we're reliant on men to bring in a high enough income (because we ourselves don't earn enough), we lose choice. Of all the social advances of the 20th century, the most profound and important was allowing women choice (of living where we choose with whom we choose, having children as and when we choose and so on). Yet even now we're precluded from some of the most fundamental choices because of low earnings and inferior career prospects. The current workplace tells us that we matter less, and because of this we are, as soon as we have children, second-class citizens.

Another area where it matters is pensions. Even if we try not to mind that our careers are less successful than our male counterparts', why should we, having worked equally hard (and often harder, after having done better at school in the first place), have a less prosperous retirement? This is a worldwide phenomenon: in the US, only a third of women in Michigan have a pension whereas well over half of men do.[21] It's similar in Australia, with a forecast that this will continue.[22]

Even if things feel okay financially now, lower pay over our lifetimes focuses itself on the level of our retirement pay. Add to this the increased likelihood that we'll have had career breaks (ie longer periods without contributing to our pensions) and less consistency of employment, plus the probability of working for employers with less provision of benefits, including pensions.

Personally, I'd like to die in comfort and, most particularly, I don't want to die cold. It worries me. I don't want to spend life worrying.

The glass and concrete ceilings

As we've already seen, girls do better at school than boys and this advantage follows through not only to higher participation rates in higher education but also to better degrees. According to commentators Burke and Nelson, in the US there are nearly as many women as men graduating from professional colleges in areas such as accountancy, business and law.[23] These graduates enter professions in the workforce at similar levels to men, but after that point women's and men's experiences and careers start to diverge. Women tend to go higher in management within sectors where there are more women further down the ladder than in more male-dominated areas but generally, women fare worse than men in career terms. There's an invisible line drawn at a certain level within organisations, known as the glass ceiling. This is the point above which women almost inevitably don't rise any higher within an organisation, a profession or a work sector. There are usually a few token women at board level, say, (though they will often be non-executive or in traditionally female areas), and the annual reports of large organisations like to show their smiling faces in full colour. The majority, however, don't progress. This is apparent to women and minority groups but often unnoticed by those to whom it doesn't apply: white male workers. In any career there are, of course, other barriers to success, such as lack of qualifications or experience. Women and people from minority groups gain the qualifications but gaining the appropriate experience near enough to the glass ceiling in order to rise above it can be near impossible. The figures make depressing reading. Recent data from the International Labour Office shows that in 45 out of 63 countries polled in a survey, women held 30–60 per cent of professional jobs in 2001–02, a level figure since 1996–99.[24] But women's share of managerial positions ranged from 20–40 per cent in these same countries, from a high of 53 per cent in Costa Rica to a low of 5 per cent in South Korea.

Senior civil servant Anne Eriksson describes the situation in her department:

> . . . about 57 per cent of the total workforce is women but at my level it's only around 26 per cent, so there's definitely something that's stopping women from progressing within the organisation to more senior levels. Whether that's through choice, and women declining to put themselves forward for promotion, there may be a bit of that. But actually when I look down into my bit of the organisation and try to pick out who are the really good performers, it's definitely 50/50; there's as many women that are identified as being 'stars' as there are men. But it's just taking a very long time.

How do women rise over this invisible line? One website offers a list of 19 actions we can take to help us.[25] These include seeking out difficult or highly visible job assignments; gravitating towards the visible, difficult, strategic tasks; and starting to focus your energy. This is sound advice, although when I had small children and was attempting to juggle work among the broken nights and potty training, the last thing I wanted or could cope with was focusing my energy or gravitating towards the more difficult tasks. But however much we try – and succeed – in focusing and gravitating, very few women break through, and most give up trying. This has brought about the use of the term concrete ceiling. Instead of battling against the inevitable, many women accept that they won't get to the top, or after years of ambition they come to realise that they don't actually want to any more. I suppose I'm one of those. Nowadays, after working hard for so long, I can't see the point any more of trying to get to the top. To do so means sacrificing many of the parts of my life that I hold precious, and what's the point? To sit at a boardroom table of loud men who might be thinking, or even making, snide comments and sexist innuendo? I would have to (according to research) use not only braying tactics myself, but also softer, feminine wiles, thus I'd need to be twice as good as the rest of them simply to be allowed to work that hard. To me, as to many women, it's not worth it and I simply stop competing.

Across Europe

Social scientists have been reporting these inequalities for decades and governments have taken some action. One of the more interesting countries to look at in this respect is Sweden, the first nation to implement social policies that assumed men and women had equal roles in society. This assumption has been officially in place since 1968 (about the time that women entered the workforce in large numbers), with the slow drip-feed of an 'equality' attitude since then. Other countries that now have similar social policies in place didn't start as early, so ordinary people's assumptions about relative gender roles remain more traditional.

I've been visiting Sweden regularly since the 1980s and know a number of families there. Although as a young working woman, before I had my children, I didn't give much thought to what was happening in Sweden in terms of social policy. As soon as I attempted to combine parenting with work I was intrigued. Later, as I had more children and tried to work more hours, I became increasingly envious. I voiced my wonderment by asking various Swedes whether they had any idea how lucky they were to have their workplace and childcare system. Of course, to them it was just how things were. When I tried to explain what it was like in the UK I don't think I was believed.

One of the first Swedish women who impressed me was a childminder. From my experience of looking for a childminder in the

UK in the 1980s the childminding role appeared to entail working from a damp and pokey basement attempting to control a handful of screaming pre-school children. Going out wasn't an easy option as there were too many lively tots to control – there was usually a baby in the mix – and of course, in the UK children don't go out on their own. The relatively few childminders who were able to operate more professionally (their circumstances – and the status they were given – allowing it) were in huge demand. When I saw the Swedish system I was appalled at first because of the emphasis we have in the UK on 'stranger danger', but, in that particular Swedish city at least, the many children in this child-minder's house, who ranged from tiny to the school-starting age of seven, looked after each other and went out together into the local neighbourhood play area. All around them were the safe homes of other families. The city's transport system was designed around the bicycle so traffic danger was low. The childminder herself could spend time in her home with the babies knowing that the older children were ranging freely and safely around the communal gardens and neighbourhood. She kept the children from very early in the day until the final parent finished work and everyone seemed happy. Perhaps she was an exceptional example, but the system allowed her to be. In the UK this simply wasn't happening and, anyway, wouldn't have been possible.

The assumption in Sweden was that all children would be in full-day childcare until the parents were able to collect them and that all parents would be in work, at a time when the UK assumption still hadn't moved on to both parents working. In Sweden, social policy (and State finances) allowed the establishment and subsidising of a range of childcare and education facilities which encouraged both parents to be in work knowing that their children were safe and happy and that it wasn't costing them a fortune. There are many other policies that make Sweden a relatively easy place to be a parent: there's an assumption that you'll go home to look after an ill child without any penalty (this is only now being mooted as a possibility in the UK). Financial inducements encourage you to have more children close together. It's not just Sweden – the other Nordic countries follow suit. 'There's a big difference in benefits,' says author and researcher Jonathan Grant. 'In the UK for example maternity benefit lasts for 26 weeks. The first six weeks is at 90 per cent of full pay and subsequently at £108/US$216 a week. If you go to Norway, maternity benefit is 90 per cent of full pay for 12 months after birth.[26] (For up to date information on UK, US and Australian allowances and legislation, see the Appendix.)

Social scientist Catherine Hakim is researching the long-term effects of these social policies in Sweden.[27] She agrees that it's true: Sweden does provide more maternity leave, better pay and more flexible working opportunities for working mothers. But she also says that 'Swedish women don't have it made – they still end up paying a price in terms of their career or employment.' She's found that there's is a pay threshold in Scandinavian countries; 80 per cent of all men are above it and 80 per cent of all women are below it. As well as that, the glass ceiling is as much a problem in Sweden as in the US and the more family-friendly policies are put into place, the greater the glass ceiling problem has become. 'In Sweden 1.5 per cent of senior management are women, compared with 11 per cent in the US,' says Hakim. Her research also shows that the gender pay gap is roughly the same in Sweden as in the UK – about 20 per cent. Belgium and Portugal both have a pay gap of only 8 per cent – and neither of those is known for its family-friendly social policies. It goes on to show a huge disparity between the sectors where Swedish men and women work. Private employers can't afford the flexibility and maternity packages that legislation insists on, so have reduced the number of women they employ, who now work predominantly in the public sector. Take up of paternity rights has also been surprisingly low in Sweden.

The UK is finally starting to get its act together with regard to family-friendly social policy. New legislation on paternity rights is now coming into effect for the first time; there are rumours that the right to part-time work will be debated in parliament. Australia is currently debating all these issues. The looming worker and skills shortage is forcing governments to put social policies into place to allow women to have real choices about the way we lead our lives. So these Swedish research findings are alarming. Researchers aren't concluding that these social policies are pointless but that they're not making the difference we'd hoped and perhaps assumed.

All this change: what has it meant?

The influx of women into the workplace has coincided with and brought about many changes. Some are subtle; some are huge. Some are fundamental to the economy, others to our social structure, yet none stands in isolation; they weave together like strands of twine in a fishing net. The commentator Nuria Chinchilla summarises the social changes that women coming into work has brought: with the mother going out to work as well as the father, families have an additional source of income.[28] This has brought about a greater economic and legal interdependence within the family, along with a change of values and priorities due to new workplace obligations. This has lead to more stress, particularly for women, leading to a fall in birth rates. It's ironic if this very fall in birth rates, brought about in the first place by women's increased participation at work, is forcing governments to change social policy to help women be in work. And so it's easy to conclude that changes within work have given women even more to do than we had before with, in many cases, no real advantage over the old set-up. We have become working mothers who are paid less, have worse careers, work harder, get less benefits, are poorer in retirement and have the raw end of the deal compared to men. We have a traditional, unproductive workplace managed by presenteeism rather than by achievement.

Here's what happened to Frances, mother to sons aged two and four – not a headline-grabbing story, just one of thousands of similar tales that occur every day in our workplace:

> When I first joined the company, I was held in high esteem because I'd come from external lawyers. I worked there a couple of years until I became pregnant. During my pregnancy it was still fine, there was no negativity at all. But then I had my first son and I had thought, I won't take too much maternity leave because of the money, so I decided to only take four months off after he was born. It was a bit daft in retrospect. I wanted to come back to work part-time. I came back to work too soon, really, for my own mental state. It was very hard to leave him at nursery. And then they wouldn't let me go back to the job that I'd left. They forced me into a role that wasn't appropriate for me and wasn't really what I was trained in; bearing in mind I'd just had a baby it was really quite an onerous role as well.

And now, instead of contaminating the physical environment, as mankind has done from the Industrial Revolution onwards, we now pollute the social environment. We're learning (slowly) how to clean up the former but we've barely thought about cleaning up the latter.

If researchers are finding that even strongly family-centred social policy (such as that in Sweden) doesn't make as significant a difference as hoped in the way women are able to perform at work, then what's causing the ongoing imbalance? Think of the biggest, strongest, most powerful child in your class at school. Did that person want to relinquish power and adulation – and the ability to strike fear – to make the class 'classless'. Did he want to give it away and suffer near the bottom of the pecking order with us losers? Of course not. But at the same time, he might have been a decent person, fair (within his own parameters) and without a sense of guilt or inequality. He didn't see it any other way, because that was simply the way it was. He may not have been a bully (although he might have been) but he was in charge and was going to stay there. If one of us had challenged him, he might have tried to listen but he wouldn't have understood. And the chances are that he'd simply have quashed the rebellion.

In the same way, the people who have always been at the top of the workplace don't really get it. The prejudices are so deeply ingrained that it takes an unusually insightful top person (and usually the top people are middle-class, able-bodied white males) to appreciate how unjust it is. It's obvious to the women reading this book (unless you're young and still assume the career/motherhood combination will be plain sailing). What many men, and some childless women, don't get is that having a family is a full-time, all-consuming responsibility for at least one person, and the chances are that this one person is going to be the female partner. It's not that we can't buy in childcare, education, extra-curricular activities and the like (assuming we're paid enough to be able to do that, and that adequate provision is available in our area, neither of which is entirely likely). But this doesn't mean that we can (or would want to) hand responsibility over to bought-in carers and agencies.

For many professional women with supportive partners who have full-time childcare and can afford as much as it takes to keep their families' wheels oiled, issues that the majority of UK women struggle with (finding childcare that's safe and nurturing, paying for childcare, paying the mortgage, perhaps doing it all alone) are insignificant. So why don't these women succeed in their careers, reach the top and even out the gender imbalance? Because having a family is more than just slotting an equation together. It's more than nanny plus school plus cleaner plus handyman plus x, y and z equals a satisfactory solution. As well as these buy-in factors there needs to be the linchpin, the person who holds it together. Managing the troops to form the gang that handles the family is enough to do many people's heads in. To then go into a full-time responsible job and attempt to carve a career out of it . . . well, it's huge.

I think men are lovely; I admire and enjoy so much about the male persona, so I'm not having a dig here but isn't there often this tacit get out: if you don't have to do it, why volunteer? If there's someone slightly lower down the pecking order who'll do it for all for the family, then let her. For the person who does take on that role there's so much to organise and there's so much to go wrong.

Great, a North American mother, describes how it felt when she went back to work after her first baby:

> I was looking forward and I was scared, both at the same time. I wanted more than nappies and *Sesame Street* – I wanted adult company, I wanted my salary back, but I was scared of leaving my baby and of being able to cope. Getting back into the office was a shock. People expected me to be the same person but I wasn't that person any more. I was fearful, anxious and had so much on my mind. I waited for the phone call to tell me it had all gone wrong. It was easier later on but it took me years to get used to it and the effort turned me from young and energetic to tired and oppressed. I hated that.

We're resourceful, and the energy, for most of us, comes back. But not the career. Where there used to be two people in a (standard) family, and two jobs (the one that earned the money and the one that looked after the family and home) there are now two people and three jobs. One of those people is almost certainly going to take on more than one and a half of those jobs, and that person is almost certainly the woman. And who can do nearly two jobs and do them both well? There are some who can, who want to, who enjoy it, who get everything they need from it and whose children and partners are happy and well balanced, but they're few. Most people can't hack it and, in the end, don't want to. This is why we drop out of jobs and careers; this is why many partnerships fail; this is why many end up in poverty if their partnerships fail; this is why many kids hardly know their parents; this is why women are deciding to have fewer or no children. All this I understand — it's obvious, to nearly half of us. What I don't understand is why the rest don't get it and do something about it, unless of course they're the power-hungry gang leaders described above.

Are you a well-trained, well-educated woman with a supportive employer paying a good wage, supportive colleagues, a supportive partner, children with standard (or certainly, not additional) needs, good health, ambition, multitasking skills in abundance and a solid angelic streak? That doesn't describe most of us — it certainly doesn't describe me. And even if it did, all it takes is for one of those areas to weaken (employer to go bust/child to develop a medical condition/partner to start working overseas) and it gets tougher still. What we're looking at is that in a perfect world it's pretty difficult combining a successful full-time career with being the 'managing parent' within the family but in our imperfect world it's doubly-well-nigh-impossible; women often decide that their family and health are more important; women drop out of the career workplace; women fail to 'achieve'; men continue to; the cycle continues. (For more detail on these issues, and to take them from the present day into the future, look at Chapter 8.) This has lead to impoverished people, jeopardised relationships and it chips away at society to the extent that we're stopping having children. How daft is that?

3

Unjust Governments

Sweden may not be perfect but it is at least partway along a tortu-
ous road towards equality. As this journey started with equalities
legislation in the 1960s and things are still fairly skewed then
perhaps we need to hurry and strengthen our own legislation so
that we can travel further along this road — and perhaps do it
better? As women we have a lot to offer in (amongst other things)
nurturing children and running countries. We're allowed to do
one but disallowed from the other. But if we were to form an equal
part of governments, would the methods, manners and results of
these governments change? This chapter looks at two issues: why
women aren't there and then, if governments were gender-
balanced, what might change by way of legislation and the
difference this could make to working mothers.

Governments don't do anything unless it suits them. They tell
the electorate what they want to hear, produce detailed figures to
underpin proposed policies, get themselves (re)elected, then do
whatever they choose. Sometimes they seem to go out of their way
to do the opposite of what they were elected to do, such as waging
war (electorates rarely want to do this), and whenever lobbied by

groups with strong political muscle (ie those whose revenues support the government), they cave in. This inverse law of government can be seen worldwide over the ages from the first elected caveman (probably, though evidence is sketchy) up till now. Electorates have come to expect nothing more, which is sad, but given human nature, hardly surprising. The appeasement record improves in the run-ups to elections, for obvious reasons, then plunges immediately afterwards. Just look at your own government over the past few decades and see for yourself. What stands out above all else is that the people in power don't mirror the people they serve. Politicians look, talk and smell different. And they're men. More than half of their electorate is female yet they've barely addressed women's issues.

But cynicism doesn't have to equal complacency – the more we understand, the more opportunity we have. And women understand things in a different way to men (if you disagree, have a look at Chapter 5). So could it be that a gender-balanced government, with as many women as men, bringing women's reasoning to issues alongside men's, would bring about sexually-equal policy and lead towards the beginning of true equality? If that's the case, we've a long way to go. In 2005, the greatest ever number of women served in parliaments around the world yet this relatively large proportion only accounted for 16 per cent of the total number of parliamentarians.[1] This compared to a minimum target of 30 per cent women serving in parliaments worldwide, set by the UN Women's Conference in Beijing in 1995. Some countries (such as Andorra, Burundi and Tanzania) have reached this target, but it's still relatively few.

Membership figures for the European parliament (2004 election) show that nearly a quarter are women (24.4 per cent).[2] Sweden tops the European league tables with 45 per cent of its MPs women, down to Hungary with 9 per cent. Rwanda has the highest proportion in the world, at 49 per cent (these figures are the percentage of women holding office in the lower or single house of the national parliamentary body). In 2005, women made up 32.2 per cent of New Zealand's parliament, compared to 28 per cent in 2002. The United States ranked 69th in the world, with 66 women in the US House of Representatives (or 15.2 per cent) and 14 female senators, or 14 per cent. So although women have made steady progress in elections since the UN Women's Conference in Beijing when women made up only 11.3 per cent of the world's lawmakers,[3] men still run the world.

In the UK, before the 1997 general election, the proportion of women MPs in parliament was 9 per cent. This rose to 18 per cent after that election due to the all-women shortlists adopted by the winning Labour party. This shortlisting policy was later found to be unlawful, and the following general election in 2001 saw the lowest proportion of women MPs for 20 years. It rose again to 20 per cent in 2005 following legislation to allow 'positive measures' including training and mentoring, 'twinning' (where two constituencies with the same likelihood of winning are paired, with a male candidate placed in one and a female in the other) and 'zipping' (where male and female candidates are placed alternately on candidate lists), in addition to all-female candidate lists.

In Spain a new sex equality bill has just been passed requiring that in national elections, political parties must present candidate lists containing at least 40 per cent of each sex (as well as requirements for business and electoral lists).[4] Positive discrimination is a difficult issue. Surely everyone needs to be judged on their merits, not offered a job based on their sex? But women are unable to succeed on merit alone in most elected assemblies because of discrimination in the selection process.

During the 1997 UK general election half of the shortlisted candidates in each safe Labour seat were women but only one in ten local parties selected a woman as their candidate.[5] When there's such a clear male bias in the selection process, and plenty of evidence that when the working hours and the general working culture are reasonable, women make as good a job of being MPs as men, then there's a case for measures that allow women a chance for equal representation. I can see why men don't want this – the perceived emasculation of men in many areas of life is bound to make men want to hold on to their remaining power. I daresay if I had a dick and balls I'd feel the same. Positive action is the only way that women are going to be 'allowed' into the political arena until social values and perceptions catch up, which is still a long, long way off (and is, anyway, determined in part by the normalising of women into senior roles, as much in politics as anywhere else, something that won't happen until we start getting there in sufficient numbers).

Research by Leni Wild in 2005 suggests that there are two possible approaches to getting women into power in sufficient numbers to make a difference: equality, and an approach made on the basis of difference.[6] The first is centred on women being entitled to be in politics in the same numbers and on the same terms as men and competing within the same rules. To succeed in this way, women must effectively become 'political men' – examples might be Margaret Thatcher in the UK in the 1980s or Condoleezza Rice in the US in the 2000s. Neither had young families while in the senior political scene, and both made 'tough' their motto. This tactic effectively precludes women who want to combine motherhood of young children with a political career. The second approach requires the rules themselves to be changed; something that's only likely to happen once there are sufficient numbers of women already in power to bring in positive legislation to enable and continue this. Both are necessary, as one feeds into the other. We need to get into politics in the first place if we're going to change the rules.

Would you bring up a family and work as an MP?

Can all this zipping, twinning and whirligigging make any difference to the day-to-day lives and careers of mothers? It might, if women bother to vote, and we do: women now sometimes cast their vote as regularly or more often than men in the UK, reversing the trend up to 1979; women might even vote more often, as shown in research on postal voting. In the US, more women than men vote overall,[7] and of those, there's a trend for more women to vote Democratic: 'In the pivotal states of Missouri, Montana, and Virginia, exit polls [for Senate elections] show that a majority of women cast their ballots for the victorious Democratic candidate, while a majority of men voted for the Republican opponent,' says a press release for the Center for American Women and Politics.[8]

Academic Susan Carroll adds:

> Women voted for change in this election. The exit polls provide compelling evidence that Democrats would not be in control of the new [2006] Congress without strong support from women voters.

This didn't result in a landslide for women representatives because so few were available for election; it does show that this more liberal (and more women-centred) political party gains women's vote – even if only marginally. It isn't yet the norm, however, for women to be as politically active, formally or informally, at most levels. Yet the chance to vote for a woman MP does increase our likelihood of turning out to vote.[9] Do we therefore vote for women solely on the basis of their sex, and, more to the point, should we? I guess this depends on whether, once women are in parliament, it makes any difference to the policies that those parliaments bring in: the Thatcherite years in the UK (1979–90) certainly didn't help the standard woman reach an equal level in the workplace.

Persuading suitable women candidates to run isn't always easy. Traditionally, 'much of the explanation of US women's political under-representation has been rooted in the notion that American women just don't seem to desire political office as much as American men do,' according to researcher Louise K Davidson-Schmich.[10] Although a study in 2001 found that the US electorate was increasingly receptive to women's candidacies for governor, the study concluded that women need more political experience at a high level and to be able to draw on available support systems in areas such as fund-raising and other daunting political activities.[11]

Perhaps we feel so fiercely independent that we won't ask for help, in contrast to men who are prepared to grab the help that's going. Without wanting to take advantage of help when it's offered, we're not going to get enough high-level experience to succeed. That's part of it. But another part is what it's actually like once we're there: apparently, the term 'melons' is an all too familiar cry of male MPs in the UK parliament at Westminster. What self-respecting woman would want to be there to listen to it? This baying was reported in a recent book by Boni Sones and Margarat Moran based on interviews with female MPs of the Blair era and it makes astounding reading.[12] And here's why: 40 per cent of MPs, for instance, are lawyers. Lawyers, particularly those old enough to be senior MPs, generally emerged through the public school system (the British private schooling of the upper middle classes) largely in single-sex environments. Privilege, a lack of understanding of the opposite sex and of anyone else who isn't part of the system, and consequent prejudices, all feed the injustices inherent in this ancient system. But I assumed that men have generally got enough common sense not to let others know how they think. Surely MPs would be hounded out of their workplace for demanding to 'roger' (have sex) colleagues, for juggling imaginary breasts and for crying 'melons' as women try to speak? Apparently not.

Add to this the cultural expectations we all have, men and women. We're not going to participate in something that's counter-culture unless we're pretty spunky people. Even to come near political office at a national level we need first to have experience in local politics and this can be pretty daunting to gain and keep. Research from Australia shows how some obvious constraints keep women out of local politics: timing (just when careers are taking off, milk is seeping) and the lack of childcare available, especially for single parents who comprised over 21 per cent of families in this particular study, 90 per cent of which were led by a mother rather than a father.[13] Evening meetings were seen to conflict with a woman's domestic responsibilities, with distance and the lack of public transport adding to the issues, particularly for women in country towns. Evening meetings could be difficult for older women who can be afraid of going out in the evenings alone. Then, the way that men often dominated meetings suggested that when women attended, many either deferred to the men or lacked the confidence to stand up and speak out. Much of this constraint is organisational but it's also based on how we feel deep down – the expectations we have of others and of ourselves. This quote from historian Gavin Long is enlightening: 'Australians have always treated their women a little worse than dogs.'[14] Harsh words – which were hopefully always an exaggerated generalisation. Times move on, yet underlying cultural feelings and expectations run deep.

Despite all this, there are still many politically ambitious women around and many who hope to combine a political career with motherhood. Yet it's when the family's needs kick in that real problems begin. These needs are well-known to most of the female electorate, mainly ignored by the male electorate and more importantly, by male-led parliaments. Until 1989, UK governmental debates usually began in the afternoon and ended after midnight. Barbara Follett, MP, explains why: 'Parliament was organised this way so that Victorian gentlemen MPs could work as lawyers and stockbrokers in the morning then run the country after lunch.'[15] She gives an example of how it worked:

> Big Ben was striking 2.00 am somewhere above my head. In the
> tea room, another member of the world's oldest parliament
> came staggering up to me, drunk as a skunk. He put his arm
> around me and said: 'Come and have a drink with me, darling.' I
> stood up to leave. 'No, thanks,' I said. 'I'm going to lie on the
> couch.' 'Let me lie on the couch with you!' he said as I walked
> away. I made my way down the cold corridor . . . lay down in the
> Lady Member's Room and covered myself with my coat. Seven
> other women lay around the room in uncomfortable positions.
> What would our constituents say about this? . . . what chance
> had we of solving their problems if we could not even get our
> own working hours sorted?

In the 1990s the House of Commons introduced earlier finishes so that MPs could go home at 10.30 pm after sitting an average of eight and a half hours a day. As Julie Mellor, chair of the Equal Opportunities Commission, says:

> The real issue here is not that current parliamentary working
> hours are too long but when they happen – outside normal
> working hours. When we surveyed would-be Parliamentary
> candidates on their experience of the selection process,
> Commons' working hours and methods were seen as a signifi-
> cant deterrent from coming forward as a candidate. That
> doesn't mean these people aren't fit to be MPs; it just means
> that they don't see why a life in politics means working in the

middle of the night . . . We don't want a Parliament that in effect says to MPs who are parents: 'choose between your political career and your family life'.[16]

This phenomenon isn't restricted to the UK. 'Parliamentary politics in Australia is a competitive domain,' says a report on women in parliament in South Australia, 'which has been set up for men, by men with no regard for women and which reflects male values. In common with many other institutionalised systems, parliament is characterised by a hierarchy based on competition. It is adversarial and male.'[17] The report goes on to state: 'There is a perception that the loudest voice and the most truculent approach wins, and the general level of aggression has been compared to a bear-pit.' Sittings commonly continue well into the evening and sometimes into the early hours of the next day. 'It would be extremely difficult, if not impossible for a person who has a day-to-day responsibility for running a family, to be able to combine this with the job of being an elected member,' concludes this section of the report.

As well as the appalling hours and behaviour in some chambers, commentator Anne Summers shows how the Australian media depict female politicians as frivolous, and expect them to conform to outdated female stereotypes. This makes it easy for their fellow politicians to collude in treating them badly. It may not be as overt as the melon-juggling in the UK parliament but it's equally undermining. It's thought that some women's political careers have failed despite the continuing support of the electorate because of this media portrayal.[18] In the US, too, media influence is extremely strong and can make or break campaigns; eyes are currently on Hillary Rodham Clinton: will she become the first female US president? We can be absolutely certain that her campaigning takes the media very seriously, with decisions of whether to portray herself as a cookie-baking earth-mother type or a tough career woman among the most important of her campaign.

Making change

Let's assume that there are enough suitable and dedicated women prepared to duck the verbal abuse and tolerate the hours and tough life of an MP: would they make any difference to the lot of the average woman? The answer seems to be yes. In elected assemblies where there are already large numbers of women it's been shown that the policies produced are more women-centred. The regional assemblies in Scotland and Wales have a relatively high number of women participants: the Welsh assembly became the first legislative body in the world with equal numbers of men and women when 30 women were elected to the 60-strong assembly in 2003.[19] Topics such as the social economy, equal pay and childcare have been more frequently addressed.

Researchers say that it's still too early to be sure, and that these results are within the context of an elected assembly with equality built into the original rules of the institution. Paul Chaney, of the Centre for Advancement of Women in Politics, describes how in the Welsh assembly, for instance, normal working hours are defined as 9.00 am to 5.30 pm and there is a requirement to take account of family responsibilities of members and their travel arrangements, as well as the rules of debate defining what language may be used.[20] One member of the Welsh assembly says: 'having a critical mass of women parliamentarians has made a difference to what we talk about, what we prioritise, what we do, and it's made a big difference about how we do it'. Another says: 'If you look at the committees that have succeeded in working in an inclusive way, they are predominately committees where women are ministers and . . . that makes a difference'.

Dario Castiglione and Mark E Warren, researchers working in the UK and Canada who have looked at relative representation in politics, agree that 'when representative bodies look like their constituencies, they do a better job of representing the full range of experiences, perspectives, and situations in society'.[21] American commentator Elizabeth Sherman adds her thoughts: 'One might say that women candidates and elected officials are "regendering" the role of the politician,' she asserts. 'Through their campaign themes and policy-making endeavours . . . women in the Congress and state legislatures have achieved notable successes, advancing a host of issues of particular concern to women, such as family leave, domestic violence, reproductive rights, and breast cancer.'[22]

So there is some good news. Despite this, it's easy for things to slip: there's a tendency among male chamber members to return to the antisocial hours normally encountered in political fora. In addition, researchers note that other factors need to be taken into account when looking at the positive social and women-centred policies that have already come from the new assemblies. These include general shifts in social attitudes as well as the rules built in to the assembly at inception, as noted above. They also say that only modest progress has been made in involving women, in a wider sense, in politics across society. Despite all this, researchers conclude that the Welsh and Scottish experiences are informing debate on how to approach sexual equality in European politics. But how can assemblies ever look like their constituencies when so few have equality written into the rules, when the more-equal selection processes are still being challenged and when, in general, working hours and practices exclude mothers from taking part? It's bizarre and offensive to think that, in the 21st century, were I to enter parliament and speak on behalf of my constituents, I might be heckled purely because of my sex.

What women think governments need to do

We've already seen how fast the world and the workplace are changing. The job of governments' (amongst other things) is to react to this change in order to deliver soundly functioning states. With more women coming into the paid workplace and a greater need for us to do so to bolster the economy and help resolve the skills shortages caused by the falling birth rate, governments need to legislate to allow women to function fully. As the last chapter saw, there are many factors that constrain women in this respect – the cost and availability of good childcare, flexibility of work contracts to allow for family commitments and emergencies, pay that's sufficient to encourage mothers to continue in paid work rather than to give up and so on. Many young women think about these issues before they decide whether or not to have children, see that the odds are stacked against them being able to continue their careers and see that legislation isn't keeping pace with needs.

Natasha Carpenter sees obstacles ahead should she decide to have children:

> They're trying, but the whole process of passing new legislation takes so long that by the time they've actually passed something it becomes outdated and outmoded so quickly. Whatever they try and do is always five years' too late. So they . . . need to think ahead of themselves, about what women want and what they need, or what they will need in five years' time as opposed to right now.

Sarah Nias, a 27-year-old part-time drama teacher and mother of a young son, says:

> Our government tries to encourage mothers to go back to work and contribute to society again, which is great, but they don't offer us any help. [My husband and I] are on a just-below-average wage and it doesn't seem worth it for us sometimes. I know somebody who lives near me who's a single parent and chooses to work for 16 hours a week and she has lots of financial help including childcare. She and I have worked out that she ends up taking home more money than we do. You do feel: is it worth it?

Dani, a Californian woman, is at the end of her tether:

> Imagine getting the kids ready for school while you take your
> shower and dress. One child is coughing. You go to work for
> eight hours then pick up the kids. He's still coughing. You go to
> the drugstore for cough medicine. You bought the food yester-
> day. You cook for dinner tonight. You wash at least one load of
> laundry every night. You read a bedtime story to the kids. Your
> second child is coughing. You don't stop for 16-plus hours.
> Now, tell me, do you need help with childcare, medical
> expenses and some vacation time?[23]

A 1999 UK Listening to Women consultation included women
reporting these hopes:

> . . .the biggest concern is trying to strike a balance between
> home and work. However, health care, good life-skills training
> for girls, flexible employment, violence, getting their voices
> heard and recognition of their role as carers, are also near the
> top of the priority list.[24]

This same consultation listed steps already taken by government to
address these issues and the priorities for future work, which
included combating the pay gap, making the work–home balance
easier, supporting women thinking of setting up a small business
and helping girls fulfil their potential through better careers
advice. Since then there have been gradual moves forward in many
areas to support mothers in the workplace, as well as more general
help for women to achieve social equality. These have included
changes to the benefits system in the form of new children's tax
credits, and allowing childcare costs to be paid or contributed to.
State nursery provision is also increasing and therefore allowing
more freedom and flexibility for mothers in work, though you

could argue that the nursery places offered to their children are often too time-constrained to be particularly useful from a child-care perspective. The Swedish model, for instance, where state-subsidised nurseries remain open throughout the day to care for children when formal sessions are over, is still a distant hope in the UK. However, the benefit to young children of well-equipped nurseries staffed by professional nursery teachers and nursery teachers is accepted and helps many in their career development.

Governmental reforms in Australia called New Welfare to Work are intended to decrease reliance on welfare benefits and move more people into the workplace. These list one of their target groups as principle carer parents and one of the new services as additional uncapped places for 'outside school care and Family Day Care'.[25] But are these reforms enough to make a difference to women when their primary objective is to get people back into work rather than to improve the equalities agenda? The reforms have been a long time in the making and follow on from 'substantial workplace reforms of 1993 and 1996' according to research from the Australian Chamber of Commerce and Industry.[26] This research shows how opponents of Australian workplace reform believed that making change to the Australian workplace, which allowed greater freedom for both employers and employees to decide their working patterns, would disadvantage working women and decrease women's pay and career opportunities. The research goes on to show, however, that earlier reforms to workplace relations have 'led to increased job security for women, higher pay for women, less disparity between female and male earnings and greater working opportunities for Australian women than ever before.'[27]

Joan Ruddock, a UK Member of Parliament, states that the most important modernising achievement to date has been to create 'government machinery that could deliver any kind of programmes that tried to advance women's agendas'.[28] This fits with the Australian research findings above. Whether or not this is the case worldwide, there's not going to be a reduction in the number of women-friendly policies once there's a greater number of female MPs. Even if there's no immediate advance in policies, at least we can feel someone familiar is representing us in parliament rather than some boor from another era. And as evidence shows, increasing the number of women MPs will increase the attention to women- and mother-friendly issues and therefore to increased legislation in these areas.

Welfare states worldwide and how they affect women in work

It's easy to think that the whole of the developed world is roughly equal when it comes to women's rights and status, position and earnings; the movies we see indicate that life is great everywhere that has flat-screen TVs. But Brennan, an American woman from Washington, DC, says:

> I want to have children some day, but I'm afraid of what their future might look like. The middle and lower classes are all struggling to get by, while the super-rich get rewarded with things like the estate tax repeal and outrageous tax breaks.[29]

Elizabeth, from New York City, adds:

> Things have gotten so bad for all working Americans that it's not even about women's issues any more. Worrying about women's issues is a luxury we hope to have again some day. Right now, it's about basic issues of health care and job security that affect all working people.

Overall, 65 per cent of women participating in the 2006 US AFL-CIO Ask a Working Woman Survey ranked legislation to make health care affordable first or second on a list of measures that would improve their lives. Laws to improve health care and retirement security are the top two priorities of women of all races and ethnicities. White, Latina, Asian American and Native American women rank legislation to help them out with childcare as their third priority, while African American women give that ranking to laws to challenge discrimination.[30] So the US, seen on our screens as pioneering an affluent lifestyle, on closer inspection appears to be in the throes of meltdown as far as citizens' and workers' rights go. While in the UK we're enjoying the fruits of years of campaigning for paternity leave and looking ahead to other anti-discriminatory legislation, with similar advances across Europe, many US women are worrying about losing their savings, health care and how they'll feed themselves in retirement. One illness can cost a family its future. As a report from The Project on Global Working Families survey states:

> The United States lags dramatically behind all high-income countries, as well as many middle- and low-income countries when it comes to public policies designed to guarantee adequate working conditions for families.[31]

It shows how, out of 168 countries studied, 163 guarantee paid leave to women in connection with childbirth but the US isn't among them. It's one of only five countries in total, and one of only two developed countries, which lack this provision. Australia, the only other developed country which doesn't provide paid leave to mothers, offers 52 weeks of unpaid leave, more than four times as much as the unpaid leave offered by the US through the Family and Medical Leave Act. In all, of the 168 countries surveyed, 45 give paid paternity or parental leave to fathers; 76 give mothers the right to breastfeed at work; 96 have legislated for paid annual leave; and 139 have paid leave for workers for short- or long-term illness. The US has no national legislation for many of these (though some states have separate legislation covering some of these areas). US income levels are decreasing relative to the cost of living, and as the women above testify, it's becoming increasingly difficult to manage and to ensure provision for illness or retirement. Because there are few positive social policies in place, US parents encounter increasing obstacles to caring for their children, far more than in many countries, both developed and less developed. The US situation terrifies many of its citizens and makes chilling reading; it underlines the necessity for decent social policy.

We depend upon our welfare state in the UK, and to differing extents across the developed world. In the UK we tend to see it in terms of a safety net of health care and benefits plus education provision – state-funded schools and nursery schools. Yet we're letting it move us towards becoming a 'caring state', as researcher A Leira explains: when there was no welfare state, responsibility for all forms of caring lay largely with families (plus charities, faith groups and similar picking up some of the burden).[32] In this situation women took the primary roles as carers, whether or not they also worked outside the home.

With the development of the welfare state, additional caring provision became available outside the home. The level of, and perceptions of, this provision has varied between countries, with UK and US parents primarily seeing themselves as clients of the welfare state, whereas Scandinavian mothers see themselves more as consumers of public services.[33] This is due to the more comprehensive welfare services offered as a matter of course to parents of all incomes and social class in Scandinavia. In the UK now, we see the government moving away from responsibility for some parts of our lives. For instance, it encourages us to make our own provision for retirement, claiming that it will be unable to fund pensions for our increasingly ageing population. Yet it also needs to ensure that the youngsters in the population – those going to become parents and whose taxes will underpin our economy – have the ability to work. There's been noticeably increased investment in nursery education, increased regulation of private childcare provision to assure standards and promises of this continuing. Yet until it's led by people who truly understand what it means, will it reach the level that's required for women to be able to say – as some can in Scandinavia – that they can afford to have children because they know that the social fabric and the state provision allows them to be mothers and also to have a career?

But to what extent does the Scandinavian model work? We've seen how it has polarised the Swedish workforce by sex – women into the public sector and men into the private, and hasn't helped alleviate the glass ceiling. In Finland in the 1950s, new legislation was brought in to offer 'home help' to women who needed to work on their farms, thus allowing them to run their homes too. It became a godsend for working women whose children were unwell (a carer coming into the home to look after the child), allowing them to continue working, and now the service includes allowing elderly people to stay at home rather than go into residential care.[34] Some aspects of this are familiar. The concept of cover for sick children, however, seems too miraculous to be true – yet was present half a century ago in Finland.

This policy's later development allowed women to build careers once they'd moved away from farm work. The other part of Finnish social provision that's allowed women to participate fully in their careers has been out-of-home childcare. Half of Finland's social services expenditure goes into daycare. This stems from 1970s-Finland, when part-time work began to recede, with full-time work taking over as the norm for everybody (this full-time working model was unusual, even in Scandinavia). In this situation, adequate childcare was essential. This was in an environment where women had worked the land equally with men and where the concept of 'housewife' was alien, rather than the more usual gender split role stemming from industrialisation, which divided roles early on. Politically, then (and with a social democratic government), it was simpler than in some other nations for Finland to find a way through the childcare and housework issues once labour moved from the farms. With our more highly defined and separated roles in much of the world, and with the social attitudes reflected in some MPs' behaviour and in tranches of our society, governments need to move further in creating a social backdrop that allows women fully into the workplace.

The Finnish model of social policy was built on a strong economy but in the 1990s, recession hit. Along with high unemployment, it brought a dismantling of, and a new cynicism about, much of its social provision.[35] Although legislation remains in place for local authorities to provide social care, financial cuts make this difficult. Its economy is, like all in the developed world, dependent to a large extent on foreign trade and international markets; multinationals need to be based in countries with stable, educated workforces such as those with developed welfare states. So isn't it best to keep the social provision? The initial reasoning may seem straightforward, yet balancing the economy is anything but. The Finnish example shows that it's not so easy, and for governments to weather economic downturns as well as booms, perhaps there's an element of luck involved. But whichever way the luck blows, getting skilled women into the workforce in adequate numbers is essential for economic development. The Finnish government says that recent structural reforms in pensions, public spending cuts and higher employment now allow a better financing of the welfare system.[36] Finnish women say that 'it is obvious that power and money are still controlled by men.'[37] With only 37 per cent of the Finnish parliament female, perhaps that's unsurprising.

Sponsored babies

When governments really wake up to issues, they act. Take the fall in the fertility rate (see Chapter 2). Although in the UK this couldn't yet be termed a crisis, in some countries governments have felt the need to take action: in Japan the government has sponsored speed dating to encourage new couples and consequent progeny. In Portugal the more children you have, the lower your pension contributions. In South Korea in vitro fertilisation treatment is reimbursed. Other, looser family-friendly policies encourage us to have more children by helping out in a more general way, such as the child credit and benefit system described for the UK, echoed across the world as tax incentives of different forms, as well as parental leave and government sponsored or subsidised childcare. Yet in the UK we rely on work–life balance and child support policies (and immigrant labour) rather than overtly going all-out to increase our fertility rate (which sounds like much more fun).

Population expert Jonathan Grant says:

> As a society we've got some stiff options to face. Do we really want to maintain our current welfare state? Or are we going to ration it, or are we going to pay more taxes? Because if we pay more taxes then we can address some of the issues of population ageing. Or do we want to maintain our current living standards, and if we do then we're going to have to think about trying to increase our fertility rates.[38]

The government estimates that getting women to participate more fully in the workplace, and at the right levels, would increase the contribution to the UK economy by between £15/US$30 billion and £23/US$46 billion a year.[39] This makes up for the lost contribution of quite a few unborn babies. You can see why the government is suddenly liking us so much.

Back to the chopping board

Family-friendly legislation isn't the only type that aims to support working mothers. Another problem many women face is trying to get back to work after a complete break or after working part-time. We might no longer have family responsibilities. We might need to start again by retraining, or find work with another organisation. Yet research shows that, depending on how old we are at this stage, it might not be so easy because of age discrimination.

A study by the Chartered Institute of Personnel & Development shows that workers have only five years of freedom from age bias during their working lives. 'People between the ages of 35 and 40 are the only group unlikely to be deemed too old or too young for a job,' the reports says.[40] In the UK we've banned age discrimination from 2006. Will legislation make any difference? One American worker, Brian Meadows, quoted in the report, thinks not:

> Here in the US, age discrimination is illegal, and has been for some years. All that happens is they find other 'reasons' when they find out roughly how old you are (you don't put date of birth or age on an American resume). I drove 200 miles to an interview within Pennsylvania, only to be told that 'they wanted to appoint a local candidate' . . . All that the age discrimination legislation will mean in the UK . . . is that you'll get to hear some more inventive reasons if employers think you're not the 'right' age.

The legislation that Brian's concerned about, the Employment Equality (Age) Regulations 2006, covers discrimination in employment, training and education and applies to the self-employed and well as the employed, former employees, students and former students and other categories of worker.[41] It's too soon yet to say whether Meadows is right.

As Patrick Carroll of the Pension and Population Research Institute points out, when women are competing for top jobs there's more workplace pressure on us to have less children, so the birth rate will fall further.[42] Governments could extrapolate to decide that women shouldn't have that choice, that men should continue to be the top earners, women continue to take the career breaks and that more women at home in this way will lead to a rise of the birth rate. Surfing the internet shows that there are plenty of people out there who think this is a great idea. That's one way of seeing it. The other is that demographics are pushing governments — even the more blinkered ones — to get older workers and returners back into the workforce, and this entails passing the sort of legislation that's going to help, not hinder, our coping and hence our careers. That's the optimist in me talking.

4

UNJUST PERCEPTIONS OF MOTHERS

We know we're good. Our line managers confirm it; research underpins it (even if some MPs can't accept it). Yet we're paid less and have fewer opportunities to do the work we want to do. Research from the United States General Accounting Office[1] into women's earnings and work patterns concludes that in the US many people just don't think that women should be treated equally at work and shouldn't get to senior positions at all, certainly not once we have children. These perceptions automatically lower the chances of gaining responsibility and promotion.[1]

Previous chapters have alluded to people's perceptions of women in the workplace and how strongly these contribute to the collapse of our careers once we have children. This chapter looks more closely at what people really think of us.

If you haven't had kids and you work in a company full of younger people, there may be real parity between the sexes. Twenty-three-year-old media worker Natasha Carpenter of London says:

The money's crap; everyone I know is on crap money; everyone in the industry is on crap money, both women and men. On the lower levels there's no distinction between the sexes when it comes to salary in the media.

As Alison Wolf, a professor of public sector management, says:

For women who work as men traditionally do – in comparable jobs without taking breaks for childbearing and without going part-time – being female has become irrelevant to career success.[2]

If we're one of the younger careerists, do we ever stop to think why some of the older women in the organisation are doing more minor roles, and earning significantly less, than us? Bob, a neighbour of mine, has recently taken early retirement to run the family home. Talking about his wife, who works in the public sector, he says:

Mandy's a team coordinator, something that sounds responsible, and she does many different tasks that require certain skills but she's paid only £7/US$14 an hour. Her organisation is full of women with families doing these responsible jobs for little more than the minimum wage. Employers depend on them but they don't have to pay more than that because there are so many women looking for flexible work. They have their pick of them.

Employers who assume that experienced and skilled women will do this work for low pay have, so far, been proved right and so their perceptions continue unaltered. But the jobs are exhausting, not simply due to the responsible nature of the work but because there's no motivation, no prospect of promotion (while still retaining the flexibility), no reason to do it apart from the wages. Perhaps some of us, while rushing to chair the next meeting, don't realise that in 20 years we ourselves could be doing that part-time admin job. And perhaps our current assumptions, based on the social environment we grew up with, are helping to perpetuate the inequality that, later on, we may ourselves be swallowed up by? So in reading about others it's good to remember that we all have a base level of bias in the way that we think.

Employers' perceptions of mothers

Like the MPs described in the last chapter, many employers are of the generation that thought women should be at home. And when their employees go on maternity leave or leave early to collect the kids it's a real pain and they see it biting into the bottom line. There's some interesting research being done on this. Shelley Correll has spent 18 months looking at US employers' attitudes and why working mothers' salaries tend to decrease with each additional child. She's called her findings 'The Motherhood Penalty'.[3] She started by writing two fictional applications for a marketing director post then asked a group of undergraduate students to look at them and decide which applicant they would choose. Each had equivalent qualifications and experience and no indication of sex or family status: the students marked them as equal candidates. She then gave the same applications to a new set of students to evaluate but this time she indicated that both applications were from women and that one of them had young children. The childless women 'got the job' 84 per cent of the time, the mother only 47 per cent of the time and, when preferred, was offered a starting salary of £5,500/US$11,000 less than the childless women. Then Correll went to employers to test it further. Using 300 pairs of CVs and covering letters she 'applied' for a number of mid-level marketing jobs. Both were from women; one was relocating 'with her family' and it was clear that she had young children; the other was simply relocating. The fictional non-parent was invited to twice as many interviews as the fictional parent. Correll is kinder to employers than many of us would feel: 'It's not that employers don't like mothers,' she says, but that 'cultural ideas of motherhood are seen as pretty incompatible with cultural ideas of the workplace.' A committed worker, she concludes, is expected to devote enormous amounts of time, drop everything at a moment's notice and work late and at weekends. She adds that 'the cultural logic of "intensive" mothering in US society . . . assumes that the "good mother" will direct her time and emotional energy towards her children without limit'. That the young students felt the same way points to at least one further generation of bias ahead.

Economist Professor Richard Berthoud has also looked at how employers' prejudices become clear during the UK recruitment process.[4] His research shows that mothers are about 40 per cent less likely to be offered a job than an average white, able-bodied man. He looked at 'penalties' for various types of people, going from the norm of the white male. Against that yardstick, Pakistani and Bangladeshi women have a 'penalty' of 29 per cent; the disabled have a penalty of 16 per cent, women with children under 11 who have a partner have a penalty of 37 per cent and lone mothers with young children have a penalty of 41 per cent.

A 2005 survey of UK recruitment agencies (which locate candidates for posts on behalf of employers) carried out by the umbrella organisation The Recruitment and Employment Confederation found that 75 per cent of agencies said that they had experienced discrimination by employers against pregnant women or women of childbearing age.[5] A third of these agencies said that a good proportion of employers showed this discrimination, even though it's illegal, and nearly half said that it's highest among smaller employers. Nearly two thirds said that the situation was either remaining static or getting worse. This 'small employers' finding is interesting.

Sarah Veale, the UK Trade Unions Congress' head of equality and employment rights, confirms that:

> Employers exercise prejudice against people who have competing demands on their time outside the workplace, such as mothers of small children. While larger companies are better about hiring people who need to work flexibly, small firms tend to be more nervous.[6]

And this makes sense. If we're running a small organisation we have fewer staff to step in to cover an absence, we have a thinner spread of skills and less resources generally. Anti-discrimination legislation worldwide only applies to organisations above a certain size because it's understood that very small enterprises simply can't afford, for instance, to place wheelchair ramps throughout the premises. An example from the US: when Congress passed the Pregnancy Discrimination Act in 1978, barring employer prejudice in hiring, firing or treatment of women who are expecting a child, it applied only to companies with at least 15 workers.[7] The introduction of maternity rights and pay has understandably been difficult for some of these employers. With paternity rights now on many nations' agendas, how, they ask, are we to cope? Yet can governments tell smaller employers that they don't need to offer these benefits? Many growing employers consider whether it's worth expanding above the national thresholds of staff numbers and therefore needing to provide additionally for their employees (ramps, stakeholder pensions, etc) so that perhaps it's better not to expand at all. Which is bad news for the economy. So when Veale continues to say that 'Ministers should encourage employers to allow job-sharing in senior posts and expand affordable, good-quality childcare,'[8] she may be right, but is it practical to the average employer and more than that, does it seem sensible to the average employer, whose perceptions are perhaps a little off the 21st century mark? For most, just keeping up with legislative requirements is difficult enough. Adding an in-house crèche and the organisational complications (and in some employers' perceptions, added costs) of job-sharers can be a non-starter.

Cultural norms

US economist Evelyn Murphy describes how employers think that women change once they become mothers: '. . . managers assumed their work-life conflict would slow them down. And if they did ask to work part-time for a while, their salaries and career possibilities were penalised far out of proportion to the time they put into their kids.'[9] Murphy goes on to argue that although some women would make the choice to become lower-paid workers with less responsibility once they had children, this is a choice that should be made by the woman herself yet frequently it's made via the assumptions of the employer. Murphy finds that US perceptions and values are rooted in the 1950s. So what should the 21st-century perception be? Is it reasonable to state that becoming a parent makes no difference at all to a woman's work and productivity?

Here's 38-week-pregnant Anna, who's just started her maternity leave:

> Mentally I did start preparing myself to leave. I think perhaps, in some ways, my heart went out of the job a little bit towards the end. It's like when you're going on a really long holiday you almost start winding down, don't you? The difference was I was out of the door by 5.30 every day. I didn't work late any more because rest is really important when you're pregnant. So your priorities do start to change. I did get a bit stressed and my boss was like: 'It's not worth it, think of the baby, don't get stressed.'

Of course there's going to be a tugging of loyalties at times, and a need for readjustment – but this has to come from both sides. Employers who throw their hands up in horror without looking at the broader picture – of what the recruitment market's doing, and what mothers can bring to the workplace, are blinkering themselves from opportunities. Anna's employer had a more caring – and rational – approach.

As described in Chapter 2, employers also base their perceptions of workers' productivity (and therefore our worth) on the amount of time they see us. If we're not in ready view we lose some of our worth. This is backed up with research into the pay gap which shows employers' prejudice. Women are more likely than men to take any family care time allowance (some UK employers offer a number of working days a year as a maximum that parents or carers generally may take to look after their children or elders when sick). Men generally try to fit such responsibilities into flexitime, annual leave or their own sick days. Employers see that an absent worker is conforming less to their ideal worker norm and so give other workers preferential treatment when it comes to promotions and pay increases whether or not the hours worked are in fact the same.[10] Some parents work a slightly shortened week to achieve the same outputs then see colleagues who work longer hours to the same outputs preferred over them. It rewards inefficiency.[11] These employers aren't meaning to be prejudiced, they just can't see as much work is being done and forget that a day spent working from home may well be more productive.

Our broader social expectations of a woman's role push us further away from job success in many cultures. In Spain, for example, normal working hours include an early start, a lunch break of several hours through which many women are expected to cook, eat, then sleep, and then a late end to the working day. How is this reconciled with school hours or global working hours? How can working mothers operate within and outside this 12-hour working day? And how can they do more than simply operate when for a successful career they also need to carry out the networking and additional graft necessary? Given this, it's amazing to find that 97 per cent of Spanish women still feel that the family is 'an essential value'. This is against an infrastructure where national spending on the family is only one quarter of the European average, with a political structure of different autonomous geographical regions making it difficult for overarching research to be carried out and policies to be introduced. Perhaps it's unsurprising that Spain's birth rate is so low as to have reached crisis point (fertility rates are down from 2.8 to under 1.2 children per woman from 1975 to 2002). It's kept even at that low level only due to massive immigration into some regions (one region reports half of its children being born to immigrant families). And all this despite 36 per cent of Spain's families saying that they haven't had the number of children they would like to have.[12] It's simply too difficult.

Employers talking

The surveys above show how employers react to the prospect of employing a mother. Because it's illegal for them to show discrimination, they're not generally forthcoming about their feelings. There are some roundabout ways of gleaning their inner thoughts. A US lawyer, Eve Markewich, who works with employers, doesn't feel that discrimination is increasing in the US despite statistical evidence to the contrary. She says that the increased level of complaints reflect instead the attitudes of modern working women who are higher paid and better educated than their predecessors, with more at stake when they lose a job. They're also increasingly conscious of their ability to sue for perceived discrimination. Another US lawyer, Will Hannum, presents the employer's side by saying how employers sometimes have to make difficult decisions about which employees to keep and which to lose. 'If you're pregnant or if you're disabled, you've got rights,' he says, 'but as an employer, trying to respect those rights while running a business can be a real challenge and it may be that employers are getting tripped up on that,' he says.[13]

Graham works as a human resources director of a medium-sized sales-based company based in southern England. He describes how his company tries to balance work/parenting issues:

> We had one saleslady who wanted part-time work. We were happy to accommodate this but because all the other sales staff had to work weekend and evening shifts we required that this worker also had her fair share of weekend and evening shifts. Weekends for her were particularly difficult and she said, 'Well, I just can't do them'. She felt that we were discriminating against her and went through a long internal appeal process with us. In the meantime she'd come back full-time with us to protect her employment but she only spent one day with us before she went off sick with stress so that exacerbated the difficult relationship. We'd been in dispute with her for four months, all that time she'd been off sick, we parted ways and she went to an employment tribunal. The result was unsatisfactory for both of us because by the time she brought a sex discrimination complaint against us she was out of time. She was being legally represented so she should have been properly advised but she wasn't. What that left us with was the sex discrimination part being thrown out by the tribunal. We never knew whether we had discriminated against her or not; we would have liked to have known.

We asked Graham whether, where it's worked and mothers have come back successfully into the business, this has created any additional advantage, such as increased loyalty by the staff concerned: 'I'd like to think that if you help a mother to re-enter the business that she would be loyal. I've not seen much evidence of it,' he says. He then describes women who've come back to work and been highly successful as well as those who have re-entered the business on a part-time basis and then six months later have left because they've decided that they don't want to work:

> For small employers of six people, say, having to cope is very difficult. My attitude is that you just have to do the best you can to accommodate the person who's returning. We try very hard to protect our employees from our nastier instincts, our business instinct.

Women as employers

And it's not just male employers and managers. Suzie, a British woman, says:

> My new line manager is very ambitious and encourages everyone else to be like her: to come in early, work late and work evenings and weekends at home. No male line manager in my organisation would try to get away with what she asks of us but as a woman she seems untouchable. It's making my life a misery, eroding the balance I've tried so hard to achieve between my work and home lives.

Another woman describes how her female boss arranges meetings late in the day and inevitably requires her to spend her one home day a fortnight sorting out work issues. The boss herself has two teenage sons. 'I don't understand,' says this worker, 'how she can be so hard-nosed, when she knows exactly what it's like to work and raise kids at the same time.'[14] Although few of us think of each other as 'the sisterhood' in some 60s feminist way, it's still shocking, at some level, when women aren't supportive towards other women.

Nicki Defago looks at the issue of bosses (male and female), colleagues, mothers and work in her book *Childfree and Loving It!*[15] She says:

> Some childfree people have big chips on their shoulders and their bleating that 'it's not fair' is redolent of the children they're bleating about. To others, a few extra hours in the office is a small price to pay for the freedoms bestowed by not being permanently bound to a school timetable. Most aren't whingeing, they just want their own lives to be respected in the way that parents' lives automatically are.

In other words, it takes all sorts. Defago goes on to describe parents who take any child-sickness leave as their own sick leave where non-parents don't have that opportunity – or choose not to take advantage of the system.

Senior civil servant Anne speaks about the part-time workers in her department:

> Part-timers are a very good deal for employers because they try to do the same job in fewer hours. Peter [her husband] is doing the same job as he did full time but doing it four days a week. Part-timers are very productive; they tend not to stop for long chats, they don't take doctors' and dentists' appointments during working hours. Often they're very focused and do a very good job for employers.

Male and female, employer and employee: there's a huge variety of attitudes and actions right across the spectrum. We can be pleased that legislation is increasingly in place to protect us from the 'nastier instincts' of employers. It's also worth remembering that it's not always a clear-cut case of 'us and them'. Some employers try very hard; some workers don't.

'I know that as soon as I start a family,' says Sheree, a US worker, 'my employer will do the minimum that they can get away with. I've seen it happen to other women who've been sidelined and have eventually left. My company won't break the law but they'll break me.'

Australian Melissa Kemper, a general manager at an IT consultancy, says that:

When I was looking at returning I was apprehensive about telling employers I was a new mother. I wasn't sure if I should bring it up. Because of my past experience with my previous employer, I was concerned that I'd be put on the bottom of the list. There's a perception that you'll either get pregnant again, or your child will get sick and you'll need to take more time off.[16]

But the fact is that our children might get sick, and we might need to take time off. Lee Lusardi Connor, in a US article, relates how 'asking for a change in schedule to accommodate your family obligations can give you a quick image makeover – from player to worker bee'.[17] She imagines how our work contracts are rewritten to state: 'We'll let you have a life, but you can forget about career growth.' Marcia Brumit Kropf continues in the same piece: 'Working on a flexible schedule can get you labelled as being uncommitted or regarded as less valuable, which is interesting, because the reason you get these arrangements in the first place is that you are valuable.'

There are contradictions at play. On the one hand employers can't manage without us – imagine losing such a substantial and committed proportion of the workforce if we all stopped trying so hard to make it work. Yet employers stop counting us as key players because of a few missed hours and more than that – in the expectation of a few missed hours.

Sue, mother of three and full-time in-house IT consultant, says:

It's crazy – they're expecting me to fail. Yes, I do work fewer hours some weeks, but hardly ever. And I get more work done as I'm driven, committed and more than that, I'm good at my job. They thought that for ten years, and now suddenly they think the opposite. When are they going to wake up?[18]

Other organisations are more open to the equality agenda. Jenny Bell, manager of a community farm, describes her employer's approach:

The company I work for are really good, they're very sensitive to women, the needs of women workers and mothers, and also women getting ahead in the job into managerial roles. They encourage women to go on courses which are specifically for women and how to deal with a male-dominated workforce, etc. I work with a woman who brings her children to work sometimes if they're ill or if she can't get a babysitter. They sometimes come into the office which is really nice to see.

Good employers

What does this actually mean? Various websites designed for working mothers have sections listing 'good employers'. One of these, a UK site called Mothers@Work, seeks nominations for 'employers who have a good work–life balance attitude and who have demonstrated their commitment to this'.[19] It goes on to describe these employers as those who have 'a positive and personal attitude to individuals' needs, whether that be flexible working, part-time working, job shares, childcare provision, home working – things that take them over and above the legal requirements of the UK.' The US magazine *Working Mother* lists its top 100 employers each year. One of these, in 2004, was Harvard University, where flexible timetabling, 'family and parental leave, and child-care options, including scholarships to defray the costs of day care . . . full medical benefits to employees who work half time or more and tuition assistance programs that enable employees to continue their education' are all available.[20] The magazine has a number of rigorous criteria for selection to the list in the areas of: flexibility; representation of women, particularly in upper management; child care; advancement of women; family-friendly corporate culture; and leave for new parents. Chapter 8 looks in more detail at what some employers are providing for parents. As a taster, here's what Peter Eriksson, who works in the public sector, has experienced:

> The department . . . allows all sorts of flexible working. My part-time is flexible to the extent that I don't have a fixed day a week and I plan two or three weeks ahead. I don't have to be at home on a particular day to do a particular thing, it's just that one day a week it's very useful to be home to cut the grass or clean the house or do the ironing; be here when the gasman comes. Sometimes it's a Monday or sometimes a Friday and I put that in my diary at work so everybody knows ahead when I'm not going to be there.

This type of flexibility sounds unbelievably wonderful, even to many of us working in the public sector. His wife Anne Eriksson is at a more senior level and explains how it works for her:

> Seventeen years ago, part-time women were still relatively rare but I was always quite disciplined about saying 'no, I'm not going to a meeting with someone more senior than me at 4 o'clock on whatever afternoon'. I'd have gone home by then. And they were okay about that, perhaps more so than many

organisations would be even today. If I need to leave early and be home for a parents evening, as long as I'm not doing it every week, then we're fortunate to be in jobs that are flexible enough to allow that. And you're working all the hours you're supposed to; it's not as if you're stealing time from your employer. There are lots of people, fathers and mothers, who work flexibly around things like school appointments.

So there are employers out there who take this seriously and put thought and money into making it work. There are good reasons for this. The US-based Childcare Partnership Project says in relation to an employer providing childcare for its employees' families: 'Childcare is central to the economic well-being of families, businesses, and communities.[21] According to recent surveys, businesses with childcare programmes report workplace improvements and bottom-line savings.' It cites the following benefits: boosting recruitment, reducing staff turnover, lowering absenteeism, increasing productivity, strengthening the business image, as well as helping to prepare the children to be tomorrow's workforce.

How colleagues see working mothers

We know our bosses (sometimes) have problems reconciling our divided loyalties when we have children. But what about colleagues – the people we work with rather than work for? Is it any of their business, do they care, and if so, what are they thinking?

Katerina, a US project manager, surprised herself with her reaction when she had to cover for a colleague who became pregnant.[22] During the maternity leave period Katerina took on most of her colleague's workload with no additional pay and found herself resentful. Then the colleague worked reduced hours when she came back to work after having her baby. Katerina says:

I felt so guilty. I can't imagine how tough it must be to work and have a baby. I really wanted to support [her]. But to be honest, I was also angry. I felt like she was taking advantage of me.

In that situation, although it's our bosses' responsibility to redress the workload balance, where this doesn't happen colleagues understandably feel put out. Alan, a UK worker, sees it this way:

I don't see why people with families get all the benefits. I'm middle-aged and have worked hard to get where I am and I'm exhausted. I could do with the flexible working that my company gives people with families but they don't extend this to me. I have to keep working to pay off a huge debt of my ex-wife's but don't get any of the benefits of a family or family life.

Frances discovered that people saw her differently once she was back from maternity leave:

I've been there longer than anybody else now, but because I've had these absences (I took a year off with my second son because I realised the error of my ways with the first [only taking four months]), you're not held in the same esteem. You also lose out on pay rises; you're bound to fall behind because you've had a year and a bit out, but it takes a lot of hard work to get back to how you were perceived before. The people who've arrived since then or during my absences, I get the feeling they don't really understand who I am or what I can do.

On the other hand, Shenagh, a senior civil servant working in New Zealand, finds that:

I have always felt totally supported and that having children has been something everyone has been proud of for me, interested in me for it and positive. If anything I have enjoyed the company of my male colleagues of work even more, when we talk about things other than children. We have an extremely supportive environment here for mothers, but in all my workplaces (perhaps slightly less so at [a private sector company]) I have felt the support as a parent.

Some work areas have their specific problems when it comes to colleagues' perceptions. Academics who are also mothers feel a 'particular form of attribution bias', according to Joan C Williams in her report 'Hitting the Maternal Wall'.[23] Before academics have children, while they're away from their places of work, colleagues assume that they're at conferences or writing. Once these women have children and return from maternity leave, colleagues assume that any absences are spent looking after the children, even if they're working elsewhere:

> Childless women are understandably pained when they are asked to countenance a shift in workplace norms that would make it easier for women to have children. For those who feel they sacrificed having a baby themselves through what author Sylvia Hewlett called 'creeping non-choice,' this wistfulness can easily turn to anger if they are asked, for example, to take over for a colleague out on parental leave.

Even those who made a solid choice not to have children get caught up in it: 'They may feel that policies that help mothers reinforce the perception that all women are mothers, which in turn feeds the perception that women without children are unnatural,' says Williams.

Women undergraduates see women academics all the time during their studies. The students tend to think, unsurprisingly, that the academic world is gender-equal. But things are far from how they seem.

Jill Lebihan of Sheffield Hallam University, says:

> The assumption is that women are not discriminated against . . .
> I find that incredibly shocking. They think they have equal pay.
> They see the increasing number of female academics and feel
> reassured, but they don't realise that most are hourly paid or on
> short-term contracts. They have no idea about the hierarchy.

Lebihan's comments are from a feature in the *Times Higher Educational Supplement* called 'Women are still 15 per cent cheaper',
showing how the pay gap applies equally on campuses as off, for
the same reasons, and leads to a false sense of security among
young women students.[24] The feature goes on to quote Lebihan in
the context of young women's marks going down in the second
year of study: 'The women move in with men and they start doing
all the housework. It's depressing.' The male undergraduates
perceive the women as the house workers; it seems that the
women themselves see it this way, too.

Those women academics who continue working after having
children and career breaks are continually hit in their pay, then in
their research results and therefore later again in their pay. Too
few female academics have research records good enough to be
included in the prestigious assessment of universities' research
achievement, the Research Assessment Exercise (RAE). While 64
per cent of men were selected by their managers to have research
work submitted in the last RAE, only 46 per cent of women were.
This difference wasn't because of gender discrimination by
managers but by work failing to reach the required standard
because of 'deeply rooted' inequalities in higher education, such
as the failure to properly take into account the effect of maternity
leave on research careers.[25]

Scientists have specific issues to overcome as well. The
Australian scientist Jane Curry has spoken to female colleagues

who've been unwilling or unable to fight the particular culture of long hours, set deadlines and research protocols, even before health and safety issues around pregnancy in the lab are taken into account.[26] Curry talks about one former colleague who was planning to stop work altogether once her baby was born.

> It turned out that my colleague, the perfectionist, didn't see science as a worthy career when she couldn't give it 60 to 70 hours over 6 days a week. Part-time wasn't an option, because you can't do part-time science. And even if she could, she didn't think her supervisor would let her. Did she ask, I countered? Yes, and she wasn't convinced that it would work.

This colleague had found a lack of understanding for parents who try to balance the rigours of scientific research with family demands. 'If an experiment doesn't work, I don't want them to automatically think that I didn't put enough time into it because I ran off to the sitter at four,' said Curry's colleague. Professional respect, undiminished after six years in the lab, was important to her. 'And no experiment is going to be as important as my child.' Another of Curry's female scientist colleagues is going back to work but into a corporate role, not back into laboratory research. Her reasons are slightly different but hit the same notes. Implying that part-time just won't work out, she says:

> I'm tired of fighting the long hours. I asked, and they said they didn't have a policy, and I was welcome to try, but I'm not so sure. I probably wouldn't be able to keep my project because it would take too long for me to publish, and another postdoc would take over as first author.

She's being asked to give a definite time for returning so that her computer time can be scheduled five months in advance. But 'I've never done this before,' she says. 'I'm supposed to know how long it will take for the baby to sleep through the night, and how tired I will be, so that I can schedule computer time five months in advance?'

Our partner's perceptions and predicament

The researcher Scott Coltrane tells us that husbands and wives live in different worlds and that every marital union actually consists of two distinct marriages: his and hers.[27] This is from looking at men's and women's perceptions of who does which chores around the home. He finds a marked disparity between what women feel that they and their partner do, and what men feel. There are interesting reasons for these different perceptions (our recollection of the tasks we perform varies according to how commonplace they are, how much they are felt to 'contribute' and other reasons) which are useful to bear in mind. While we may be seething at the relative inequality of the sharing of the chores, he might not understand this and might genuinely feel that his contribution is equal, or greater, than ours. As well as that, other contributions such as bringing home more money, staying more hours in the office or mending the shelves might, to him, make up for our collecting the kids and attacking the ironing pile. When our partners see their contribution to domestic work as being equally balanced while we feel that we're drowning under a pile of additional chores and responsibilities, it needs talking about. But one consistent characteristic within couples who become parents is that communication changes – there's simply less time to spend quietly getting into your partner's mind frame and see how s/he's doing. It's easy to make assumptions and come to conclusions ('he's a selfish bastard!/she only works half the week!') when, if it were possible to talk fully about it, the reality is that he genuinely doesn't see it.

Jenny Bell, yet to have children, feels that men are aware and considerate of these issues:

I think especially as you see more men playing more of a role at home looking after children, and women going out to work instead, I think we're going to see some quite interesting developments in relationships and how men and women work together as a partnership to both earn the money they need to earn and bring up children.

For Anna, pregnant with her first child, the support of her partner is essential:

Housework was pretty much 50/50 while I was still working. But now I'm not working, so I'm quite enjoying doing most of the shopping and cooking and cleaning and washing and I think he appreciates that, but I think in two weeks when the baby's born then everything will change. It will go back to being 50/50 or even 90/10 with him doing everything. Because I'll be breast-feeding every two hours and won't have the time to do anything, especially in the first few months and hopefully then it'll get easier. You need a man who's going to [be supportive]. It's got to be a joint thing that you both want, unlike the old-fashioned view. In my parents' day my dad wasn't even in the hospital when the baby was born and he hasn't changed a nappy in his life. It's got to be even – it's got to be something you both want and if you both want it you've got to be willing to put everything into it.

Recent court rulings giving increased alimony awards to the divorcing wives of wealthy couples have raised debate. People's perceptions leap from the newspaper page. For instance, Dan Bell writes about how women want to stop working to spend time with their families, whereas men have no choice but to get out there and earn the cash.[28] In these cases, why are the ex-wives awarded money as though they had made a life sacrifice whereas in fact they have been privileged to have been supported thus far? He continues:

> Men are in a double bind. They are expected to support the decision of their wife to become a mother, but are then told that they are chauvinists for standing in the way of their spouse's career. They are required to work long hours to be providers, but then held in contempt for not being fathers. The upshot is that they are respected and valued as neither.

These views echo those of the divorced fathers, now made to pay more. Of course, these aren't the attitudes of every father but it does remind those of us who take the 'new man' for granted, in his unthinking acceptance that women and men are equal and working together towards a fair family unit, that the old-fashioned views still pervade.

Researcher Esther Dermott recently found that, contrary to our impressions of many fathers as 'new men', new fathers not only continue to work the same hours as before but most of them want to work those hours.[29] Another report states that, in fact, new fathers start working even more.[30] As Sarah Veale says: 'Employers exercise prejudice against people who have competing demands on their time outside the workplace.'[31] Although many employers do carry prejudices against women/mothers in work, of course there are many more who don't care at all about sex or status, they simply want someone reliable to come in and do the work. There's been a lot of talk following recent legislation on paternity leave for fathers. As described earlier, many small businesses (as well as some larger ones) find this constant chipping away of the time (and perceived loyalty) of their workforce difficult to cope with and not just in the female workforce, fathers face this discrimination too. Research on pay shows that it's not only working mothers who suffer the pay gap (see Chapter 2): although men's pay rises slightly with each child, working fathers are paid less than men who are not fathers, though the gap is much smaller than the gap between average men and average women or mothers. It used to be that a 'family man' worker had the domestic support of his wife – in effect, two people for the price of one. A husband could count on his wife to buy, wash and iron his clothes, pack for his business trips, provide a hot meal at the end of the day and a clean and tidy house to sleep in. When wives also go to work this system is strained. Without this support, working, childless husbands are on the same footing as working single men but once there are kids in the mix, unless the father ignores them completely, there is more competition for his time at home in the evenings and at weekends. If the father is also caring for the children during the working week (which the average father with a working partner is bound to do, even if only sporadically) then the pull away from work increases. Father-workers then find themselves less available, less present, perceived to be less committed and are therefore less likely to be promoted. It's like being a 'little mother' in its effect on salary and career. And as Veale says, it's the competition for a worker's time that's important.

Men who take on the primary caring role and let go of their work outside the home ('house husbands') can find it a shocking experience.[32] They can find themselves socially isolated and barred from the usual peer groupings of parents: mothers' groups. They also tend to find that they lose their sense of legitimacy. So, many of them hold back from this, the status quo continues, and mothers' careers continue to suffer more than fathers'. Philip's a good example of this: he actively chose to take the caring role when his two children were born. His wife, Su, went back to her job in IT. She was content with the arrangement but Philip found his himself increasingly unhappy: 'I was never accepted in any of the activities for parents with younger children. I made a couple of good women friends and would spend time with them, and that kept me going, but it wasn't enough.' Once the children reached the ages of three and five and could attend the local nursery and primary schools, Philip went back to work full-time in his former role as a management accountant.

Young women's perceptions and expectations

As well as interviewing parents for this book, we made a point of speaking with a number of women in their 20s who were yet to have children. Some are wonderfully idealistic, reminding me of my own energy and ideals at that age that life has since shaken more than once. Others were more pragmatic. I felt I could gauge how much life experience each had had, how realistic they were, how much some yet had to learn . . . but also, I came to realise, how much I could learn from going back and seeing life through those eyes again. Here are some of their thoughts.

Jenny Bell explains how she would feel about becoming pregnant now:

> If I did, I guess I would carry on with my job until I had to take maternity leave and have the child and hopefully my job would be supportive and I could take time off and go back.

Asked whether she felt that freelance work is more conducive to being a mother, she says:

> I personally would want to spend a lot of time with my children so I wouldn't want to give them to a nanny or childminder and go off to work nine till five. I would want a job where I could either bring the children or work from home or do both.

She would expect to go back into her job at the same salary and level, even if she was given more flexibility from her employer. She sees how much the world of work has changed in recent history:

> Women are participating in fulfilling careers and there's been a big change since my parents' generation. It's become a lot more flexible and its only going to improve in terms of women working and raising a family and fitting it all in.

And so . . . ?

Research concludes that there is discrimination. Society presumes that the woman has the primary responsibility for any children and it's the woman who takes account of these responsibilities by (for instance) working part-time. Even though some women who work part-time would prefer to work full-time and would do so if they didn't have the childcare responsibilities, underlying societal discrimination often prevents this. According to a report from the United States General Accounting Office, 'employers or clients may underestimate women's abilities or male co-workers may resist working with women, particularly if women are in higher-level positions.'[33] But the report also goes on to say that there's discrimination against working fathers:

> Due to their family responsibilities in terms of hiring, promotions, and terminations on the job . . . discrimination may occur if employers enact policies or practices that have a disproportionately negative impact on one group of workers, such as women with children. For example, if an employer has a policy that excludes part-time workers from promotions, this could have a significant effect on women because they are more likely to work part-time. Other experts suggest that workplace practices reflecting ideal worker norms – such as requiring routine overtime for promotion – could be considered discrimination. This could impact women more (particularly mothers) and may result in a disproportionate number of men in high-level positions.

I once recruited staff into an organisation that paid lip service to equality in the workplace. The preselection and interview structure was geared up to equal opportunities legislation. When it came to the process itself, interviewers scored candidates on several criteria, one of which was: 'how well would this candidate fit in to the department?' This seems a reasonable question but it allowed us to exclude anybody who didn't look, act and speak like us. Unsurprisingly, we were a uniform troupe. When in the future there aren't enough candidates, interviewers will be forced to look seriously at all candidates and sometimes to recruit those who might formerly have been rejected. In the meantime, even the most well-meaning employing organisations are underpinned by individuals who may have no understanding that a diverse mix is an asset in the workplace and that recruiting people with the advanced skills gained during the juggling of work and home can give a team an edge.

A US summary of research finds evidence that men and women have different life priorities, and that some women choose to prioritise home and family and in doing so knowingly give up their potential for higher earnings. Yet the same summary reports other evidence that men and women are no different in their life priorities and that the low earnings of women are based on discrimination in society or the workplace. Kate Bellamy and Sophie Cameron agree with the latter. In their report for the Fawcett Society, Gender Equality in the 21 Century, they say:

> These 'gender gaps' cannot simply be attributed to women's choices. Research has found that discrimination is a major contributor to the sexual pay gap, suggesting sex discrimination legislation is not working effectively.[34]

I'd agree with that: when I think hard about my own presuppositions and prejudices and find how difficult they are to eradicate, I see how we're all riddled with them, at some level and in some form. There are many facets to the enormously complex issue of our collapsing careers but most of these are symptoms rather than causes. The pay gap, for instance, doesn't merit its own chapter in this book because it, like the glass ceiling, is an 'effect'. The workplace could be equal almost instantly (within a decade, say) if people's perceptions and expectations changed. Unfortunately, and as each of us acknowledges if we're honest with ourselves, these run very deep indeed. So if equality ever arrives it'll be via evolution, not revolution. Each generation brings new mixtures of genes and new upbringings; whatever other action we take in remaking the frameworks for our careers, it's worth remembering that we're the people who are raising the next generation of employers.

5

WHAT MOTHERS HAVE TO OFFER

Women are different from men, and it's not just the wobbly bits. The debate of these differences has lead to the formation of university departments; we argue in the pub and the bedroom whether there's any real difference; the pros and cons; the rights and wrongs. Because women are different we bring different skills and use them differently.

One of my first jobs was in sales. The company's managing director told us, in a rambling speech, that women make better executives than men. At the time (the early 1980s) sales jobs were usually done by men. The real art of selling (as opposed to taking money at a till) was supposed to require the more assertive male mind. But in my experience, salesmen were often arrogant, loud and stupid. The director of my company was agreeing that this masculine approach didn't work or, at least, not as effectively as a feminine approach. I was taught that selling is about listening, empathy and intelligent conversation – not what you'd expect from your average second-hand-car dealer in those days.

Two decades on there's more research into selling and listening. This stems from and feeds our increasing interest in psychology – of the academic and scientific types as well as pop psychology in the press and on TV. People are intrigued about gender in new ways, including what women can bring to roles traditionally held by men. Where organisations are forward-thinking enough to risk it, many find that including women in a traditional male workforce has unexpected and positive results. It's not simply about direct work skills: a mixed workforce has many positives for the culture of an organisation. Even the British Royal Navy sends women to sea these days.

Male and female

There's a genetic difference of only around 3 per cent between men and women – that's the proportion of our DNA that differs. Yet we see life from a woman's point of view, we think 'woman', we eat 'woman' and we have sex 'woman'; this difference is intrinsic to almost every aspect of our lives, not just 3 per cent of them. Because the difference is in our DNA it's in every one of our cells – so you could say that we're 100 per cent different. It underpins and helps to dictate each part of us, creating layers of differences we don't necessarily see but feel, hear and usually accept which stem from our bodies, our minds and the way they think. These are the differences that are most interesting in the workforce (although in some jobs physical strength or endurance are paramount). Researcher Doreen Kimura explains the differences in non-physical/reproductive abilities between men and women which occur, it's thought, due to the different hormones whooshing around the body while the brain is developing:

> Major sex differences in function seem to lie in patterns of abil-
> ity rather than in overall level of intelligence (measured as IQ),
> although some researchers . . . have argued that there exists a
> small IQ difference favouring human males. Differences in
> intellectual pattern refer to the fact that people have different

intellectual strengths. For example, some people are especially good at using words, whereas others are better at dealing with external stimuli, such as identifying an object in a different orientation. Two individuals may have differing cognitive abilities within the same level of general intelligence.[1]

So our minds work in subtle but measurably different ways. These differences then flood into every part of our culture. We've become used to thinking of some attributes as being masculine or feminine and we describe them as such. When we meet someone who seems counter-gender we remark on it: 'that man did a very feminine thing' (or perhaps 'what a wimp'). The attributes described as masculine are thought to be analytical, rational and quantitative, whereas the feminine are synthetic, intuitive and qualitative.[2] To look at this further, scientists set up experiments tracing the patterns within people's brains when carrying out tasks. Working with psychologists, they've been able to put together 'pictures' of two different forms of thinking. There are many popular books, magazine and newspaper articles which underline these traits so we've become used to thinking Mars/Venus, or whatever terminology and ideas are in vogue at the time.[3] Scientists have underlined these popular notions by finding that in general men are more: competitive; targeted at achieving objectives; action-based physically; likely to retreat away from discussion when things go wrong; and likely to feel needed, while women tend to be: more interested in, and good at, interpersonal relationships; interdependent; cooperative; appreciative of the process leading up to achievement, rather than just the achievement; action-based verbally; needing to talk things through; and wanting to feel loved. Of course, these are huge generalisations. As someone with a science degree who prides myself at having a logical, structured approach to things, I sometimes wonder whether I'm more 'masculine' than 'feminine' within these definitions, but then I read more and think that yes, there are particular traits and ways I have of doing and analysing things that I don't see in the men I know.

Professor of Developmental Psychopathology Simon Baron-Cohen estimated in the 1990s that around 60 per cent of men have a 'male' brain, around 20 per cent a 'balanced' brain and about 20 per cent a 'female' brain. Women show the same figures but the other way around.[4] (These differences are independent of differing sexuality.) People also spend hours arguing the nature/nurture argument: are we like this because of our genes or because of the way we were brought up, and to what extent? The discussion suffuses religious and political fora as well as research centres, coffee bars and common rooms, but although interesting (and perhaps, ultimately, insoluble?) what's relevant is less how we became what we are, but that there exist accepted differences between the sexes in terms of skills and approaches to work.

Women at the top

That being the case, there's an argument for workforces to contain a balanced mix of men and women in order to capitalise on our differences. Scientist Peter Lawrence argues that while it's difficult politically to talk in these terms, if there's a certain type of work where the male brain delivers a better worker, surely we would, and should, expect there to be more men in that field? Talking about the obsessiveness that he considers important for scientific research, and that this is considered a more male trait, then 'if males on average are constitutionally better suited to be this kind of scientist, it seems silly to aim at strict gender parity.'[5] He goes on to give another example, this time favouring the female brain:

> For example, among current student members of the British Psychological Society, there are 5,806 women to 945 men; and

among graduate psychologists, 23,324 women to 8,592 men. Of those who practice as chartered psychologists, the ratio has fallen further (7,369 women to 4,402 men).

Yet it's the Fellows of the Society (there are 428 men to only 106 women) who are honoured for their research, who have the highest standing and presumably, the fattest salaries. So even if he's right, it doesn't get over the basic inequality that underpins these differences: even where the skills required are predominantly female, pay and status are ultimately awarded to men. Lawrence redeems himself, however, when talking about the need for a mix of gender at the top of his scientific research profession. He gives three reasons why women and men should share the top jobs: that these call for a mix of skills, to include the 'female' ability to nurture younger talent and not solely the 'male' drive to obsess over a small research area; he then says how a balanced mix of men and women at the top would make for more contented and productive workplaces (motivation arising from a supportive environment as well as well as a competitive one); and finally, that younger workers need role models; if there are no senior female role models in a discipline then young women won't feel encouraged to create their careers there.

His conclusions are echoed by Burke and Nelson, who conduct research into organisational behaviour and industrial relations. In the light of falling birth rates, rising educational achievements of women and the advantages for an organisation that has a broader approach to issues (gained by recruiting women with their differently wired brains), they looked at whether women should be considered more often for roles of responsibility in work. They concluded that supporting women who want to rise through organisations makes sense for these reasons: organisations would obtain the best people for leadership positions; it would give the chief executive officer experience in working with capable women; it would provide female role models for younger high-potential women; it would ensure that companies' opportunities for women would be noticed by both women graduates in recruiting and women customers; and it would guarantee that all ranks of management would be filled with strong executives.[6]

What mothers bring

All of that was women contrasted with men. Yet there are additional skills that mothers bring. This is one of the ways that Frances finds being a mother has changed her:

> As a mum, on the one hand you're more emotional but on the other, you're kind of hardened to things on another level. When people are being prats at work I find it much easier to deal with now because I just see them as being pathetic. I think 'Why are you getting so worked up, can't you see this is the way to work it out?' But they get all overexcited. It seems easy in comparison to looking after children when they're kicking off.

Mothers learn a whole range of skills that many men, even fathers, don't have. Again, there are plenty of fathers who are hands-on not only in the day-to-day caring for their children but in the organisation of the family and the home and who also gain these skills. Parents know that many non-parents have absolutely no idea of what's involved. The demands on each parent are, of course, different; some have plenty of support from their partners and families and others have none at all. I'd advise recruiters, if they know that their female interviewee is a single parent, to think of the skills she brings with her: she has to manage the budget (probably very tight) and navigate all the financial areas of family life – tax returns, benefit forms, financial planning of all types – as well as perhaps project managing a property, organising maintenance after reviewing its condition and the available options. She will have learned to be strongly independent (a self-starter) yet also learned the value of strong relationships and the support they give (teamwork). She'll have learned the social skills necessary to persuade the benefits officer to review her case early while suffering from sleep deprivation (sales skills and endurance); she'll have kept fit (energetic), taken on and coped with huge responsibility and will be motivated to move her life on. Those happily partnered will have been able to share that responsibility (to some extent) but still have myriad skills – and maturity – over those who live their lives without the responsibility of a family. And there's a whole range of additional skills that older parents bring to work simply because of their longer life/parenting experience. The days of workplace ageism are over (in law). How much more does a parent returning to the workplace after a break to bring up children know, over a younger worker? Even if specific skills are rusty, life and transferable skills are greater. Specific workplace skills can be learned where people are motivated, and returning parents are certainly that.

There's a new skills agenda: we used to need literacy, numeracy, IQ, punctuality and all those old transferable skills. They're still important yet, as Chapter 2 saw, there's a new set being floated to support the knowledge economy, covering areas such as entrepreneurism and creativity. The former is something many new mothers learn fast: how to make a bit of extra money while the children are small and we're working part-time. Many turn their minds to small-scale business, such as becoming agents for home-selling products. Some go on to think up their own versions, make their own products, set up new organisations, perhaps only in the short-term before they start applying for employment again. A few continue, and their entrepreneurism fuels new careers working freelance or perhaps becoming employers themselves. But those who come back into the employed workforce offer a majestic outlook on work: accustomed to seeing what works and what doesn't and to performing most aspects of the business themselves, they make well-rounded, multi-skilled and creative employees if used to their full. Creativity of thought or the ability to see outside the box is second nature to those who are already outside the box – parents who have been working part-time perhaps, or taken a career break, and can see the workplace anew. And parents have more to their lives than work: someone with a decent sense of work–life balance is going to achieve more, long-term, than someone who's a bit haphazard because they don't care about work, or someone who's work-obsessed and can't get perspective. Parenting certainly offers perspective.

The mothers I know rarely stop working. Not only are their domestic responsibilities heavy but they also gain a new work ethic which disallows them from skiving, taking longer lunches, playing computer games when no one's watching or generally putting their feet up. Gemma Childe is a 30-year-old mother of a 3-year-old girl; she and her husband juggle their lives to maintain the family. She describes returning from a two-week holiday 'to be faced with 150 emails, 3 deadlines, daughter starting pre-school, birthday parties, new business potential, housework and a fortnight's worth of washing to do.' She worked as a journalist for five years then worked for a graphic design company for four years before having her daughter. Now she works part-time in an office and from home in the evenings while her daughter sleeps:

I definitely work harder now. When I had a full-time job I switched off at 5.30 pm. Now I work in an office from 9.00 am – 2.00 pm; when I am in the office, I get my head down and do my work. Then I rush home to be a mum and housewife, do all my chores, and check my emails when I get the chance and then I work from the moment my daughter goes to bed, until I am ready to drop! My husband Matt and I share looking after our daughter between our working hours. He works afternoons and late into the night so that's why it works well.

And employers feel the benefit of hard-working parents. Tanya is a 27-year-old recruitment consultant in northern England, and is the mother of two sons, one of nine months and the other of three years. Her partner is the full-time carer of the children. We asked her whether she works harder now than before she had her children:

> Yes, because it's important to do the best that I can. I have the least number of sick days in my workplace, whereas before I had the children it was all about going out and phoning in sick . . . I do exactly the same job I did before, I don't leave any earlier or have more time off. [When I was pregnant] I still took only one sick day off each year. I still did the same 50 hours per week as everybody else, and had the out-of-hours mobile, the quality of my work did not change – except maybe in the last few weeks: I had such terrible pains sometimes I couldn't speak – which ruled out sales calls!

Employers would give a lot for employees like Tanya – the motivation to carry on at that pace in a job that, as a trained musician with aspirations for a career in music, she describes as simply a means to feed her family. This is the type of motivation that places many parents among the most worthwhile of employees. Not all are so productive, of course – bad luck can strike: a difficult pregnancy, lack of support at home with young children needing a parent's attention, or other issues. Yet those who are creating homes and futures for their children have a lot to work for and little to gain by skiving or working at less than full capacity. Those employers who lament the passing of the Protestant work ethic should try tapping into the parental work ethic.

Research backs up how hard parents work. A US study by Hochschild of a corporation with strong family-friendly policies showed that of workers with children aged 12 or under, only 4 per cent of men and 13 per cent of women worked part-time.[7] Being a parent made remarkably little difference to attendance records at work. When considering why parents don't take more time away from work, the study suggests that they can't afford to. It also suggests that people (some of whom didn't even take all their vacation entitlement) who worked these long hours did so through choice, not because they were worried about being seen as shirkers. It seemed strange, in this study, that a large corporation was offering family-friendly policies, such as the right to work shorter hours or flexitime, yet these options were hardly being taken up.

With such a predominance of well-qualified women coming into the workforce, more companies are seeing the need to offer these policies in order to attract women – and yet they're barely used. These policies are also seen to benefit employers in terms of lower sickness rates and other factors. The study asked whether the hardcore middle managers, who were those who implemented the family friendly policies, were obstructing usage of them, but found that no, it was simply that workers weren't applying for more time off: even when the middle manager was known to be family friendly, there was little take-up (though slightly more than the norm). Some women felt that they needed to work long hours in order to prove that they were worth their promotion, not just to their managers but to their colleagues. But even those who didn't feel this way still worked long hours. The study concluded that people simply don't want to work less hours, and cites evidence to underpin this. So, although we find it hard to juggle all the demands on our time, and we say that we want to work shorter hours, when faced with the option many of us simply don't want to work less.

If this is true, and if parents have this increased skills base, have more dedication and don't even take up the flexible approaches to work offered by their employers, shouldn't we be top of every recruitment shortlist? Employers who remember the times they've been let down by parents might like to remember the research about domestic responsibilities outlined in Chapter 4 showing how husbands genuinely feel that they are making an equal domestic contribution, whereas all studies show this isn't the case.[8] Perhaps it's easier to remember, and scowl at, the mother who had to run home to look after her child than the worker who simply didn't work very hard at all.

Researchers had a look at some early studies into women and work.[9] These early studies, which accepted stereotypical gender-related roles in a way that we wouldn't today, came up with two opposing ideas. One, dated 1974, was called the scarcity hypothesis. The author of the work (Seiber) argued that we only have a certain amount of time and energy, and that if we try to fit more into our lives (as with mothers having jobs as well as running homes and families) then something is going to suffer, whether it's the children, the job or the husband – shock, horror. This was balanced in 1977 (by Marks) with the role expansion hypothesis, which asserted the opposite: that time and energy expand to meet the demands of multiple roles. One is judgemental about people's abilities (and makes assumptions about set roles) and the other says that, simply because it used to be a certain way doesn't mean it can't change. The study also showed that although the multiple roles taken on (primarily by women) can lead to stress, multiple roles in themselves didn't necessarily lead to stress. It reminds me of the adage: if you want something done, ask a busy person.

6

IS IT WORTH THE FIGHT?

A question was posed to Jane from Germany, a worker in a family business and mother of three children, aged 14, and 13-year-old twins: 'Do you work harder now than before you had children?' Jane's answer:

> Yes. But it's a different level and form of work. You're no longer doing things for yourself but serving, caring for and supporting the others first and then not being left with any time or energy for yourself. Priorities are totally different.

This will sound familiar to most mothers who juggle a family and work. For some of us it feels like second nature to be in a caring, nurturing role, putting others first and our own career, aspirations and leisure last. Often though, it doesn't feel so comfortable, and certainly not for the length of time involved – it might be perhaps 15 years (or more) before we can once again do exactly what we want to do when we want to do it. Of course, we knew about this before we had our children in the first place . . . didn't we? It's one thing to think in advance about a happy gurgling baby and quite another to realise, as many of us do only once the childbirth euphoria and shock wears off, what it really means. And this reality varies enormously with our personality and circumstances.

This is Frances' experience:

> I definitely don't feel as confident . . . the girl I work with started whilst I was on maternity leave and she's full-time and a bit younger than me. She's just been made head of the department, even though she's got less experience than me. She hasn't got kids; she's a single women. She is capable, she may well be better for the position anyway. But, had I been full-time and not had kids then that probably could have been me. But you have to accept it and to be honest; when you're a mum you have different priorities.

Some of this we can determine in advance but much of it, however hard we try, is fluid and out of our control. We can choose the very best partner in the world who we know will not only make a fantastic co-parent to our children but will support us in our careers every step of the way. However, we never really know how long that will last — there is always the possibility of separation, even death — leaving us to do the whole caboodle alone. This isn't meant to put shivers of apprehension and dread up prospective parents' spines. Rather, it's here to point out the reality that many of us will be less supported in our parenting than we first envisaged. But hopefully that won't apply to you: what's more within our control is how we ourselves approach our lives and our parenting. Will we feel the need to be there for our children after school every day or is it sufficient for a carer to do this? Or the other parent? Or a grandparent? Does the concept of 'quality time' mean we can reasonably take only half an hour out of each day to be with the children? Does it mean we can go on long business trips? There are as many answers to these issues as there are parents and it's something each of us needs to work out for ourselves and our families — children vary so much, that in one family a parent who sets aside four hours a day to be with the children might find themselves ignored for most of that time by independent children who want to go off with their friends or play alone, while in other families that time together might be an essential underpinning of everyone's lives. It's something that most of us work out as we go along, which by definition means that we can't know in advance how it'll be.

In researching this book there do appear to be women who find it easy to be fairly separate from their families, and others who need to be with them much more. To that extent some women might find it possible to say from the outset, with some degree of confidence, whether a career will succeed or might need to be put on hold. Researchers Gordon and Kauppinen describe how 'domestic circumstances and the main responsibility for housework and the care of children still affect women; they enter the labour market with one hand tied behind their backs.'[1] The first half of this book has shown this to be true. Mothers experience it and women without children begin to understand it as they watch peers begin the family/work struggle. This chapter asks: is it so tough? If it is, is it worth having children and if you do, is it worth trying to have a career too?

A woman who's managed both is Shenagh, now in her 50s, a senior civil servant and mother of four who lives and works in New Zealand. She describes her career:

> Twenty years ago, I ran a mental health service and an alcohol and drug service part time. I then started working full-time some 60 kilometres away so did a full-time [health management] job in four ten-hour days, staying away from home two

nights a week but having a full day at home in the middle of the week — my daughter was under two years old at this time. I then moved on to be a general manager in a strategic health organisation full-time and we moved to be nearer my work. We then moved and I had six months off work and then worked full-time for a private sector company. I progressed to director in this company then I got a job in an office similar to the Cabinet Office in the UK where I worked for three to four years and then became the equivalent of a permanent secretary in the Civil Service. I have worked full-time for the last sixteen years, with the first three years on a four day week.

How did she manage to do all this with four children?

With my first child, I took six months off; with the other three children about two months and with one of them I think I was only away for six weeks. This was quite a long time ago. The overall impact on my work life is that I remained part-time for a good deal of time and I feel that my career broadened rather than went upwards. My experience was that when I did return to full-time work (when the youngest was two) my career developed very quickly. I was mature and experienced and confident and I do not believe that those years part-time deeply disadvantaged me in the long term, even though it did in the short term and I needed my husband's earnings probably to keep being able to spend time at home with them.

Throughout my working life I have taken time out of the working day to be with the children — taking them to music lessons, visiting their schools, going to their camps and even home schooling one for one year and taking two afternoons off a week as part of a flexible work package. As you can see, once I worked a full-time job four days a week. This was 16 years ago, before it was the norm, but I just had to ask confidently and it was agreed – and I was not that senior or that precious to work then. I just believed it was possible, and it was.

She finishes by talking about her family:

My children . . . went to different part-time childcare and to school. Most of the time my husband also worked part-time, but at times we were both full-time. They are the most important part of my life, but they have overall benefited from my working, despite sometimes feeling pressed and guilty and knowing that at times they would have loved to have me at home when they arrived from school.

Compare this with Sue's story; she lives in Devon, England, and has brought up three daughters:

When I married for the first time I thought it'd all be fine. I'd give up the job that I had and look after the children and my husband would earn the money. I never contemplated divorce. I thought marriage was forever so I thought that was the family unit, where you stay at home to bring your children up and your husband goes out to earn the money. I had to fit in with my husband looking after the children so I did waitressing in the evenings. Then I started to shape up a bit and went into Montessori teaching but tried to fit it around the children, so my youngest daughter went to the Montessori. I then became a lunchtime supervisor because that fitted in with her and my middle child. Then I got divorced . . . and realised I couldn't flit about trying to combine the whole picture so I then branched out. I had to leave my youngest at a friend's house while I went to work as a laboratory technician at another school. I still thought it wasn't going to earn enough so I went on to do a teaching degree at Bath University. My children had to then fend for themselves a bit more; to get themselves home and make their own dinner.

When I remarried I was back to square one. My husband said he didn't want me to work and he'd take care of everything. I finished my course halfway through. But then I had his four girls to look after too, the youngest being three years old at the time. I had them for four days every week so I couldn't combine it with going off to college everyday, though I had enjoyed it and seen it as another way of life. But after a while I had another shot at work, I did part-time estate agency work at the weekends for four years. And then when I got divorced again and it wasn't enough, it didn't hold together to make a neat CV. Computers had come in, and everything had changed so much. Then I was out doing anything I could get. I tried lots of different jobs: call centre, factory work, cleaning. But they aren't big money earners and aren't of any consequence as such.

If I'd realised that I was going to end up getting divorced and bringing up the children on my own I would have rethought the whole thing. I definitely would've concentrated more on my career. I would have realised that I needed something substantial that I could fall back on once I'd had children. I would've gone back to work. If I'd thought about it properly, it would probably have been better to have had my children and gone back about one year after they were born and I would have kept it going so that I could fend for myself, and my husband's income would have been a bonus rather than the only income.

I would now strongly advise my children to get in there and get a career. You have to be financially independent; you can't rely on anyone else. My children did break up my career but I'm not bitter because I set out to have children. I can just now say with hindsight that I handled it badly. And now its: 'oh dear, if only!' but I deal with it. I may be at the bottom but I have three lovely daughters and all I can do is emphasise to them to get out there and do something with their lives.

Sue's and Shenagh's lives could hardly be more different. But both still feel that their children – now grown – are central to their lives. Like Sue, Shenagh says:

I have a marvellous relationship with my young adult/teenage children, who still come and live at home at times, help with chores and are always lovely with me. The house is like a youth hostel, but basically in my control. I have masses of friends and my job provides me with a structure that makes every day good. I have intellectually developed enormously over the last 20 years while in New Zealand. I work and play very hard, but the salary I get cushions me. I feel I have been a very good mother and that my children appreciate the fact that I work. I am very busy, but have a lot of energy.

When Sue started working life she didn't have huge aspirations. To her:

Life was all about the way my mother had done it and you just brought up a family. That was just the way of life and I never really thought beyond it.

This norm of the 1960s is reflected in the small numbers of women now nearing retirement who hold senior posts such as Shenagh's – although Shenagh's story feels more modern, she was, of her time, exceptional. This career/family mix is now the expectation. Sue goes on to describe her peers, dividing them between those who gave up work and their marriages succeeded, so they continue to have a reasonable standard of living, and those who fend for themselves and have the training and experience to earn well enough to support themselves, some part-time as they get older. Not many women nowadays would make the same early assumptions Sue made about giving up everything and living on their husband or partner's wage – would they? Few would be prepared to take on a stepfamily of an additional four children and give up work to care for them, as Sue did. We're now brought up to be independent and to earn our own livings. But that's not to say that the conflicts have been resolved.

Sarah Nias is the mother of a 16-month old boy, and works part-time as a drama teacher. She says of her current situation:

I'm choosing to be with him. I could choose to take on [work] opportunities and he could go to nursery but basically I'm choosing not to work full-time at the moment. I had him for a reason and there's no point in having him if I can't spend some time with him. I'm choosing to do that.

It's too soon for Sarah to know whether she'll end up a Shenagh or a Sue. And how's she to know how to draw that line between family and work? As Shenagh puts it:

Most of my working life I have worked very hard, but only rarely over the top. I like to extend my work into the evening if I need (ie bring work home) if that enables me to get time during the day to do chores, see the children if they call at my office, see friends etc. But my husband did not like this – he would prefer me to be 9.00 to 5.00 and then entirely focused on the home and him. I work harder when I do not have children to get home to, look after or be with, definitely. They put limits on the amount I work because I both have to be there for them, and want to.

Shenagh is now single. Might her hard work (that her husband resented) have contributed to the break up of that marriage? Might Sue's lack of work outside the home have lead to the break up of hers? These are impossible questions for the people involved to answer, let alone an observer. But they're exactly the questions Sarah Nias and others need answered if we're going to decide whether it's worth battling so hard at both work and home, how, and in which direction.

The personal costs of working as well as having children

From the perspective of an 'older mother' I've been surprised at how many of the younger mothers we've interviewed for this book aren't as committed to work as they once were. I'd forgotten how all-consuming it is when you have young children, and how for many people this changes their life view completely.

Gemma Childe, a journalist, says:

> I find it much harder to focus on work now I have my daughter, and I think my priorities have changed. I am now only working to pay the bills rather than to build a career for myself. If money wasn't an option I would have never returned to work. I may have considered a little freelance work to keep the brain ticking over, but on my terms. I just want to be happy and feel fulfilled, but these days my satisfaction comes more from family life than my work life.

Sarah Nias describes that she works much harder now than she did before she had her son:

> It feels like it! I only work part-time [now], but you don't just come home from work and slump and that's the end of your day. Your day keeps going until your child goes to bed and then

you've got to turn round and do all your household things. So I'm working harder. Just juggling that is hard work in itself.

And Sarah, who was once an ambitious actor with a burgeoning TV career, describes her current approach:

My ambition is just to earn enough so we have a comfortable life and to add to my husband's wages so things aren't hard, so we can enjoy life, take the children on holiday. Not all the riches in the world, but to be comfortable.

Are some of us giving up our careers and then letting go of aspirations because we know that our decisions to date (in setting the partnership agenda, and in having the child) preclude ambition for the foreseeable future? And so we tell ourselves not to want or hope for too much?

Here's Sarah Nias again:

[My child] does have an impact on the other side of my career. I can't really go for auditions now and take on possible opportunities of getting parts in things, which is what my degree was for, because I live in the countryside. As such I'd have to take a whole day out of life to go for auditions as well as finding childcare and then if I got a part it could mean a month away filming on a set somewhere – I feel with children I just couldn't do that.

Tanya has put her ambitions on hold for her family too:

My work is a means to feed my family. It's a job with good prospects but it's not what I envisioned. Nobody would have had me down as an office, suit-wearing type, but I can't do what I really want as I would have to give up work.

Prior to this, Tanya trained as a musician:

> I did a Higher National Diploma in Music Performance. I dream
> of doing what I am good at – writing and making music. I'm a
> creative person and a job like mine suffocates me. I don't mind
> because it's a sacrifice happily made for my children, but I do
> believe I can and will be successful in music thus giving us all a
> better life. Right now I'm in a rut – not enough pay to buy our
> own house, but I can't quit to chase the career that would give us
> that.

What is it that makes Sarah and Tanya feel this way? Surely they
could still act, write and perform if they really wanted to. Shenagh
seemed to have climbed over huge obstacles while caring for four
children (and later, stepchildren). Why don't we all?

The answer comes down to what makes us, firstly, people and
secondly, women. We fight hard for our families and the people we
love and we're prepared to make sacrifices for their sakes – as do
men. And yet the very qualities of nurturing, caring, homemaking
or, in the academic language of Chapter 5, of being 'synthetic,
intuitive and qualitative' pull many of us away from the hard-line
career aspirations that the (male-led) world expects us to have.
Twenty per cent of us (according to research) are more 'male' in
the way our brains think. Among those 20 per cent, perhaps 10 per
cent have the energy after the toll of childbirth, breastfeeding and
sleepless nights to be able to work at the pace Shenagh describes
whilst also caring for four children. Perhaps half of those also have
a husband or partner who's prepared or able to work part-time to
support our work . . . that leaves us with very few women who both
want to and are able to carry these ambitions forward during these
early parenting years. A huge proportion of women feel they have
more important things on their minds during those years.
Research by social scientists Fenton, Bradley and West shows that

'over half of young women see the ideal family situation as one where mothers either work part-time or not at all.'[2] Some of us, when marriage or partnership, work and luck is on our side, can look forward to a decent living and/or newly resurrected career later on. For others, the cost of trying to juggle everything is immense. And for almost all of us, it slings us into the role of unpaid – and unappreciated – domestic slave.

Laine, the mother of one-year-old twins, says:

> The twins have given me a sense of purpose in a strange situation; they have become my work. What I do resent is that housework is lumped together with bringing up babies. In my mind cooking them healthy food, stimulating them, making sure they get enough exercise, that they are secure, that they develop properly – that is my 'work'. Laundry, vacuuming, dusting, etc, is as much an extra for me as it is for my husband whose work is further away from home. What I am trying to say is that the children have been a beautiful – exhausting but beautiful – impact on my life but the relegation to domestic servant status which seems to be insidiously lumped together with 'mother work' has impacted very negatively on myself and has caused a lot of resentment and anger.

Laine also sees that motherhood, being such a creative process, saps creativity from other areas:

> The thing about childbearing is that it is the creative process for a woman and that somehow, by having children, the creative juice for other passions is significantly depleted. For female writers it seems to be either one or the other and, if not, one is affected by the other . . . It is impossible to be wholly anything else once you are a mother.

Laine describes the sheer exhaustion that being a parent of small children brings. Young children are mind-stoppingly all-consuming. People who've never experienced this rarely understand how debilitating it is to be woken consistently at night, to be up early and on your feet for so much of the day. Add to that the mental and emotional toil that goes into child-rearing and running a home and family. I have single, childless colleagues who go home after a (not really so long) day's work and need a sleep – to me, I'm less tired now than I have been for 20 years. Those early years consume everything we have – and that's before we go out to work. As many parents say, sometimes we go to work for a rest. But the cumulative effect of doing both is so exhausting that it goes right to our core. When Allison Pearson wrote a chick-lit novel called *I Don't Know How She Does It*[3] about a City worker who's also a mother, and focused on the balancing act it entails, it became an international best-seller. Exhaustion is a central theme. Readers either identified with it or found it flippant and irrelevant – those who identified, judging from reader reviews on Amazon,[4] were, unsurprisingly, those in the same situation as the protagonist: 'how do we do it?' these people ask. 'We don't know, but at least someone else is in the same boat as us.'

We're (generally) young, fit, motivated and pretty tough. We do work at it, we do put in the slog, we get through those early years and hopefully find ourselves employable and able then to start building a career again or carry on more easily with the one we never left off (Chapter 7 looks at this in more detail). The cost of having a family, for the majority of us who step back to some extent during those years, is going to be with us for the remainder of our lives in terms of lower career attainment and lower pay. Is it worth it? It depends on how you feel about your family and the children you've brought up.

So don't have kids

The media labels issue after issue as 'the last taboo' – surely stating a wish that we hadn't had our children must be the absolutely final taboo? We've tried unsuccessfully to find a mother who'll tell us in an interview that she regrets having her children. Yet I was once with a group of mothers talking frankly (and a little drunkenly) about our lot when one of our number said then that it had been a mistake and she wished she hadn't had her two kids. Of course she loved them but it wasn't right for her and she was miserable, felt trapped, her career was over and she couldn't see a way out. She'd have been much happier, she knew, if she'd said no to the children that her partner had wanted more than she had.

There's a groundswell of women who make this decision after listening to their feelings, talking to and reading about mothers and motherhood, discussing work and understanding more fully what motherhood might really mean. An increasing number of media articles and books are emerging on the subject, and statistics underpin that more women are choosing not to become mothers.[5] And for those who've found it tough, when they reach their mid-years and look back with a broader perspective they question whether having children really was the right thing to do.

Sue (whose story runs parallel to Shenagh's, above) describes her current situation after three divorces, with no structured career that allows her to fall back on:

> I work for myself cleaning private houses. I'm just scrabbling around trying to keep my head above water now. I'm absolutely way out of touch; I couldn't even get a decent CV together, as my working history is so sporadic and spans 30 years of bits here and there having spent my whole life bringing up children.

We asked her what she would now do if she had to choose between children and career. Perhaps surprisingly, this was her response: 'Children, definitely.'

Here's the opposite view – this time from an American woman, Jacqueline Passey:

> My mother deciding to have kids may have benefited me personally, but I'm still sad for what it did to her own life. She is a very smart, politically savvy, charming and talented person . . . she decided to have children, and stay home and take care of them. Then my parents got divorced, and she became a single mother . . . it was very difficult for her financially and socially. She also had to go back to college and restart her career, and her career options were forever limited after that because she had kids to worry about. Also, although she made lots of sacrifices for me and my siblings my life was still pretty bad. I spent a lot of my time stuck in some awful childcare situations – creepy babysitters, religious day camps – and my school experiences were absolutely terrible . . . She was trying to have both a career and children, and ended up doing a half-assed job at both . . . Raising happy, healthy (physically and mentally), responsible children is a more-than-full-time job – even more so in places like the US, where the public education system and most of popular culture are actively working against you to make your children unhappy, unhealthy and irresponsible instead. I feel that someone has to be willing to give up their life for 15 or 20 years to do that job successfully. Maybe there are women out there that have so little going for them otherwise that the opportunity cost of giving up their life isn't that much. But my mother could have done so much more with her life – and instead she wasted it by doing a not-so-great job raising kids.[6]

'Nani' responds to Jacqueline's blog with:

> Our lives changed a great deal when we had children, but
> neither of us feels that we gave anything up because of it.
> However I can see how a lot of people would think that we gave
> up a lot. We made choices that allowed us to spend a lot more
> time with our children, and therefore 'gave up' a lot of potential
> income. To us, it has been more than worth it. Those who do not
> value the intangibles that having children bring over the tangi-
> ble income will not find the experience worthwhile . . . If this is
> how you feel, then do not be a parent, because anyone who feels
> this way will make a mess of it.[7]

Most women have children and most mothers find a compromise
solution which allows them to work. As mother and part-time
teacher Sarah Nias says:

> Even though I do enjoy my job, I do it to live. Because if I had the
> choice I'd have all my time at home while they were young,
> before school.

There are many women like Sarah who don't have the financial
choice of giving up work in those early years. She's grateful that
she can choose a hybrid, part-time model:

> Some of the teachers come back full-time . . . I feel I couldn't
> do that. I cannot see how they can have a happy medium.
> When they get home they're knackered and their kids get
> dropped off by the childminder; I just don't see how that
> works. (Various ways people have of making this work are
> discussed in Chapter 7.)

What working parents do to children

One of the first things that we learn as parents is that we're never going to do a perfect job and to be content that we're doing the best we can, hopefully without beating ourselves up over it. Far better than succumb to the destructive guilt that creeps over working parents is to look at an overview of available research by Sacks and Marrone, which shows that the effects on children of having a working mother are mostly positive, particularly when these effects are measured by academic test scores and social skills.[8] The effects vary with the sex of the child, marital status of the mother and the social status of the family. Some studies show that middle-class boys with employed mothers fare less well, though not all. Among working-class married families, the most disruptive children come from families with working mothers. Otherwise, children with employed mothers fare better in academic and social tests than those with mothers who don't work. Girls whose mothers don't work have more need to be in control (if their parents are married) or are shyer (in single-parent families). Children's perceptions about women's sexual stereotypes vary with whether or not the mother works, though boys still feel traditional stereotyping of male roles holds true, whether or not their mothers work. Girls tend to have less stereotypical views about male roles whether or not their mothers are working.

Some studies show that children with early care outside the home are more aggressive and non-compliant, while others disagree. However, it's the nature of the family, rather than whether or not children go to day-care centres, that has the greatest effect on behaviour. Psychology researchers Hoffman and Youngblade explain how children whose mothers work are usually looked after in a series of nursery settings, away from home and maternal/paternal influence, and so they develop personalities which allow them to thrive in these environments.[9] If this means more aggression in early years (though minimally so, and sometimes unmeasured or reversed) then this is a reasonable adaptation and a fair trade-off for better academic and social scores later on. But in any research on this type of issue there are reasons why, for instance, the mothers do or don't go out to work, and these reasons can have a great impact on the child's development. So although it's easy to form conclusions, the researchers say, we need to be wary of doing so.

There are many perfectly happy and well-adapted children whose mothers stay at home to look after them, and many whose mothers go out to work. There are many whose parents choose one of a variety of compromises. What matters is that the child is adequately cared for and feels a sense of self-worth and love. Most families provide this, whatever the personal or work circumstances. The majority of parents put this as their top priority and will try to change the world if they feel it better enables their child to flourish. It's easy to find ourselves in one camp or the other in arguments on this sort of issue. In the heat of insufficient sleep and looming deadlines we panic, wonder and question. But we can put this aside knowing that if we love our children, we'll work out the best solution for our family that will deliver happy, fulfilled parents as well as children. More than this, those of us who choose or need to work full-time, or full-time plus, are helping to fuel a change in social perceptions of the role of women in society and in the family, and that has to be a good thing for the future enabling of women generally.

Those of us who choose to give up work and career altogether are becoming rarer creatures and because of that are often looked down upon. You may be stopping work for your children's sake, your family's or your own but the chances are that it's been a difficult decision with risks and costs involved, and you've been brave to make it. Getting away from society's expectations, not just of what mothers should be doing, but of the high standard of living (in terms of material goods), suits some families. Getting back into work later may be harder for these women, but it doesn't have to be: there are ways of keeping skills up to date and developing new paths, while also spending time with the children.

What working does to a marriage

'Guys,' says Michael Noer in an article for *Forbes* magazine, 'a word of advice.[10] Marry pretty women or ugly ones. Short ones or tall ones. Blondes or brunettes. Just, whatever you do, don't marry a woman with a career.' The piece goes on to explain that research shows career women are more likely to get divorced, be unfaithful and less likely to have children. Those who do have children are less likely to be happy about it. Some men are bound to think like Noer: what's happened to their cosy little world where wifey waits at home to welcome them with warm slippers and hot food? Life was once so . . . so . . . settled. Now, who knows what's happening? It certainly doesn't feel comfortable. For women who are happy to be dependent, great. The problems begin if the marriage or partnership falters or crumbles and leaves us vulnerable. And in that type of old-fashioned marriage this is increasingly likely to happen because, even if we grow up with these patriarchal attitudes, having kids often makes us realise that women of recent generations are hybrids: we're not Victorians but neither are we yet truly equal in the 21st century. So we're more likely to want change than we might have a few generations ago. And, because it's now acceptable behaviour, the men are more likely to chuck in the haggard, worn-out wife for a newer model.

Antonia Douie sees her husband as the 'brains and breadwinner'. She says of her transition from working woman to full-time housewife and mother of two small children:

> I couldn't have done it without [him]. I don't even want to think what my life would be like without him supporting us emotionally and financially.

Many such marriages work magnificently. They are dependent, though, on the woman's dependence. If things start to feel wrong, from either perspective, within that sort of relationship then where can they go? I remember being told, 30 years ago, that the most successful marriages were those in which the wife was at least slightly dimmer than the husband. This matches the slip-per-warming, food-preparing wife described above. In this age I'd hope that marriages work best when both partners are equally matched. I like this from writer Elizabeth Corcoran:

> The essence of a good marriage, it seems to me, is that both people have to learn to change and keep on adapting. Children bring tons of change. Mothers encounter it first during the nine months of pregnancy, starting with changing body dimensions. But fathers have to learn to adapt, too, by learning to help care for children, to take charge of new aspects of a household, to adapt as the mothers change.[11]

The effects of two careers on a marriage is a book in itself. It's one of many factors that need to be considered in this whole issue of working mothers – marriage needs to be planned as carefully as the trousseau and then layette, then reconsidered and adapted over time by both partners, as well as with the children, if it's all going to work.

The financial cost of having children

'Unfortunately we live in a country where returning to work as a mother of three is all but out of the question unless you're drowning in cash or have a supportive and well-positioned family,' says UK columnist Mariella Frostrup.[12] In the UK each of our children costs us an average of £165,000/US$330,000 to raise to the age of 21.[13] This is without adding in the existing house, car or the price of taking maternity and/or paternity leave. Children are most expensive between the ages of one and five (when over £50,000/US$100,000 is spent) because of the increased need for childcare. Each baby costs us around £7,716/US$15,432 by the time it/we blow out the candles on its first birthday cake. A survey by the Daycare Trust in 2006 put the average cost of a week's nursery care for a child under two at £142/US$284, with some parents paying up to £400/US$800 a week for full-time nursery care.[14] There are other options: childminders, au pairs, family members. But for many these aren't workable: would you leave a new baby, or a tantrumming toddler, with a new, young, inexperienced au pair? Are your mother or father available and willing to start over again with another 10 or 15 years of childcare?

This huge figure covers obvious items such as baby clothes and equipment, toys, outings, trips and books, and associated costs such as ongoing loss of earnings. It also covers the less obvious such as additional insurance, life cover, a larger car and a larger house. It covers university costs too, though by the time today's young children get to uni it's thought that more students will be expecting to cover that cost themselves with a loan paid back over subsequent years, US-style, so perhaps it's unfair to add it in. It also assumes the little dears go to a state school: educating them privately will cost an extra £78,430/US$156,860 each for day pupils and £122,713/US$245,426 for boarders. The total figure has risen 18 per cent in three years largely as a result of the rise in university costs (which are set to rise further), though nursery places have also risen, by an average of 27 per cent over five years.[15]

Getting the children off to school doesn't end the need for childcare, of course: arrangements for after-school need to be made, as well as the school breaks. After-school clubs cost an average of £40/US$80 for 15 hours a week and school break play schemes cost an average of £77/US$154 a week, rising to a high of £225/US$450 a week (that would add £1,300/US$2,600 to the cost of your family's summer for each child). Good news for Londoners though: average costs are £48.90/US$97.80 a week, down from £58.35/US$116.70 a week in 2005 due to subsidies by local government. Other government help towards these costs include the childcare element of the Working Tax Credit, which averages at £49.80/US$99.60 a week (per award, not per child).

In the US, urban high-income families spend over £140,000/US$280,000 to raise a child to age 17, though this figure drops to £67,000/US$134,000 for lower income families. It excludes costs of medical bills, private schooling or lost earning while taking a career break.[16] It also excludes the cost of university, which is included in the UK study. Between £6,000/US$12,000 and £16,500/US$33,000 of this cost goes on childcare and education; there's a childcare credit (when both parents work full-time) which allows a dollar-for-dollar reduction in the tax bill within certain limits. This also covers domestic help needed because you're out at work. There's also a child tax credit allowance of around £500/US$1,000 for lower and medium level earners.

All this assumes that your child is well and able-bodied: it costs three times more to bring up a disabled child than a non-disabled child. Parents of a disabled child are a third more likely to work part-time than other parents and to earn almost a fifth less than those from families where the children have no disabilities. Eighty-four per cent of mothers with disabled children aren't in employment, more than twice the rate for mothers of non-disabled children. They are also seven times less likely to return to work after the birth of their child. When they do, the average hourly cost of childcare for disabled children is £5.50/US$11 an hour, £2/US$4 higher than for non-disabled children.[17] In the US, the childcare credit is available to parents of children with disabilities even if they're not working full-time, which redresses the financial balance slightly. As journalist Annie Shaw points out, it's a good thing most of don't add it up in advance of preg-nancy or the human race would probably die out.[18]

Postponing children

So perhaps we can help offset the massive cost of having children by saving in advance? Though, realistically, the average 20-something isn't thinking this way.

Anna describes it like this:

> Matt and I had eight years of partying and having fun. I think we've got too many choices in life now: how good it is to travel and have holidays and go out and we just kind of weren't ready [to have children] really. You can't ever be ready, but certainly we enjoyed our 20s living it up!

As we remember our 20s most of us will have some similarities with Anna; it's not generally a time for being overly sensible. Yet recent data from the Banks Automated Clearing System (BACS) in the UK show that 66 per cent of 16- to 24-year-olds always try to save some money each month, and that in general this age group has more control and is more knowledgeable about financial matters than in the past.[19] Over the last ten years the number of young adults with a current account has increased by more than 10 per cent and only 24 per cent believe they're disorganised when it comes to bill payment compared to 34 per cent a decade ago. Direct debit usage has also increased by 6 per cent. So some of us might perhaps save a few thousand pounds and get ourselves onto the housing ladder where, with a bit of luck and planning, we can capitalise by moving areas when we have the children. But it still won't go far towards the £165,000/US$330,000 for each of our children. So, many parents have come to think that the best financial ploy is to increase their earnings as much as possible before having children. Those of us in a good position career-wise, who are skilled in a workplace short on those particular skills and with the contacts and a good job to go back to, are in a far stronger position financially than those who a family start earlier, or who haven't developed a career that far.

So a generation of parents-to-be have postponed their families, waiting until they've had their fun or worked their careers in their 20s, and are settling down to parenthood in their mid- or late 30s. Fertility rates in women in their 20s have dropped by a quarter in the last decade (this means the number of children that women have, not how able we are to have them), while fertility rates in the over 35s are increasing, with the number having babies in their 40s doubling in the past decade,[20] but analysts don't yet know whether these families will stop at one child or go on to have more. In addition, the fertility rate researcher Jonathan Grant, says:

> There could be an issue that they're postponing it so late that they can only actually have one child before infertility sets in. And that means we will have more families only with one [child] and the consequences of that on fertility would be a further decline of fertility rates. There is an increasing proportion of women aged 45 and above who don't have children and that's increased from around 16 per cent to 20 per cent over the last few years.[21]

Grant describes research showing how teenage mothers have a harder start, and find it harder later to enter the workforce. However, leaving motherhood until later has its dangers in terms of fertility as well as, earning higher salaries, they have the most to lose in cutting their hours or taking extended leave. There's also the health and disability issue: it's riskier giving birth as you get older and the chances of the child being affected by a disability such as Downs Syndrome or spina bifida increase with maternal age and autism with paternal age.

The costs of going back after a break

Once you've had your baby – earlier, or later – you'll almost inevitably be heading back to work at some stage. As US website smartmoney.com advises, it's wise to 'crunch the numbers' first.[22] A worksheet encourages us to look at our potential earnings not in terms of gross salary but at the bottom line after taxes and general work expenses have been taken into account as well as the more obvious childcare. Work-based expenses include clothes and accessories (such as make-up, a decent briefcase, perhaps, and the ongoing number of small items that add up), commuting costs and so on. Commuting incidentals can be higher than you think: a friend of mine estimates his annual commuting costs from his town into London, England, at around £6,000/US$12,000 a year, despite his train annual season ticket only costing £3,500/US$7,000. The remainder goes on coffee, newspapers and magazines, drinks after work (which he didn't have when he worked locally) and sometimes an overnight stay when he has to work late or there's a winter of floods and fallen leaves on the line. Hard-up parents could manage without some of those costs, but not all of them. Families also spend more on food and other shopping when there's less time to plan, to look for bargains and to shop ahead and in the sales. The message: you might not be improving your finances by as much as you think when you go back to work.

Recently, a distressed mother cried to a British newspaper agony aunt: 'I have three wonderful children and a great husband, and yet I feel like a complete failure!' The columnist, Mariella Frostrup, responds, tongue-in-cheek:

> Pull your socks up, you lazy woman! With only three young children pulling at your apron strings, are you trying to tell me that you don't have time to squeeze in an Open University degree, start your own business, write a best-seller?[23]

This particular anonymous mother can't afford to go back to work despite being well educated and on maternity leave from her job because the cost of childcare is too high. Her husband feels she should be enjoying the role of housewife and mother – indeed, he says he would like to do that himself – yet she's desperately unhappy. Perhaps her feelings are tied in with the way we manage our children, with nuclear families putting young mothers into lonely isolation and with the expectations that we put on ourselves stopping many of us feeling fulfilled unless we have a career galloping away at full speed. Although this chapter is asking whether it's worth the continuing battle to have a career while our children are young, for some women it's not an option. And where that's the case perhaps it's better not to get hung up about it – if we can. On days when that feels harder, remember the conversation between Alice and the White Queen in *Alice in Wonderland*:

> Alice laughed: 'There's no use trying,' she said; 'one can't believe impossible things.'
> 'I dare say you haven't had much practice,' said the Queen. 'When I was younger, I always did it for half an hour a day. Why, sometimes I've believed as many as six impossible things before breakfast.[24]

Ambition-wise, what happens to us when we have breaks from our careers to be at home with the children? Research from the Institute for Employment Studies shows that a small minority (7 per cent) felt that they were more ambitious following a break, about a third (33 per cent) felt that they were roughly as ambitious as they had been beforehand, 20 per cent said that their career would have to wait, another third (30 per cent) said that they had lower career aspirations and 10 per cent were less committed to their career and had lower levels of ambition still.[25]

Peter Eriksson, who has spent less time in paid work over the past 15 years than his wife so that he could care part-time for their children, looks ahead to the rest of his working life:

> I've got out of the habit and, age-wise, missed the boat really in
> terms of having a career that stretches me. I don't know whether
> I live to now regret that and think 'oh well, the girls have left
> home, what am I going to do?' because at the moment they still
> fill up an awful lot of time.

With two salaries and pensions to look forward to, his question is in the context of how he'll spend his time rather than how to earn enough. But it raises an issue that many of us don't consider in our early parenting: what, exactly, will work and life be like for us once we get properly back into it?

Researcher Suzan Lewis asks whether it's equality we're looking for, or equity?[26] She looked at previous research on dual-earners who sought either equality ('equal sharing of the same roles and entitlements') or equity ('fairness which can include different but equal roles'). Lewis found a number of different models identified by researchers such as Hertz, who described three approaches to childcare: the mothering approach (where the mother is seen as the best person to raise and care for the children), the market approach (where considerable amounts of childcare is delegated to paid help) and the new parenting approach (where family and work are centred around the children, with both parents highly involved and where time is created for both fathering and mothering).[27] Barnett and Lundgren describe how work–family decisions and strategies are 'influenced by a complex multiplicity of factors.[28] Workplace flexibility is important, but decisions still have to be made about whether this will be taken up and by which partner(s)'. They go on to suggest four different models we could choose from; other researchers see it from yet more angles. If we're feeling glum about the difficulties we face it's worth having a browse through the internet or library for some reassurance that really, there are as many models, as many methods, as many combinations that allow for anything that works – for us and our family. To have this gut feeling underpinned by academic research can be reassuring.

So, is it worth having children and if we do, is it worth trying to have a career too? Shenagh and Sue, who started this chapter, demonstrate two opposite approaches. Both had family issues, both are now single in their mid-50s, and both report strong relationships with their children which underpin their lives. Is it worth juggling everything, working so hard and putting yourself last? If you believe in your relationship, if you're not so bothered about a career, and if you believe the state will look after you if it all goes wrong then perhaps it's not worth all the hard career work that Shenagh put in. But if you love (or can tolerate) your work, you're at least partly independent at heart and you're a realist, then it looks as though your career needs some attention during those early years (if only milk-sodden occasional meetings with your employer, attendance at conferences and reading the trade press while on maternity leave) followed by a well-aimed dive back in when time and responsibilities allow.

Here are three quotes to finish off a chapter on a subject that doesn't have wholesale answers.

Sarah Nias, a young mother:

> I feel I've got to keep working part-time so that when he's at school, I've got it, it's there, still in my lap, still there for me, whereas if I think it's not worth it and give it up it'll be harder to get back into when he's started school. So that's why I do it.

Researcher and writer Catherine Hakim talks firstly about the irresolvable conflict of career and family:

The bottom line is that as far as investment in a career is concerned, policies actually don't make that much difference. The major investment required is one of time and effort: if you are seriously interested in a career, you don't have time for children and if you are seriously interested in bringing up more than one child, let's say, you don't have the time, effort and imagination for getting to the top of a career. The fact is that children are a 20-year project and a career is a 20- to 40-year project and there is an incompatibility there.' [Over the past eight years Hakim has written six books and she says] 'There's no way I could have done that if I had had children.[29]

And finally, newspaper correspondent Barbara Holtz, responding to an article written about 'The Mommy Wars', writes:

So live your dreams and talents – in the boardroom or at home – love yourself, your life and the choices you have made. I hope that will help us be the mothers that we want to be.[30]

Is it worth the fight? That depends on who you are, what your career's like, who your partner is, how much money you've got, how much support, how you'll fare in retirement and what you want. Easy, heh?

7

HOW TO BALANCE YOUR LIFE

The baby's been up half the night, the au pair's homesick and school's closed for a teacher-training day. There's a nasty stomach bug going round the office. You haven't finished the annual report because the slimy toad of a data manager won't give you the figures you need. Your partner's gone on a three-day business trip and the children are fed up with peanut butter in their sand-wiches. Your bank statement is shrieking that a chat with the bank manager would be a good idea. There's no milk in the fridge. And your mother-in-law's coming to stay for the weekend. Apart from recruiting a House of Windsor-style brigade of staff, how are you going to cope?

We do. Somehow, we hold it all together and make it work. Sometimes this feels more like luck than judgement but, in fact, we build a vast array of management and coping skills that tick away gently then come into their own in a crisis. At least there is an au pair in the house – so someone's thought to recruit and engage with her, even if she's behaving (understandably) more like a child than an adult. You had advance warning of the school closure day and the older two children are going to friends', being walked there by the weeping au pair. A bit of fresh air will cheer her up. The baby's childminder is lovely and accommodating and above all, adores the little darling. Now all you've got to battle with is the fridge, the bank, the report and the in-law but you know you can leave all of this to your partner because you chose someone who takes equal responsibility for these things. In the meantime the family can cope with boring sandwiches and black coffee. And if the au pair and mother-in-law work at it together they can look after the kids on Saturday evening and the pair of you can go out for a romantic dinner. Getting to this state of muddling through and then one step further, to having the energy and verve to enjoy both work and family, is an art form at which we become extremely talented on our journeys through parenting. Usually without any training, we work out the best way for us and our families to be and to operate and when the time's right, to re-form our careers. This chapter looks at some ways of doing this.

I eavesdropped on a conversation between two young women discussing how they, and their respective boyfriends, behaved on dates. This is what they said:

Girl 1: My boyfriend doesn't like it if I pay for dinner so if we're going Dutch or I'm paying, I slip him the money quietly.

Girl 2: My boyfriend doesn't mind, and anyway, I don't want to do that. I want us to be equal.

Girl 1: Oh yes, we're equal, just that he wants to look like he's in charge.

I know how the first girl feels because I used to think like that, aged 14. But these girls are speaking in 2007, not 1977, and more, they're students at a university known for its radical politics. Perhaps I should have intervened and given Girl 1 a talking-to. But she wouldn't have listened; she'll find out for herself in time. I give her ten years. By then she'll be in a male-dominated professional workplace and might have started her family; she'll have woken up to the facts and will herself be throwing off the paternalistic attitudes her parents taught her and understanding a little more about life's realities. Will it, by then, be too late for her? Will she have chosen a partner who comforts her by his resemblance to her father, and have settled into domestic life where she does a little more of the housework than he does? It won't matter at this point; she might even enjoy having the freedom to furnish and look after their new home spending their joint money. She'll set it up how she wants it, with his tacit approval.

It's not until she bores of this and her hormones and a baby kick in that the trouble starts. When she asks him to do the washing up, the vacuuming and to get up alternate nights for the baby, he won't understand. And why should he? His whole life, including his marriage, will have been underpinned by women taking on those roles. He'll do some of it, hopefully gladly, but the core responsibility will be hers. She'll struggle to manage the baby alongside full- or part-time work for a couple of years but deep down they both want more than one child. Just as it's becoming easier she'll become pregnant again and although she now knows how to care for a baby, so in this sense it'll be simpler, in every other sense it'll fall to pieces. She'll slowly become tired, less willing to engage in the marriage, her work and her social life — not because she doesn't want to, but because she can't do everything. Something has to go, and the chances are that (at this stage) it'll be the job. She might even give up work completely on the assumption that her high-earning husband will continue to support her and the children for the rest of her life. All fine for as long as both partners are happy with it. But how can it be called a partnership when one is free to enjoy his career and the support of his wife while the other puts the home and family before the career and gradually gives away her independence? Perhaps later, a combination of her resentment and her need for freedom, or his free and outward-looking approach to life, will mean an end to the marriage too. If so, she has no safety net. She's probably on the breadline, despite her degree and professional experience.

Girl 2 stands a better chance; perhaps she won't marry at all. Maybe she'll find a man (or woman) whose gender perceptions are closer to hers. It won't be easy, but it'll be fairer. That basic sense of justice will keep her – and them – going through the tough times. She'll earn more in her lifetime, her partner will reap those benefits over the long term, the children will have happier (and hopefully more stable) parents, and when it comes to retirement, it's more likely to be a waterskiing accident that kills her than hypothermia.

Hearing that conversation shocked me: have we still not, even today, woken up? Middle-aged men in offices may still have old-fashioned perceptions that lead to the snide comments and discrimination discussed in previous chapters, but surely not today's educated young women? And if we ourselves don't see it, how can we expect it to change?

The place where equality goes wrong

In that sense we can say that sexual inequality in the developed world's workplace is our fault: if we go along with it, we reap what we sow. By tacitly approving of sexist and unequal attitudes we condone them. By choosing to have a family with someone who expects our role to be the main carer for the joint progeny, we accept that our lives will be ridden with injustice. So what if there aren't enough 'new men' out there? In my time as an undergraduate at the same university in the 1970s I don't remember anyone speaking like Girl 1. We were gentle, caring, silly, loud, foolish, brash adventurers who enjoyed all sorts of relationships but we'd never have dreamed of pretending that boyfriends were paying for the meal just to save face. Despite this, my cohort has since, largely, taken on the traditional gender roles that were more prevalent back then. The women have generally stepped sideways in their careers and many are now waking up to the inequality of it, even though at the time, and through the years of caring for the family while working part-time, they may have been happy. Their pension projections aren't causing glee. One overheard conversation is hardly objective evidence – surely it can't be worse now than it was then? There must be thousands of young women on campuses across the UK and beyond who feel differently. I hope so.

Chapter 2 described 'work' as the place where equality goes wrong. In a sense it is. At a broader level though, it's the home where it goes wrong, and the wider sense of that: community, and society. And while we're shooting ourselves in the proverbial foot, it'll stay that way.

Choosing a partner

One of my 1970s group of university friends swore that he'd only ever work for a cooperative, or be a house husband. He was offered a job in finance for a multinational corporation and spent the next 25 years earning more than the rest of us put together, accumulating his nest egg and suffering due teasing from his loving, if sometimes unkind, friends. Then he gave it up and now lives as a house husband and father to his child while his wife works for an international agency. He has the money behind him, a pension in place and a wife who's dedicated to her career. Perhaps, all along, he knew what he was doing. American professor Linda Hirshman would agree.[1] My friend's family has done what Hirshman notes as being essential if the mother is to continue in her high-flying career: they only have one child and the father is willing to put his career second. Hirshman's research is based on women who, coming from educated backgrounds and with successful early careers, managed to retain their presence on the career ladder, as opposed to those who dropped away. In 2003 and 2004 she interviewed a group of 'educated and accomplished' American brides of

1996, who at the time of their marriages were working in high-flying careers such as a vice president of client communication, a gastroenterologist, a lawyer, an editor and a marketing executive. She found that seven or eight years into marriage 90 per cent had children. Seventeen per cent of the mothers were still working full-time, 33 per cent were working part-time, though often a long way from their earlier career paths and half the married women with children were not working at all. She noted that those who remained successful and whose careers blossomed had married 'loser' husbands. This 'loser' is an intelligent man who doesn't see a successful career as a demonstration of his penis size. He could be an artist, a writer, a musician – anything arty-farty would do. He might be into sport, or computers, or collecting diverse types of umbrella. The reason for marrying the 'loser' is that if you're to maintain your standard of living there's no choice but that you continue with your brilliant career. If he can't – or won't – go out to earn a decent living and you have children and a mortgage to support, it's down to you. The politics of the marriage would have to be fairly precipitous if the husband in this scenario insisted that you were the one to stay at home and look after the children while he painted a few unsaleable oil paintings in the garden shed. That's not to say that he won't be working: he himself will be beavering away with his own interests, and perhaps making some money, even forging his own successful career which emerges over time. The point is that he accepts the default position of main carer so that when the children get chickenpox or teen pop stardom he's the one to drop everything, not you.

Journalists Roger Dobson and Maurice Chittenden have put together a number of examples and quotes, including this from UK writer and broadcaster Claire Rayner:

> A chap with a high IQ is going to get a demanding job that is
> going to take up a lot of his energy and time. In many ways he

wants a woman who is an old-fashioned wife and looks after the home, a copy of his mum in a way. The bright girl, on the other hand, remembers that old saying, that at first she sinks into his arms only to spend the rest of her life with her arms in his sink.[2]

Rayner cleverly found her husband, Desmond – an actor who gave up his career when they married: a man with brains whose ambitions aren't directed at the workplace. If you believe the stories and statistics, men like this are rare. In addition to the need to spot a rarity, Paul Brown, a visiting professor of psychology and an expert on relationships, says:

What we are finding is that women in their late 30s who have gone for careers after the first flush of university and who are among the brightest of their generation are finding that men are just not interesting enough. It is a really difficult issue. Women want independence but we are all hard-wired into wanting to be into relationships. The paradox of the post-feminist position is how we create a social system in which both independence and inter-dependency can flourish.[3]

So we need someone who's both interesting enough to engage us, yet at the same time amenable enough to drop his ambitions and allow us ours. The question is, who we're going to find – and whether, if we don't find the right person, we're prepared to give up thoughts of partnership and family. The figures bear out that this happens: clever women are less likely to marry than clever men. A study of 900 men and women which measured their IQ at the age of 11, then revisited them 40 years later to find out whether they had ever married, discovered that schoolgirls with high IQs were less likely to marry than schoolboys with high IQs.

As Claire Rayner points out above, professional men prefer to marry women who remind them of their mothers and who will provide the domestic support while they go out to work. There seem to be plenty. Ambitious women, though, find it difficult to find men willing to sacrifice their careers to become house husbands. A relatively large number of the girls in this survey didn't marry at all; I wonder how many of them married as a compromise, finding men who they felt 'would do' rather than those they knew were right for them and their ambitions. Even Nicola Horlick, dubbed 'Superwoman' for her juggling of high-flying career and family, has since separated from her husband.[4] 'Maybe you can't necessarily have a happy marriage if you end up being a very high-powered woman,' she says. 'It may be that men find it difficult living with a woman who's forging ahead.' She's also refreshingly open about her projected superhero status: 'Look at someone who has no help at home and holds down a job. Or look at me with my nanny and my secretary. Who would you call "superwoman"? The first one.'

Christine Northam, a senior relationship counsellor with Relate, says that 'IQ measurements are frightfully judgemental, but it is true that men do not want women more intelligent than themselves.[5] It bolsters their position if their partner is not too challenging.' But this is a generalisation; Sarah Nias seems to have it under control. We asked her how she juggles work with family and what support she has from her partner:

The nature of my work is freelance. I dictate my own hours, and because we can't afford much childcare, yet need to earn money, we have to work it around when my husband gets home. I then go out and do some of my teaching and he looks after [our child] so we do a swap over. We have to support each other. It's like working as a team, we don't see each other all the time and we have to make certain sacrifices.

I'm supporting him as he's supporting me. He's contributing to most of the mortgage and I'm topping that up, so I don't see myself as behind him or in front of him or subservient to him. I just see a good balance. And I know that when I go back to work, potentially I can earn more than him because I'm slightly more qualified and have more experience but that's good for us. I don't compare my career to his.

Although Sarah is compromising as well as working extremely hard, her husband is compromising too. Peter Eriksson is another example of a father who's happy letting his career take a back seat; while his wife Anne Eriksson says, 'it's a fact there are very, very few men working part-time or turning up at school groups with young children, though I think men do take a greater interest in children than they did a generation ago and are more heavily involved.' Peter adds:

> Some of that might just be a bit of show: they do that when it suits them. It's that background hard graft that goes on constantly [that counts] – you know – picking up the socks, the washing up, etc. Taking them out for a push around the park on a nice day is quite pleasant but it's the day-in day-out chore of it that's the tough side and I suspect that not all of them are totally up to their neck in that.

And how do we find this person who is both bright enough to provide intelligent conversation and yet prepared to teach the kids to tie their shoelaces? In the words of dating coach Sam Van Rood, 'finding a husband these days is like finding your perfect home or job. It's going to be a lot of work and there are going to be disappointments along the way.'[6]

One thing you'll find in abundance on the internet is dating advice. Some of it's probably sound and perhaps worth looking at. Yet it's easy to be carried away by the romance and passion of an early relationship without thinking whether this person will match you and your ambitions well enough. With feminism still the 'F' word, these sites don't usually consider these longer-term aspects of the partners' career aspirations. It feels deflating to set them beside the red roses and champagne. Yet if we go into it without keeping these areas high on the agenda we've only partly ourselves to blame if we find our two ambitions – work and family – mutually thwarting each other by the less than helpful approach of a dinosaur of a partner.

Once we've found Mr/Ms Right, the relationship needs sustenance and those of us who take the 'male' approach and dedicate every waking thought to our careers and then expect our families, like pets, to be available and well-groomed on demand, are living in a dream world. If we want both we need to compromise to make it work. Marital compromise in one direction creates the old-fashioned relationships where women end up without careers. Find a mate who'll compromise too. If you want to be a career high-flier, find a house husband and have only one child. If you're prepared to, or want to, go part-time and bide your time until the children are a little older before returning to a full-blown career then you need a partner who supports you in this. If you want to take the risk of the full-time housewife option, there are plenty of men out there for you but try to choose one who truly believes the promises he's making. We each need to decide what we want, to be realistic, find the person who'll do this with us (unless we decide to go it alone) and work bloody hard. Then it might work.

Get educated – in the right thing

We may find our partners before – though more probably during, or after – school or university. What's vital is that alongside our romantic quest, we get educated. The UK is behind many other developed nations in the number of young people who go through university-level education (and the government is quietly dropping its recent 50 per cent participation target) but if you want a top career in employment (rather than self-employment) it's more or less essential that you're one of these near-50-per-cent. As women, it's more likely that we will go to university – and succeed there – than our male schoolmates, but what should we study when we go? There are different views on this.

Linda Hirshman says to study something that gives you the vocational leg up.[7] Forget archaeology – loving a subject isn't enough. Get qualified in a subject that's in demand from employers and that gives vocational skills ready to slot into a career with good earning potential. We need to look at what the top recruiters are asking for in their graduates and plump for that, or an equivalent that matches our aptitudes and will get us into a good apprenticeship with a solid employer – enough to get us onto the springboard. This thinking is borne out in the movement away from traditional, non-vocational (academic) university subjects towards those with a more vocational leaning. UK university applications to traditional subjects such as classics, music and history have fallen in recent years and those to vocational subjects such as maths, pharmacology, social work and nursing have risen.[8] When Hirshman advises us to keep away from arts-based degrees, she's looking at successful US businesswomen: cultures and workplaces around the world vary and you need to take account of that. In the UK, blue chip employers recruit from selected universities and often don't mind what your degree is in. If you're studying at such a university where top recruiters visit to persuade the best students to work for them, and if you're one of these students, then study whatever you like. Although some of these recruiters look for business studies graduates to fill their management trainee positions, many are looking for history, French or philosophy graduates with first-class degrees. It shows an aptitude in thinking, reasoning and argument as well as sufficiently high intelligence. There's a case for saying that any old person who can get to university can study their way through a business studies module but not everyone can make the intellectual arguments that a top English degree requires. The answer is to do your research: don't read just one article or book on the subject but get lots of work experience, call recruiters, speak to careers advisors, look and feel your way before you even apply for your university course.

Diane Baker is 60 and worked as a secretary before she married and had children, then worked part-time for her husband until their marriage failed. She says:

> For a while my daughter said that she wasn't going to university but then she got a job and said 'Mum, there are idiots at work and they've got silly degrees and they get more money than me!' So I said 'You know the way forward.' So she chose to go to Goldsmiths and did psychology. And now she works for research analysts at a merchant bank and earns extremely good money and is completely self-sufficient; she hasn't a family yet but she's travelled all over the world and she's done amazing things and I'm very proud of her.

For anyone still deciding whether to carry on into higher education we now have the additional question: is it worth the debt that comes after studying? A decade ago commentators were telling us that a UK graduate earns, on average, £400,000/US$800,000 more in a lifetime than a non-graduate. This estimate has come down over the years since Highter Education participation had been going up, partly because there haven't been as many 'graduate jobs' in relation to the number of graduates as in the past. Why slave for a degree simply to end up emptying dustbins? I've seen estimates of as little as a £150,000/US$300,000 difference in earnings estimated now. This still allows for the projected £30–40,000/US$60–80,000 graduate loan in the UK you'll need to repay over your working life and leaves a fair bit of change, assuming you're one of the ones to earn a decent salary. In the US, as in the UK and around the world, student debt is becoming more of a problem: the number of US students who have graduated with more than £12,500/US$25,000 in debt has tripled since the 1990s; some current students estimated their future debts at between £5,000/US$10,000 to £300,000/US$600,000, with most around £25,000/US$50,000.[9]

And remember too, that in a future workplace based on a knowledge economy (see Chapter 1), the skills we'll need are knowledge skills. The gradual whittling away of jobs that can be done anywhere (manufacturing, call centres, software and many more) leaves a need for people who can supply the new entrepreneurs – or become them – and commercial and strategic thinkers. Getting the right work experience to lead into the right career may well depend on having a degree in the first place even if your first job or two aren't exactly 'graduate' jobs.

And then choose your career. Something glamorous like media or advertising crosses many people's minds at some stage. We may groan at the thought of accountancy in the same way that 20th-century men groaned at the thought of a high-flying wife, but look at the job satisfaction statistics. The Training and Development Agency for Schools carried our a survey of more than 2,000 graduates aged 21 to 45 and found that more than half were regularly bored at work.[10] The relative enjoyment of people working in the various professions is interesting. With a 'boredom rating' of 0–10 (10 being the most boring), teachers scored the least (ie were least bored) with a score of 4. This is unsurprising perhaps in a survey carried out by an agency for schools; however, there is presumably no bias in the scores for the other professions. The ones we'd probably think are most exciting, such as media and marketing, scored 6.9 and 7.7 respectively. Those we start yawning at even before the words are out, accountancy and engineering, score 6.3 and 6.6. In other words, graduates working in these areas are less bored than graduates working in the glamorous professions of media, marketing and advertising. Administrative and secretarial work scored the absolute most tedious 10; IT and telecoms, 7.5, and healthcare, 5.1. Another UK survey, this time by City and Guilds, looked at trades as well as professions.[11] It's perhaps galling to see that almost all the trades (work that requires skills developed through an apprenticeship or similar type of training, rather than work done primarily by graduates) tended to score more highly than the professions. In this survey, the percentages of people who enjoyed their work were ascertained through interviews. This time a higher number means more fun. The highest score was 40 per cent for hairdressers and the lowest was 2 per cent for social workers. In between came chefs and cooks at 23 per cent, and media at 16 per cent. Interestingly, teachers came far lower than in the previous survey, at 8 per cent, but whether or not you're bored is a different question from whether you're enjoying yourself. A finding common to both surveys was that media-type professions were less interesting than many of us would perhaps expect, and that many of the trades, which often also involve running a small business, were more interesting. This makes some sense if you think how the more glamorous an industry, the more choice of graduates it has and the worse, in theory, it can treat them. In TV or film, for instance, you might work as an unpaid lackey for a couple of years in the hope of being properly employed but even then, you'll probably earn peanuts in another menial role for a few more years . . . you may do brilliantly but the chances are slimmer. Aim instead for a career, and prior to that, a degree, that takes you towards good employment prospects, decent pay and high job satisfaction and you're more likely to do well in all senses.

In addition to looking at the job satisfaction indices, find out what your intended profession thinks about women. A 2003 report on architecture, for instance, described how women (and men) find the profession. A combination of factors, it said, 'including poor employment practice, difficulties in maintaining skills and professional networks during career breaks and paternalistic attitudes, cause women to leave the profession.'[12] The report described the gradual erosion of confidence and deskilling caused by the lack of creative opportunities for female architects, sidelining, limited investment in training, job insecurity and low pay which lead to reduced self-esteem and poor job satisfaction in architectural practice. You could take this as a reason to avoid architecture or a reason to research it further: it is at least looking at the issue and hopeful that change can be made. Research into other professions will reveal similar reports and action taken as a consequence. Engineering will reveal a long-standing campaign to draw more women into the profession that has succeeded in doubling the percentage of female engineering graduates from 7 per cent in 1984 to 18 per cent today.[13] That's not to say that it's plain sailing for women within engineering but there is at least an acceptance that there needs to be change, and an ongoing commitment to that change.

Limit your family

Linda Hirshman, quoted above, says that we should have only one child. My old university friend has done this – many couples do, some through choice and some through circumstance. As anyone who's been a parent of more than one will tell you, there are advantages to a larger family – the kids play together and therefore make it possible to cook the occasional meal – but equally, they fight, they compete, they refuse to eat the same food, they go to different schools and the one with chickenpox becomes well enough to go back to school at exactly the point as the next one goes down with it.

Sarah Nias has one child so far and is uncertain whether to expand her family: 'Lifestyle-wise, maybe you should just choose to have one child,' she says. 'I'm not sure about that – maybe I'd feel different if I had a high-flying high-powered city career but I don't.'

A mother who's chosen to stick to one is Jennifer Baker.[14] She found it hard to cope with a child and a demanding job, and has since changed jobs to involve less travelling so that she can see more of her son. However, she also says: 'By having one child, I have the best of both worlds. I'm a mum, which is what I've always wanted, and I have a career that I'm passionate about.'

Set the domestic agenda

Chapter 4 saw how our partners often see the domestic burden as equally shared where research shows that it rarely is. Female university students get lower marks when they move in with men; a contributor to this book underlines this by saying: 'Yes, I got lower marks in my second year too. I moved in with four blokes, and I was always tidying up after them.' Our programming makes most of us yearn for a tidy home, a clean bath and not to expect men to take an equal share – or any share at all – in getting it that way. When we complain we're called nags; when we negotiate a housework sharing schedule it's often set aside and we end up doing it anyway.

Apart from labelling many men, and some women, as lazy slobs, what can we do about it? Perhaps we can remember that the house-proud values we live by are artificial. Back in Victorian times, when even Prince Albert died of illness from household sanitation problems, there was good reason to spend time ensuring that the house was as clean as possible. These days we go so far that it drains people's lives of time and energy. Experts believe we're harming our children by using antibacterial agents on everything in the home and so preventing babies from building immunity to bacteria. It also causes havoc with the environment as these bacteria-zapping potions go into the sewers and alter the biological balance. There are certain domestic habits that are essential – washing hands, cleaning toilets and trying not to eat mouldy food will all improve our health, but vacuuming religiously will only exhaust us. The oven sterilises itself each time it's set on high. Dusting is pointless. Writer Quentin Crisp lived in a Chelsea boarding house where 'he left the dust heroically undisturbed through decades: in his whole renegade life, no statement was more outrageous than his "after the first four years the dirt does not get any worse".'[15] Crisp didn't have small children with dust allergies to cope with but even so, we can lay hard floors, buy in hypo-allergenic bedding and the best dust-busting vacuum cleaner and then leave the washing up for tomorrow and the front porch full of blown-in leaves. That may test the tolerance factor of our housemates.

We all get to the stage where we notice the mess around us, and most of us then do something about it. This default tolerance needs noting and living around if we're to relinquish some of the domestic burden – our own tolerance setting, and that of our housemates' and partner's. It's not only our own lives that we ruin when we insist on being stupidly house-proud. Imagine being a child brought up in this pristine environment where no shoes are allowed and nothing can be broken: removing the joy of fun from a child's home is a great shame. I wouldn't go so far as to advocate playing tennis across the kitchen table or badminton up the stairs, as my partner does with his children in his house, because I'd prefer some of my crockery and pictures to remain intact. We all have our limits – once again, it's a matter of compromise, but if our existing way of living is preventing us from having what we need from life then we need to address it.

However fair the initial domestic share-out is with childless couples, once the children come along it's easy for the balance to skew. As Sarah Nias says:

We don't particularly share domestic duties; I pretty much do everything but that's because my husband works full-time and long hours. Because I'm only part-time, I should be doing more at home. But he's supportive of me, he's not expectant, I just choose to do it that way. I think it's fair.

It's fair now because Sarah is working part-time and can fit the chores around her child. What happens once children grow and the wife goes back to work? If these patterns are long-established, it's easy for them to continue. If we can ensure that the role models in the family and the chores that our children are required to do are split equally and not according to sex we'll bring up a generation that assumes equality. It's often easier to do the chores ourselves than to insist our children do them but it's only in insisting (and gently training and helping) that we're going to bring up a generation who will participate equally within their own relationships. Anyone looking after children will ensure that they stop at every kerb and look out for traffic; that way, they have an inbuilt sense that grows with them. In the same way, we can ensure that the childminder includes the children in cooking, clearing up and cleaning. The nanny and au pair need this at the top of their lists. And at weekends and other family time children need to learn early on that they have the same responsibility for their belongings as we do for ours and a shared responsibility (tiny to begin with, but growing) for the house. Pushing this agenda despite its difficulties only works if both partners are engaged with it; this in turn ensures that the man about the house has a day-to-day understanding of what's going on domestically, in reviewing the children's activity, even if he's not actively engaged himself that day. And to ensure that the boys as well as the girls take an equal part in domestic chores, their father has to set that example.

As the children grow and we return to work, what happens then? Shenagh has some thoughts on this:

I do not think of domestic responsibilities as work; they are hard work, but they are part of life, like paid work or work outside the home. My partner did not really see them as work either. We shared them fully. Most of the time I was happy with the level of sharing, but because of some challenges to our relationship at times it felt competitive at home and sometimes I wished we had slightly more demarcation and less negotiation about absolutely everything.

'Sharing them fully' will sound like a heavenly treat to some women yet even here there were issues: it's never going to be straightforward but it does need attention, not ignoring, if we're going to be free to engage with our work and families without that housework hand tied behind our backs.

Set your skills agenda

What if you're in your 20s or 30s with a partner chosen long ago, a successful relationship, little education or a degree in something no one's ever heard of, the wish for more than one child and a growing realisation that your career might not survive motherhood?

There are plenty of things you can to be doing right now, before the week is out. One of these relates to your own skills agenda. I've tried to avoid talking about 'skills' partly because they're impossible to get away from in the press and workplace and partly because this book isn't about career development per se. Nevertheless, skills are important and need considering. Hopefully you already have a CV. A straw poll around my office showed that yes, my colleagues did have CVs . . . somewhere . . . probably. We tend to think of CVs only as job-hunting tools but they're far more. Everybody needs to take a monthly look at their work (just as we take a monthly look around our armpits) and think what skills we've used in that past month. It needn't take more than a few minutes. Remember any training courses we've been on or given, or read, and log them in the CV under continuing professional development or as a memo that we want to do them. Create a magnificently overfull and lengthy CV that describes the things we can do and when and where we demonstrated that we did them. We'll never send it in this state to an employer; it's there for our own reference and edification and to be streamlined as appropriate for job applications or other purposes in due course. We also need to note the voluntary or community work we're doing (in the home as well as workplace community – for your professional association perhaps) and think about what skills we've used and developed there.

If we know what we've done we can present it at short notice to anyone who wants it but more importantly, we keep with us a sense of who we are and what we've achieved. It's so, so easy, in the maelstrom of the mind that is early parenting, to lose sight of how good we are at what we do. The best tip I was given in career terms was to see a CV as the basic tool that underpins my working life and to see this CV in terms of my own achievements. Cultures push women down in often subtle ways. The British traditional upbringing is to be 'seen and not heard': we're certainly not encouraged to crow about what we're good at. We're not going to get anywhere until we find the courage to write our achievements large within our CVs and learn to think achievement in our daily working lives. Inside, we may be quaking and thinking that really, we're not good at very much (a trait often exacerbated by childbearing). Remember that many of the people who do well in the workplace around us aren't actually very good at what they do; what they're good at is self-promotion. I like this comment from *Marie Claire* magazine: 'We'll know we're equal when lots of "very average" women are running the government and the economy (just as lots of "very average" men do now).'[16] 'Very average' may not be enough for you in the long-term but if it works in the short-term, go for it and shout about what you can do (on paper too). Read it on bad days and add to it on good days.

Do as much community work as the little darlings allow. I somehow manage to include on my CV: running a community play scheme, meeting the Prime Minister, appearing on BBC prime-time news and securing public funding for an innovative social project, all through voluntary work. I was working part-time, the kids were around for some of it and on childcare-swaps the rest of the time. The reality wasn't nearly as impressive as it sounds (shhhh . . .) but it's all true. It's certainly helped me, in bad times, to be able to look down my list of experience and skills and brainwash myself that I am actually quite good at stuff.

Along with the hard-hitting CV need to be the basic personal development tools – things like time management, assertiveness, all of the standard things that perhaps we learned once and didn't think much about, and certainly don't now there's a trail of puke running down our shoulder. When someone interrupts us, do we stop speaking or do we carry on regardless? – all that sort of thing. We practise it at work but once we're out of the everyday work-place, it's surprisingly easy to forget. It's simpler to join a group of people who are re-learning it together – a group-aggrandisement process. There will be a number of these running in cities and large towns, or try the internet. Groups such as the European Social Funded Career Action for Women, with free classes and funded childcare and travel costs, might be running in your area and will bring together groups of women in a similar situation to learn together how to move ahead into education and work.

Another thing to keep up with is networking. This again may be the last thing on your mind when on a career break but it pays dividends. Go and see colleagues – with the new baby if you must but far better to go in regularly on your own at lunchtime or at the end of the day and join a group or selected individuals for a drink. Talk about anything except babies – even when asked – and display some ongoing knowledge of the sector, gained by skimming through websites regularly; even the headlines will be enough to give a hook for conversation when you can't find time to gain in-depth knowledge of current issues. If you don't have a workplace, why not join a networking club? There's one local to me that meets for business breakfasts. I was invited to join one the basis of a freebie piece in a community paper – they didn't have a writer in the mix and felt it would be mutually beneficial. Whatever avenue you can find, track it down and do it, however hard it feels. And write it on your CV. There are plenty of websites with advice such as this – a quick Google will get you reading about some of the strategies you can employ to keep your hand in. You don't have to do much but it's important to be doing something.

And lastly – look after yourself. You're not the family's lackey, you're one of the linchpins that hold the family together and as such you're one of the most important members. Your child will almost certainly be fine without home-made meals/ designer clothing/visits to additional-maths-for-three-year-olds classes. You won't be okay unless you feel good in yourself. Part of this is getting and staying fit – put exercise into your week even if it means jogging around the baby for 20 minutes 4 times a week; better still if you can go swimming with friends or find a new exercise class to make new friends. Buy new clothes (especially underwear), have your hair done, keep talking – to friends or your therapist, though the former are cheaper – and prioritise going out socially.

Get a community

The best – and worst – communities we have are our extended families. If we're blessed with the best then parenting becomes a relative cinch. Parents with supportive family around them often take this for granted and can't imagine how it is when there's no one to take the strain when things go wrong. It's also easy to complain about the presence of this support net; unsurprisingly, our own parents often want something in return, not simply to be treated as unpaid childminders. A little appreciation, the odd Sunday lunch . . . even though Sundays are so precious? It can be a difficult mix and it doesn't always work. It can leave us feeling totally pinned down – by our own kids, by our work and then by our parents, aunts, sisters. But when so many of us leave home to go to university and then stay away, or marry someone from a far-flung location and settle elsewhere, we lose what most generations before us, and what most communities around the world, have.

Family comes at a price but what it gives is also immense. I know several working mothers who couldn't do their jobs without their own parents to step in when the children aren't well enough to go to school – it would be either them, or their partners, who had to keep missing days at work, and in most jobs that simply can't happen. One of those careers would have to go. So even if you currently live a long way from family who are keen to support you, might it be worth relocating so that you can take up this support, and get involved in the family community again?

I thought I had a community around me until my marriage failed. I've now come to understand that what I had was a group of peers. I'd moved away from my home community when I went to university, and then moved again to follow various jobs. When I settled and had my children, the people I became friends with were all, like me, parents of young children. I did have some older neighbours but didn't pay them much attention.

When I was suddenly on my own with the kids I found that I was living too far away for the instant dropping-in that I wanted to do to my friends and for the kids to be in each other's houses as they grew. I was so busy with my three young children that it was difficult to find time, without a babysitting partner and while working as much as possible, to gather up the kids, walk or drive to the friend, who anyway might be too busy with her own kids, be out, etc. I needed local, drop-by people to come to me, or neighbours I could drop in on. There were few older or younger people with spare time within my own self-formed community who would support me at that time. My friends were as loving and supportive as they could be within their own family constraints and problems while I found myself difficult and prickly on one hand yet desperate for companionship and community on the other.

I realise now that community is more than a group of people of our own age and stage; it's about a cross section of people who will support others as and when needed and accept support when they themselves need it. When everyone else is knee-deep in nappies and trying to keep their marriages and careers going, however well-meaning they are, there's little time to give that support.

So, which communities aren't underpinned solely by people 'just like us'? We gravitate naturally to people we identify with: our friendships are almost always with people of our age and stage. If we can extend that through any form of more diverse group then we insure ourselves, to some extent, against disaster and provide ourselves with a support network when we need an emergency babysitter so that we can make that presentation after all. So, out of our already impossibly busy lives, can we spare time to rent an allotment-share and join the allotment holders' group? Join a sports club where there'll be a cross section of people? Join a faith community? Have an open evening in our homes for people in our street and follow that up by dropping in to borrow a cup of sugar now and again? And of course, doing what we can to support other people in return.

Try different ways of working

Taking maternity leave or a career break can be an opportunity for reflection. Many use this time to realise that the old ways and places of working simply don't suit the changed people we become. If there's pressure on us to return to earning as soon as possible and the old job is the only way we're going to earn at that level then it's not so easy. But if there's any flexibility in the sums and the structures, why not think about some of these options?

Most of us work part-time for at least a short while. Most mothers are familiar with patterns such as term-time working, short days and job shares as well as the simple shorter working week. What's it really like to cut back the hours, and how feasible is it?

American Tracy Hahn-Burkett is a writer and former advocate for civil rights and civil liberties. She muses in her blog:

> It has been made abundantly clear to me that should I wish to work full-time in my former profession, I could choose from numerous job opportunities in less time than it takes to say, 'Hi, here's my resume.' But as soon as I utter those ominous words, 'part-time,' I can almost hear the screams as the purveyors of those would-be jobs scramble to put as much distance between me and them as possible. Of course, I do know several women who work part-time, in arrangements cobbled together after they had their first or second or third child. But in almost every case, these women already had full-time jobs, and were able to approach employers who already appreciated and relied upon their efforts and skills and had a vested interest in keeping them as part of their teams. But for me, who moved to an entirely new region of the country when my son was 18 months old, there was no pre-existing job that I could convert. I sought a part-time job as a beginning, not a means to hang on. And as of yet, there have been no takers.[17]

My experience has been similar: after relocating while pregnant with my first child there was no part-time professional work available. All advertised work paid the equivalent of the minimum wage, which (after childcare and expenses) would have cost me money to do. Just to learn to stack supermarket shelves. That's when I went freelance and dived into community and voluntary work. There's also job-sharing: some jobs are more suitable than others, and those that are based around ongoing projects or issues with individuals in other departments or organisations aren't the easiest. That's not to say they're not possible – indeed, from now on in the UK, all recruiters must consider job-share applicants equally alongside all other applicants (see the Appendix for the new legislation). I can understand why sometimes, employers don't feel it would work. In other instances there are enormous benefits to employers on recruiting two people for one job – a new mind to the issues halfway through the week, different strengths and perceptions, and probably, overall, better value for money. I've seen it succeed in a number of roles where you wouldn't expect it to be easy. As for purely part-time work where the job only requires part of the week or the year: as the skills shortage kicks in, so employers will be forced to rethink. As individuals, we too need to think – how many hours do we want to work, at what level and pace? In what environment? Taking time during a career break, and engaging with return-to-work groups where available, helps put this into perspective.

Government policy underlines working from home as a useful model to decrease the stress on families and workers while decreasing employers' overheads. For parents, the thought can be enticing: no more long commutes, being available to pop out for the class assembly and generally being around more. Anne Eriksson gives the other side of the equation: 'I think it's six of one, half a dozen of the other,' she says. 'It depends on your character. It can be quite isolated and isolating.' And not all employers are interested. It may mean becoming self-employed. Her husband Peter Eriksson continues:

It doesn't give you the security or financial solidity that a steady job does. If you've got all the concerns about bringing up children and running a house, knowledge of a solid income coming in is a great benefit rather than worrying about being able to pay the bills at the end of the month.

Recent research shows that working from home's often not as positive an experience as we'd think. Psychology researcher Jeanne Moore points to the advantages of greater independence, flexibility and control over work and home life for people who work from home but she counters this with reports of work seeping into evenings and weekends and impinging on everyday family life.[18] Many of the 123 homeworkers she interviewed said that they work longer hours than they did when employed away from home, with others stating how self-motivation and remaining focused were extremely challenging. Home, for many, became a less relaxing and private place as a result of overworking. Stress levels of homeworkers overall were no lower than for average employees. Perhaps it makes a good interim step, and one where you can gather additional skills (self-motivation, ICT, remote networking) before going back to the office. For some it's a permanent move that suits them.

Working locally is another great 'plus' for parents – if it's an hour's (or more) journey to collect the children in a crisis that all adds to the stress. Anne says:

To have Peter working locally was a big ingredient to successful childcare because you need someone there on the spot. I was always in London or Croydon. I was always commuting.

Mother of two sons under four, Frances adds:

I work locally so I don't have a long way to travel. I work . . . short days, I do four days from 9.00 until 3.00 and that means I can drop off and pick up my eldest son from school everyday. I think in as far as it's possible, it's a good balance.

Women make great entrepreneurs. Many of us have the skills. What we've lacked in the past is the freedom to use them. Nowadays, being in business doesn't necessarily entail being out and about and working long hours, and women with caring responsibilities can often find a niche where starting our own businesses, perhaps working evenings from home serving a global e-market, say, when our partners can look after the children, solves the need for flexibility that isn't provided in many workplaces.

Claire Taylor is a freelance music teacher and pianist and mother of boys aged two and four. She describes how she felt the need to change when she became pregnant with her first child:

[I did] full-time music teaching at a secondary school which was exhausting, dull and inflexible. I felt like I was on a conveyor belt and craved more control and creativity in my job. I ended up resigning when I went on maternity leave. I knew that I couldn't carry on working such long hours with a child, neither did I want to. I earn a lot less now but my hourly rate of earning is a lot higher than in teaching. I take on projects (such as private piano teaching, playing the piano for weddings, working in a local primary school as a music specialist). I have also started up my own toddler music classes. I feel like I've found my niche now and don't really have a grand plan. When the children need me less in 10 or 15 years' time I might do something quite different.

Self-employment can give us much of what we strive for in our work: autonomy from a sometimes prejudiced workplace, interesting work, plus the potential for good or even fantastic earnings. The number of female entrepreneurs in the US has doubled in recent years, with 38 per cent of all US firms now owned by women.

Interestingly, the greatest recent growth has taken place in areas not traditionally associated with women's work, that is, away from the service industries, education and so on, and into construction, wholesale trade and other particularly 'male' areas.[19] In the UK, 'there are still too few women starting out and growing a business . . . If women started new businesses at the same rate as men, we would have more than 100,000 extra new businesses each year.' So says Patricia Hewitt, former Secretary for State for Trade and Industry.[20] The figures read that a quarter of the UK's 3.2 million self-employed workers are now women; 30 per cent of business owners are women; female entrepreneurs account for 6.8 per cent of the UK's working population, double the figure for 1979.[21] Compared to the standard female population, women aged between 35 and 44 are more entrepreneurial; so are women graduates and those from higher income groupings.[22] Fifty-four per cent of women start a business so they can choose what hours they work, compared with only 35 per cent of men.[23] In Asia, women are starting businesses for the same reasons found in the West: autonomy, flexibility, money and profits.[24]

Gemma Childe has both a part-time job and a young business and talks of her experience of being self-employed:

> I do this on a part-time basis and it is harder than I thought. I guess in a way I do currently have the best of both worlds, banter in an office in the morning and then working alone at night. If I was always on my own, it would become very lonely. Also it's virtually impossible to work with a toddler around, especially if phone calls need to be made. I would like to lower the stress levels. I feel I am constantly juggling my days between my morning job and my evening job. Eventually I am hoping I will be able to give up my morning job and concentrate on my freelance work from home.

Claire Taylor agrees about the hard work:

> As I now work for myself, I do not have colleagues. I miss this to
> a degree but not the politics. I don't have the time to chat to
> people these days.

We might also give some thought to changing our work personas.
A report by the International Labour Office in Geneva states how
both visible and invisible rules have been created around the
normal way a man works and that women sometimes find it difficult to accommodate this:

> Male and female colleagues and customers do not automatically
> see women as equal with men. Women tend to have to work much
> harder than men to prove themselves, and sometimes they have to
> adapt to 'male' working styles and attitudes more than necessary.[25]

Given these old-fashioned attitudes in the workplace and many
women's experience that trying to get their jobs done using mainstream skills and tactics doesn't always work, it's not surprising
that some have chosen to 'act male' in the workplace, hoping that
people will somehow forget their sex. But decades of competing
'man to man', as commentators such as Chinchilla and Leon put
it,[26] might have helped women as individuals in their particular
work environment at that time but it hasn't moved perceptions
on. This is despite many people understanding that women often
bring a welcome diversity into a workforce, and skills that are
rarer in men[27] as described in Chapter 5. Not many people seriously feel that women are less able in the workplace; it's the other
demands that certain women have on their time, or may have, that
put employers off. Employers' views will change when they are
convinced that women can perform both roles rather than when
we go into work sporting beards.

Some mothers' approach to paid work is not to do it. As Frances says, despite working four short days a week: 'it's still not that easy. I often think I wish I wasn't working as much, or even not at all.' There are disadvantages to giving up work. For most of us it's not an option financially unless we're able to exist on someone else's money (our partner's, perhaps), on the state (this can be possible) or unless we've squirrelled away enough of our own before we have the kids. And it's possible to find that the choices a good salary brings are difficult ones. Frances continues:

> Some of the girls I work with are PAs or secretaries and their salaries just wouldn't cover [the childcare]; maybe for one child but certainly not for two. Luckily for us, we can afford it. Well, I say luckily but sometimes you think, in a way, if I couldn't afford it then I'd just give up work and I'd get to spend more time with the children. I've often thought that when you're in a job like mine, which does pay really well, then you're almost a prisoner of it.

It's easy to think that giving up work would be fantastic: imagine all that time with the children, and doing the things there was never time for before. Once we've had our first child we realise that having spare time is laughable unless a nanny or another high-input form of childcare comes in the mix. But it's still a compelling thought for some. Even if it's feasible financially, there are two big disadvantages: the present, and the future. What's life actually like when you're at home with kids with no work outside the home?

Claire Taylor puts it like this:

> I did stop working for three years after my children were born. Although I did not wish to return to my previous job I felt stagnant and depressed at times. Some days I really questioned what I was doing at home and felt my life was lacking in direction.

Perhaps being a stay-at-home mum isn't all it's cracked up to be. After all, weren't there reasons why as soon as society allowed it, women starting coming into the workforce in a big way? Financial reasons were a large part of that but so too were the other benefits that work brings and that we tend to forget when we're in the treadmill of a job for year after year. I remember the pure joy of being back in an office environment after 20 years' part-timing from home. Although I'd had some success as a writer and trainer, I'd mainly done so alone and I craved the other things that work brings: a community and teamwork, a sense of self-esteem and worth in many ways I hadn't thought of before, a sense that I was a 'whole' person and that my children could see this (and thus being a model of a strong capable women for my sons to take into their worlds) and more. Some colleagues didn't understand (probably still don't) why I value my job so highly. It's not always that great a place to be and the work can be boring and/or stressful, but it's me, it's who I am in that context. Some people are happy without their own work and feel that being a mother is sufficient in itself and is more important than a career. Perhaps there's some sense of sacrifice and worth from giving up part of the self for the good of the family. I'm not saying it's wrong to do and feel this. I had some years at home when I was barely working and was happy with my role. But I would caution: look to the future. Barring apocalypse it's a certainty, yet it's easy to pretend it won't exist.[28]

Another possibility is to downshift. Author Judith Levine stopped shopping for a year then wrote a book about it.[29] On closer inspection we find that Levine does allow herself to buy the basics (she's not shooting squirrels for the pot or digging dandelion roots to grind for coffee, for instance) but decides, with her partner, to stop spending money on anything that that don't count as 'essential'. Reading her book reminded me of early parenting days when I was only earning pin money. No coffee shops, no meals out, no new clothes (except essential ones). Everything cut back to a minimum. The funny thing is that this didn't make us at all unhappy, and neither did Levine find as many drawbacks as we might imagine. There were some. But there's a certain freedom to throwing off the shackles of expectation – from the self and from others. I'm speaking about a standard of living above the bread-line; no one's advocating poverty. But within our affluent lifestyles there's often room to cut hard back in some areas without us minding very much at all.

American writer Tracy Hahn-Burkett, who spoke earlier about the impossibility of finding part-time professional work, goes on to think about the repercussions of leaving employment to become a writer and what this has done for the family's finances and for the family as a unit:

> Though we have significantly less money than we used to, we are generally able to make ends meet. I really do know my kids better than anyone else does, and I wouldn't trade that for anything. I manage to find some time to write things like this blog, which I've always wanted to do.[30]

A large part of our lifestyle is going along with our peers; our community changes as we have children and there are just as many people struggling financially but thriving as families to hook up with and share bring-a-dish dinners and babysitting circles with. As noted in Chapter 6 (when considering whether its worth going back to work from a financial point of view), simply going to work is expensive and we pay for that from our post-tax income; is it really enough to be worth the stress of keeping the career going? This doesn't get us around the problem of the long-term career and remaining skilled and employable, but it might present an opportunity to change direction.

Claire Taylor speaks above about quitting her job when she went on maternity leave. She adds:

I really felt that being a full-time teacher was not the right job for me any more, not only because of pregnancy but because of workload issues and the way I was treated as a young female by older male staff. I did not even bother to try and continue. I felt I didn't have the time or space to develop my musical skills.

South African Nadia Sitas, yet to have children, adds:

I definitely want to have kids soon and I was thinking of doing my PhD, and while I'm doing it having a child at the same time because it's a good environment for that kind of thing. You're not working but getting paid to do research, and so you spend a lot of time at home so it's a good time to be a parent. You've got the time to spend with the kid . . . the type of work I'll be doing hopefully will be a lot of fieldwork, working in very remote areas so I guess the child would just have to come with me . . . on my back.

Nadia might be optimistic about how much time she'll have for her research but even so, a new 'direction' might be lower-key version of what you're already doing, free up time and energy for the family. Peter Eriksson explains how it worked for him:

Luckily the job I have been doing is one that can easily be done from 9.00 until 5.00; it's not a sort of senior executive where you have to go all over the place. So I have kept my job deliberately fairly contained and low-key and that has been the sacrifice we've made consciously. My natural career path would've probably been back to London, something a bit more senior, but it suited us for me to keep it local in a fairly low-key job which I can now do part-time. Probably in the search of greater income, and if we hadn't have had children, then I would have gone off and done other things but I've been happy to compromise and have a combination of more home life with a job that's local and fairly easy to do.

Frances adds:

> We [did] quite a lot of planning . . . we decided it was probably the right time because the hours here are much better than the hours I was working in London, which were such long days. My previous job was in private practice law, for a big corporate law firm, and I was working on transactions which would often go into the night. It was all right for a couple of years and then I just thought 'oh no, this isn't me'. The job I have now is not so intensive and there're only two of us lawyers there. The hours are notoriously easier in-house than they are in private practice. It's a more civilised life.

Changing direction can involve re-training. It can be costly in both time and financial terms so it's worth looking at carefully. Retraining often entails leaving paid work (or leaving caring for your children) while you take a course and acquire the skills your new career will need of you. When you're already caring for children, it may be possible to do your re-training during the time that the children are at nursery, for instance, and pick up some of the skills through part-time paid or voluntary work before you make a commitment to leave your old job if it's being held open for you, or to start again. You need to ensure that any proposed training will do what it's meant to: get you into your new career. Some work areas have a minimum entry requirement in terms of qualifications, experience and skills — double-check that the course you're thinking of doing is accredited by the appropriate agency and that it'll give you the right personal and technical skills, as well as the knowledge you'll need.

It's also worth thinking about broader work issues such as unionisation. Sometimes it feels as though we've forgotten the early days of the workplace – industrialisation, child labour, factory accidents, early deaths after lives of horrendous toil. We laugh now to think this could happen again – of course, we say, things aren't like that any more. But do we honestly think that employers hand out perks, benefits, holidays, paid sick leave, safety guards on machinery, unless they have no choice? A few might, but most are either personally or corporately (via their shareholders) obliged to maximise their profits, and workers' rights cut into those. Employers have loads of rights – and if they don't have them in law they take them anyway. An individual worker, alone, has rights but little clout; the only way to have some influence over matters is in organised groups such as unions. They might sound rather too loud on the TV news during strike action but they're only doing exactly what we would be faced with if they weren't doing it for us.

I sometimes think of the parallel of immunising the kids. Child mortality has dropped to a tiny fraction of what it was (and still is in parts of the developing world) through immunisation programmes. We can prevent our children contracting killer diseases such as measles by simply taking them to a clinic a few times during their childhood. It saves their lives. Some parents, aware that measles is now rare (due to the immunisation programme) don't want to have their children immunised because of the tiny risk involved. If your child has an acknowledged condition that puts him or her under increased risk of side effects during immunisation, then fair enough. The child population as a whole can tolerate a certain number of unimmunised children before the disease starts to get a hold again. But once the proportion of immunised children drops below a certain level (around 95 per cent in the case of measles) then children are at risk again: new babies prior to immunisation, and the ones whose parents have opted them out of the process and left them unprotected (as well as many adults). Another epidemic sweeps the country and children (and adults) die.

So it is with unions: if enough of us can't be bothered then a second Victorian workplace ethic epidemic sweeps the country. Unions are our protection against being exploited. In addition they're our advocate if things go wrong: they'll take our side in a dispute and provide legal advice and representation if necessary. If you're about to become a parent, or have young children, with new legislation protecting your rights which employers aren't generally pleased about, there's an increased probability that this will apply to you. Some workplaces don't have active unions; some employers are powerful enough to ensure unions aren't involved. But where there is a union, please join it. If nothing else it'll stop your colleagues being mightily pissed off with you when you get the pay rise despite not paying union dues nor going out on strike. But this may be the last time it happens because if union membership falls too low then there won't be a pay rise to gloat over.

Another broader work issue is how we feel about ourselves. What do some of us have by the bucket-load while others spend our whole lives pretending? Whether it's natural not, we need to demonstrate self-esteem. The more we get used to having a high sense of self-worth, the more it rubs off on us and others and the easier we find the typically difficult things for women in the world of work. Often self-esteem plummets once we're faced with the reality of life and work and then again massively with a new baby and for the following few years. Have a look at websites such as The Real Hot 100.[31] This promotes the idea – and demonstrates the reality – that hot women are hot for what they do and who they are rather than what they look like and the use they are to men. I bet your bottom dollar that a good half of them have issues of self-esteem but that they've told themselves that life can go in several directions and they're determined to take it in their own. There are single mothers; people from all sorts of backgrounds with differing issues and disabilities. We don't all have to be so amazing that we're nominated for a list such as this but it shows just a fraction of the worth of a fraction of the women in the world. We're all part of that women's group and we're all as great in our own way as the people on that list. Claire Taylor puts it well: 'As I began to feel increasingly [stagnant and depressed] I decided to channel this negative energy into being creative and making my own work to fit around my new life.'

Lastly, how do we put any or all of this into action? Some of us are blessed with an innate ability to put things away and remember where that was, to plan and stick to the plan and to sort out our lives by giving them a little forethought. By dint of you reading this, I guess you're either like that or want to be, and that if you want to be it's because you can see that, as a parent, it makes things so much easier. Many people go from thinking it's anal to tidy up (blarghh – what's life about?) to realising that whatever the cost of being organised or planning ahead, it's not as great as the loss if you don't. That's what having children does for you.

Here's Claire Taylor again:

I have to be careful to keep on top of my diary. I am able to work flexibly but because I work from home quite a lot, the boundaries between work and home sometimes blur. I love my work so I don't mind that I often spend evenings catching up but I am now increasing childcare to enable me to achieve more in the day without using my evenings to catch up on paperwork. The older my children get the more stimulation they seem to need outside of the home. I am gearing my work to fit around school hours so I don't take projects on that involve working past 3.00 pm. My goal this year is to make more of a distinction between work time and family time, using childcare to help me structure this better.

Think, research, plan, set it all in motion, but as Claire Taylor says:

> Long-term I might like to do a recital one day. I'm saving up for a grand piano for my 40th. Other than that I don't think too far ahead. Having children has taught me not to.

Although no one knows for certain what's around the corner, as parents it sometimes feels that we have no idea at all. Even if planning seems pointless, it remains essential if we're going to move forward.

Anna, who's pregnant with her first child, says:

> I'm finding it hard to see how I'm going to be feeling in a month's time, let alone a year's time when I've said I'll make a decision whether or not to go back to work. Having a kid is obviously a massive thing and I want to be at home for the first year. I think that's really important and then I'll get back in touch with my company and try and decide whether or not I want to go back and if so, how, on what terms, etc. I find it very hard to be able to picture myself and what I'll want to do.

Tanya adds this:

> It took me a long time to get back into it [after maternity leave], back to the adult world. It's hard when you've been talking 'baby' for six months. I also missed my boys incredibly. I think I am back to normal now but I still yearn to be with them. It was a bit easier while Luke was in nursery as I felt he was having such a great time (which he was). At the moment he's not in nursery and I miss him more then ever — especially as he's so much fun at this age. I am also painfully aware that next year he will be in school and then my chance is gone forever.

Moving forward is about creative thinking, researching, planning, setting it going, reviewing, rethinking, reconsidering, changing tack and setting off again. There are plenty of books, sites and professionals to help with these processes. They're not difficult: what's difficult, as parents, is finding the time and then the objectivity to 'see'. Once we can do that, we can get our lives moving in the right direction, make corrections for unexpected change and keep it all moving forward. Parents' and networking groups can be helpful in this, as can courses to get us thinking about possibilities and goals again. With all of this, it's worth remembering that it takes time and reflection to work out what we really want to do. Are you succumbing to peer or family pressure in going back full-time into your old job, or is it really what you want and need? Would taking some more time to explore options be feasible financially and reap dividends in the long-term?

The parenting timeline

New parents often think that once their kids are out of nappies and can climb the stairs for themselves the work's half over. And then there's the allure of school. Jenny Bell, yet to have children, sees how parenting gets easier with time: 'In terms of going to school then I guess you have more time during the day.' Which is, of course, true. But what happens with most of us is that we set our eyes on that magical time when the kids are away for six hours of the day, and plan accordingly. Many parents find that the reality is having less time once we're back at work when the children are half-independent. It's easy to forget a few minor details: school breaks, sports day, field trips ('please deliver your child to the rural museum at 10.15 am and collect at 2.30 pm') and the dreaded round of viruses and accidents. And that's assuming our children are averagely healthy and emotionally resilient. What if your child has asthma/a disability/a fear of separation? I know a mother who spent the best part of a year sitting in an armchair once her younger child went to school. 'There's plenty of time for work later,' she said. 'For now, I'm going to have some time recovering'. She did, then launched herself back into her IT career refreshed and energised. There's a lot to be said for that approach. It's easy to panic and think we've got to carry on driving ourselves onward at breakneck speed as soon as there's the tiniest window for us to do this. That may not be the most balanced way forward.

We asked an older mother how she sees the various stages of parenting. Jenny, now in her 50s, says:

When you're first pregnant you get caught up in the wonder of what's happening. It's as though you're part of another world and an exclusive club all at once. Everything looks, feels and literally tastes different. It's impossible to get away from that and think how you used to think, and why should you? It's a wonderful time, even if it's exhausting trying to keep working and prepare for the baby while heavily pregnant.

Then the first baby comes and you become a completely different person; in a sense you are, with a new separate person central to your life. It's very easy to get absorbed in it. I wasn't aware of anything cultural, or what was in the news. I tried hard to stay close with my husband and we managed that okay I think, though it wasn't easy. I hated the lack of sleep, and the physical recovery, but loved the intensity and devotion to my little boy. I'd been working for my father's firm and went back to that part-time after about a year, but it was very hard. I had family around, so childcare wasn't an issue but I missed him and I realised how easy it would be to get back into work – which I enjoyed – and forget about the plan for a larger family, so a year later we tried for a second. It was really hard then as I was a full-time mother again and exhausted all the time, my elder son has always been energetic; with a baby too it was hard. I didn't really look after myself – I should have shouted that I wasn't coping but tried to cope; it was a really difficult time. It was wonderful too, but hard. Quite lonely outside the toddler groups, as there was a lot of housework that I had to get on with.

When the boys were both at school I started working for my father again but this time it didn't feel enough. Being part-time, and knowing we weren't going to have more children so this was going to be my work, focused me. We agreed that I'd re-train and I spoke to people about possibilities. Then I stopped working and did my speech therapy qualification. I wanted to work around people, and also children, and perhaps work for myself and it was the perfect thing then as there weren't so many speech therapists.

The boys were at secondary school when I got my practice. The school run had nearly finished me off but now the boys caught the bus to school and let themselves into the house after school if I wasn't there. I usually worked just school hours and only part-time in the holidays. Then last year I decided I'd done enough; I felt tired, and there were cuts in funding for therapists and younger newly-qualified therapists were looking for work so it was right to stop. If I hadn't had the boys and then re-trained I'd have missed those years in practice, which were wonderful, I loved working with mainly young people, a great sense of satisfaction, and working for myself too.

Regrets

Elderly people who are interviewed about their lives rarely regret things they've done: they tend to regret not doing things. We have our children later and later and it's easy to feel that, by then, we've already had the parts of our lives where we had freedom of choice about work, where we live or chucking it all in and following the surf. Yet with increasing life expectancy and lengthening working lives, we're gaining longer at the post-children end of our careers. Although with retirement ages being pushed back we're going to have to wait longer for full-time freedom, the other side of this coin is having longer to spend creating the career we want and the earnings we put on hold (as well as to stoke our retirement fund).

We asked the women interviewed for this book: what should every working woman or working mother be doing to help herself and others in her situation?

Tanya said:

Always keep hold of your dream, and if it's put on the sidelines temporarily, for example if you become a parent, don't forget to bring it out later and chase it when the time is right. Take an interest in what's going on, and make sure you have your say. If you believe you should be getting some help, stand up and say so.

Anne Eriksson:

Get a husband who doesn't want a highly driven career. It's certainly made a huge difference having that support. I go to networking lunches in London and that seems to be a common theme for women who have high-stress careers – to have a supportive partner who is there to help and provide support you need. Because you can't do it on your own.

'The main thing that women need to think about is what they themselves think is important and that life is full of compromises. I suspect that more women are more ready to make compromises around their work than they are their family. And that's really the thing that having children does; it forces you to think about the compromises you've got to make.

8

WHAT'S NEXT?

I like this selection of quotes illustrating how very wrong some clever peoples' predictions can be. C H Duell, Commissioner of the US Patent Office, said in 1899 that 'Everything that can be invented has been invented'; Lord Kelvin, President of the Royal Society, said in 1895, 'Heavier-than-air flying machines are impossible.' Thomas Watson, chairman of IBM, said in 1943, 'I think there is a world market for maybe five computers.' As the collector of these quotes, Scottish Enterprise commentator Duncan Neish, asks: 'So why keep on trying to see into the future? Perhaps because there is little sensible alternative.'[1] He then quotes The Scottish Parliament's Presiding Officer: 'If we don't think from time to time out the box and over the horizon, and rely on past experience, the danger is that we walk into the future backwards.'

Are we walking into our futures backwards? Sometimes it feels as though we have to put the world on hold: juggling our lives can turn us into zombies who glaze over when the news comes on and who have more interest in prams than politics. And perhaps that means we're failing to spot some vital imminent change, locally or worldwide, as it starts to impact. When we emerge at the far end of child-rearing into the second half of our brilliant careers, what will the world be like? We've gone from a society of extended and supportive communities to one of nuclear families and some-times-intolerable pressure on parents, from kids who did what they were told to kids who don't know what to do (and some parents who don't know what, or how, to tell them). We've gone from a workplace where men turned up, did their bit and went home to one where we're all expected to dedicate our lives. Politics has centred so that people don't see a need to vote for parties they feel are essentially all the same. Family-friendly policies that do reach the statute books are tempered by employers who don't see the need for them and certainly don't want them. Populations are changing faster than we dare acknowledge, skewing and leading . . . where, exactly? For parents, the two major variables through which we weave our lives are firstly our families and then our work. But where are they going next? Let's look at them back to front.

How work's still changing

We've seen how the workplace has changed in general terms over the past few decades. Researcher Suzan Lewis sums this up: 'the corporate world is . . . changing dramatically, with work becoming more intense, flexible and unstable.'[2] How do managers of organ-isations see the transition over the past decades and how do they see it continuing? Commentator Peter Drucker wrote about management and change during much of the 20th century.[3] He saw the 1980s as an era of transition,[4] with its changes being even more radical than those of the Industrial Revolution and the impact of the Second World War. Writing in the 1980s he drew out five social and political 'truths' that would impact on business strategy. These were: the collapsing birth rate in the developed world; the changes in the distribution of disposable income; a hard look at what 'corporate performance' actually means; global competition; and a divergence between economic and political reality. As we carry much of this change with us into the 21st century, hindsight shows us how spot-on he was. What, now, are his thoughts of what's ahead? His most recent book identifies three major trends shaping what he calls the 'new society': the falling birth rate leading to a decline in the young population; the decline of manufacturing; and the transformation of work (through the social impact of the information revolution) leading to the transformation of the workforce.[5] The first two carry on from his thoughts in the 1980s, the third, though, takes us off in a new direction. We're developing into an information society, says Drucker, within which the not-for-profit sector is becoming increasingly important, providing communities for us all and, in particular, the increasing number of knowledge workers.

Drucker is only one of many commentators and analysts, each with their own models for looking at the future of work. It's useful to consider a more hands-on approach too: Cheryl Leitschuh is a coach, trainer and consultant, and sees how organisations once focused on quality, then moved in the 1990s into an era of speed: everything done tomorrow – now – yesterday.[6] But there's a limit to the speed at which we can operate. As individuals, we need to know where we are, to be 'rooted', before we give our best and fastest, which isn't easy when our companies merge and grow so rapidly. How, then, she asks, can we continue to change in this way – become faster and faster – when there's no organisational underpinning? And this is what some organisations are now seeking to provide. By becoming 'family-friendly' they also become employee-friendly in a broader sense. They provide a stable platform from which we can operate successfully – at work and also, due to these family policies, at home. So if we want to see the changing nature of work we can look, in the way Drucker and his pals might, at Drucker's three variables: population, manufacturing and the information age, say, then see how organisations are adapting to this change via family-friendly policies, how this has impacted on their workforces and what we can expect of them. From there we can see what to expect of our home and family lives. We need to remember that these social/ work structures are available to many – but not all – of us; not, for instance, the consultant or freelance knowledge workers and others working in self-employment, the low paid workers with neither adequate income or stability, some of those doing the increasingly prevalent voluntary or unpaid work as well as the 'disabled' – those excluded from work altogether whether by a physical or mental disability, through prejudice or through having caring responsibilities which disallow them from the workplace.

How demographics are forcing change

The first trend Drucker identified for the 21st century is the changing population. Chapter 2 hinted that there aren't enough young people being born in the developed world to support our work requirements and to support us, the older generation. The UK is coping. Unemployment is low, and the economy is thriving – there are enough workers (even if a growing proportion are European migrants or illegal immigrants from further afield working in the black-market economy). Demographics is some-times counter-intuitive;[7] there can be a falling birth rate yet the population can still increase because immigration, lengthening lifespan and changing birth rates take a long time to have an impact on population size.

There are estimates that the world population will increase by another half over the next 50 years before levelling off at ten billion by 2100.[8] That sounds like plenty. But this is a global figure (with which some commentators profoundly disagree anyway) what about individual nations? Sixty-one countries have already fallen below the fertility rate replacement level of 2.1 children per woman and these countries house 44 per cent of the world's population. Many less-developed countries have lower fertility rates than the US, such as China (1.8), Thailand (1.74), the Republic of Korea (1.65) and Cuba (1.55). The average fertility rate for Western Europe is 1.7, while in Eastern Europe it's 1.36. The lowest rates are in Southern Europe, with Spain, Italy and Greece having rates below 1.3. Spain's is lowest of all with 1.15. Despite lengthening lives, populations in all these countries will eventually decline unless fertility rates rise (in Southern Europe this population decline has already started, and it'll happen in the rest of Europe over the next two decades).[9]

It's easy to see why rates are falling in developed countries; by looking at the statistics for a developing nation. In Trinidad and Tobago during 1970–75 the average woman had 6.5 children during her lifetime but this fell to 2.5 births per woman/lifetime during 2000–05. This change in the fertility rate mirrors change in the economy: recent economic growth is pulling Trinidad and Tobago towards the 'developed' bracket and its citizens are making decisions that people around the developed world have already made. Where there's the possibility of doing better as an individual or as a family in a growing economy, people aim for this; both adult members of the family will go out to work rather than the previous scenario of the mother staying at home with a larger number of children. Women's participation in the labour force in Trinidad and Tobago has increased during the same period. The fastest falling fertility rates are within the professional middle classes, whose children are most likely to be well-educated and gain the workplace skills that the economy needs.[10] It's obvious what's happening there: it's the same as has happened to us.

While on the topic of developing nations we can look at the work being done there on sexual equality generally – it's something we don't often hear about, especially if our horizons have shrunk under piles of babygros and Lego. This is an interesting thought:

> In no country around the world do men and women enjoy
> equality in economic and political participation, earning or
> educational attainment, general health and physical security.
> These gender gaps undermine economic growth and develop-
> ment and are costly to individuals and to households.[11]

This statement was written as an introduction to discussion of the United Nations' eight Millennium Development Goals, which range from halving extreme poverty to halting the spread of HIV/AIDS and providing universal primary education, and include eliminating sexual disparity in primary and secondary education, all by the target date of 2015.[12] These goals were agreed by all the world's countries and the leading development institutions and tie in with work being done since the Fourth World Conference on Women in Beijing in September 1995.[13] Though not itself the subject of this book, it's worth looking at the relevant web pages if you're interested in a more global view of women and work.

Back to demographics: researchers McDonald and Kippen describe how the recent fall in birth rate is unprecedented; in the 20th century we had the 'baby boom' years of children born after the end of the Second World War, which lead to workforces expanding by 14–28 per cent in the lowest-growing nations (France, Italy, Germany, the UK and Japan) and significantly more in parts of Asia and the immigrant nations of Canada, Australia, New Zealand and the US.[14] This baby boom generation is reaching retirement: by 2020, almost 20 per cent of the US population will be 65 or older.[15] In the past, governments have regulated their economies using standard strategies (such as setting interest rates to determine economic growth to match the available workforce) but in this new scenario, with too few work-ers, what can they do? They have no experience of it.

McDonald and Kippen go on to suggest some possible meth-ods that governments might use. Perhaps the demand for labour will fall to match the supply; if labour were to cost more (ie we get paid more – hurrah!) and productivity increased, then the equation would continue to balance. But how can productivity, which has anyway been increasing, continue to do so? Leitschuh suggested above that we will only continue to work at our optimum if we have a certain stability around us; fast, faster and fastest (or perhaps there is no 'fastest'?). And the continuing development of technology should be able to facilitate increased productivity so long as there are enough workers to allow this technological advance to continue. This technological advance will in itself reduce the current level of demand for labour to do certain tasks.

McDonald and Kippen go further to say that, in fact, rapid technological advancement and plenty of capital will create a greater demand for people to implement the technological advances. And because corporations will move offshore if the required labour isn't available at home (in the case of this research, from the US), governments will have to ensure a booming labour market – even if this means higher immigration to keep companies where they are – a growing, skilled labour force. This young skilled labour force will keep the economy afloat while lesser-skilled workers provide the labour needed for the service economy – including caring for the huge ageing population and providing their retirement services, including entertainment and leisure. These elders will also require skilled workers to support them: medical, construction and a range of other skilled 'hands-on' people who are needed right there; overseas labour won't plug that gap in the way that it can for manufacturing, IT and call centres. So although Judy and D'Amico say:

> Experience suggests that the development, marketing and servicing of ever more sophisticated products – and the use of those products in an ever richer ensemble of personal and

professional services – will create more jobs than the underlying technology will destroy,[16]

they also accept that projections of labour demand are conjec-
tural. We know for sure that developed world fertility rates are
falling but we don't know that labour demand will continue to
rise, whatever the predictions. But economies can't afford to be
caught short: the challenge for governments is how to increase the
labour supply.

It takes 25 to 30 years for any increase in fertility rate to have an
affect, therefore immigration is the only immediate solution even
if current research indicates that this isn't having as much positive effect on our economies as we'd assumed. Meanwhile,
longer-term strategies are developed as:

> Ageing and its implications are emerging as major social, polit-
> ical and economic issues . . . the long term solvency of pension
> plans – both public and private – is a growing concern across
> the triad countries (USA, Europe and Japan),

say McKinsey & Company[17] in a report by Microsoft.[18] Immigration,
though, is dependent on other nations' supply of appropriate
labour. With rapid development across what we once saw as the
'third world', growing economies will be looking to contain their
own labour forces, not let them go west. And corporations like
Microsoft are interested in these issues for both production
and marketing reasons: the same report estimates that, if trends
continue, growth in household financial wealth will slow by more
than two thirds. This slowing, driven by ageing, will cause a global
wealth shortfall of £16/US$32 trillion by 2024, meaning people
will have less available cash to buy Microsoft's products. According to The Tomorrow Project, the UK is well placed to take
advantage of global growth; 'International markets will expand for

many of the things that Britain does well . . . and strengths probably outweigh the dangers'.[19] And for a change, it's not the US that's
providing the extreme example of a developed nation: McDonald
and Kippen go on to show how almost every nation's economy will
have a worse labour supply that the US, where much of the
research has been carried out and where conclusions are drawn
for the Judy and D'Amico work.

Demographics and the 'quantity' of skills

With working populations, it's clear that it's not only size that
matters but also whether the pool of workers is qualified to do the
available work. The Microsoft paper concentrates, unsurprisingly, on ICT skills, and shows how European universities are
unable to recruit enough new students in computer sciences (UK,
Dutch and German technical universities showed a fall in
computer sciences student numbers of between 5 per cent and 20
per cent between 2001–05, with some drops as steep as 40 per
cent).[20] So European governments won't have enough home-grown
computer sciences graduates, but their assumption that they can
recruit from the emerging nations' workforces may be flawed.
China, for instance, created over three million new graduates in
2005 but it's thought unlikely that more than 10 per cent would
have the skills necessary to work in a foreign company. The same
can be said of Indian graduates. These top, potentially mobile,
workers will mostly be absorbed by their own nations. And anyway,
a large population size isn't in itself a prerequisite for economic
success. Skills are high up in the equation but skills development
in a population depends on the success of its strategies. Many
smaller nations, through directed economic management, high
productivity, successful business strategy, innovation and special-
isation are more successful than larger ones. Finland, for instance,
was rated highest for growth prospects in 2003, compared to the
US' ranking of 50th.[21] Our UK skills situation is summarised in

research by the Leitch Review of Skills, which made its interim report in 2005:

> Over the past decade, the skills profile of the working age population in the UK has improved. For example, the proportion of adults with a degree has increased from a fifth to over a quarter of the population. Yet over a third of adults don't have a basic school-leaving qualification – double the proportion of Canada and Germany; five million people have no qualifications at all; one in six adults do not have the literacy skills expected of an 11-year-old and half do not have these levels of functional numeracy. Looking ahead to 2020, global, demographic and technological change will place an even greater premium on the UK's skills profile.' The report goes on to state that Government's targets include improving UK skills by 2020 so that then, the proportion of working age people without any qualifications will fall to 4 per cent and the proportion of adults holding a degree will increase from 27 to 38 per cent. Even if this were to happen, four million adults still wouldn't have the literacy skills of an 11-year-old, and 12 million wouldn't have the numeracy skills of an 11-year-old. The Leitch Review believes that 'the UK must urgently raise its game and set itself a greater ambition to have a world-class skills base by 2020.'[22]

Manufacturing

The second of Drucker's trends was the decline of manufacturing. It's in the news all the time; another factory closes, production is transferred to the Far East and so on. And yet unemployment isn't so high and the economy is buoyant. Chapter 2 pointed out that manufacturing is being replaced by other sectors such as services and information-based work. And the former Secretary of State for Trade and Industry's declaration that 'Manufacturing in the UK has a strong long-term future,' along with rising output, doesn't prevent this continuing decline of employment in manufacturing, with the sector contributing less and less to the national economy. The number of people employed in manufacturing will almost halve in ten years' time to just over two million if current trends continue, and its contribution to the economy could carry on shrinking. Does this matter? And if it does, then the service industry and brainwork will fill the gap . . . won't it? A 2003 survey of 100 UK firms, carried out by the Institute for Manufacturing, asked whether they thought production would continue to leave the country and whether research and development would start to leave too.[23] Over three quarters said they thought production would accelerate out of the UK, and a third thought that design and development (which is different from research and development, but often considered together) would leave in the next ten years. This is contrary to what many commentators are telling us: that we'll keep the knowledge-based, high-value design/research and development type activity even if the lower-skilled work goes elsewhere. As the Institute for Manufacturing states, the role of research and development is key to economic growth. 'Under capitalism, innovative activity – which in other types of economy is fortuitous and optional – becomes mandatory, a life and death matter for the firm.'[24] With 80 per cent of UK business expenditure on research and development carried out within manufacturing firms, will this level of spend continue as manufacturing workers are lost? The UK's target of 3 per cent of gross domestic product being spent on research and development doesn't look likely with the 2004 figure at only 1.9 per cent and the continuing immersion of research and development within declining industry.

There are innovative approaches to counteracting this loss of manufacturing. The UK company Rolls-Royce plc is an example of how a change from manufacturing to service can be captured within one organisation.[25] Initially a manufacturer of cars and aircraft engines, the company has geared its recent growth towards service by underwriting airlines' risk in terms of the servicing costs of their aircraft engines. Initially it offered airlines a guaranteed maximum cost per flying hour rather than simply selling spare parts and performing overhauls, which was the traditional support offered. As airlines became more anxious to reduce the uncertainty involved with engine mainte- nance, Rolls-Royce developed a choice of service options for its customers including the Rolls-Royce 'TotalCare' service option, which 50 per cent of its clients now sign up for, with expecta- tions that this will rise to 80 per cent. More than half of Rolls-Royce's £6/US$12 billion annual sales now comes from services.

The changing nature of skills – a transforming workforce

The third thing that Drucker sees is a changing workforce. The requisite skills – and attitude, which is in itself a form of skill – are changing. So although the excerpt from the Leitch Review, above, commented broadly on the UK skills situation, over time it's not only the 'quantity' of skills we have, it's also their nature that counts. Drucker says: 'success in the knowledge economy comes to those who know themselves – their strengths, their values, and how they best perform.'[26] Organisations can succeed by generating these attitudes and skills in their workforces: a 1997 survey of 55,000 US workers compared the success of companies to the attitudes of their employees.[27] The research found that four specific attitudes were prevalent among workers in certain companies and that these attitudes being present correlated with a high level of corporate profit. These attitudes were:

1. workers felt they were given the opportunity to do what they did best every day;
2. they believed their opinion counted;

3. they sensed that their fellow workers were committed to quality;
4. they made a direct connection between their work and the company's mission.

This fits with what Cheryl Leitschuh was saying earlier in this chapter about needing to feel grounded and safe in our employing organisations. It makes us feel better so we work more effectively and our employers benefit. Skills increasingly in demand are the interpersonal and judgement skills – hardly defined as 'skills' from the viewpoint of the traditional industries a few decades ago, but required in the knowledge economy. What use are we unless we can collaborate, partner, communicate, persuade, make decisions, reflect and use this active bundle of abilities in our everyday work? In the old days accountants could get by on technical skills and bad haircuts. Now, their organisations are in partnership with a host of others, they are required to be a part of the interface with these outside agencies (collaborators and competitors) as well as liaising internally to form part of a coherent 'whole' of workers who know things. Knowledge workers need to know how the money works or at least, where to go to find out. So team working is essential, and to do this we need to be effective communicators. We still need the technical skills, but we now need to be able to use them in a whole range of new situations.

Emotional literacy, once a niche and wacky concept, is becoming mainstream both in work and education. This is why top employers will remain interested in good graduates in any of the arts disciplines: bright young things who can empathise, deduce and communicate can then be taught how balance sheets work. Traditional techie-type graduates who know how to mix compounds in a lab may not necessarily be able to learn to explain this to the rest of the development and marketing team. The former will be the high earners and the latter people who can do only the technical stuff, despite their technical competence, will be left behind. Those who don't have any developed skills will be increasingly polarised in terms of pay and status from those who also have the soft skills and the adaptability (a skill in itself) to use them. As this gap widens between those who do well at work – in pay and skills – and those who don't, it will become increasingly difficult to close.

What about those who aren't succeeding in the knowledge economy? Those factory workers whose jobs are now in China? Those part-time carers who can't go to work because work is full-time? Those middling graduates forced to take non-graduate jobs because their degrees aren't in demand? And what about those among these groups who are forced to change direction but find that, being self-employed non-mainstream workers, they can't access the benefits of employment provided by companies or institutions? Those who want to re-train who find that there's no government support to do this so must bumble along on a mini-mal wage despite being capable of earning more in the knowledge economy if they had the skills? This is where the not-for-profit sector comes in, which is examined later in this chapter. But how is all of this going to polarise society, and with what repercus-sions? The word 'flexibility' crops up again here; it's used throughout our economic and workplace discussions as being vital to allow economies to develop and succeed. Researcher Robert Taylor points out that European policy makers see the effects this is having in the US – where employers are allowed the 'flexibility' to hire and fire their workers as they wish – and are refusing to allow European legislation to follow:

> Such flexibility is deplored as a cruel example of what they
> regard as the dark side of the American model – uncaring and
> insensitive to the needs of employees. They reason that if

workers are treated as disposable assets by companies, they in turn will display little loyalty and commitment to the place where they are employed.[28]

This ties in with the Gallup research, above, showing that where workers feel part of the mission and part of the corporation, profits are higher. And anyway, in nations like Finland there is far less of this 'employer flexibility' than in the US yet its economy is set for greater growth. There's no evidence that such 'employer-benefitting-flexible' employment practices help the economy yet plenty that it devastates its workforce. In much of Europe – countries such as Sweden, Spain, Italy and France – employers are required to cushion their workers when mass redundancy is considered essential. Companies must negotiate, their decision-making must involve the workforce's consent; they must support former employees with social readjustment programmes. This slows the whole process and so allows time to resolve issues without the levels of conflict sometimes found in the US and UK. Together with legislation, these voluntary agreements lead towards workplace innovation while still allowing companies to respond to market conditions. Although the legislation required to allow this hasn't yet come to the UK, other working practices have changed across the whole of Europe and the developed world. In many of the old UK industries that still survive, partnership agreements are being negotiated with workforces to allow multi-skilling and team working linked to lifelong learning and vocationally-based training. Taylor, who describes this trend, calls it 'an underestimated quiet workplace revolution in the UK, at least in export-sensitive manufacturing.'

So we're going to be involved in the whole process and to learn our whole lives through – that's brilliant news. Taylor also points to research that yet again underpins the benefits to companies of what might be seen as a more humanitarian approach to its workforce: where in Europe there's legislation in place to prevent the hire-and-fire found in the US, this is accompanied by an acceptance by all stakeholders – including workers – of the inevitability of workplace change. He shows how companies which give their employees more security are more easily able to introduce ICT, new HR techniques and formalised systems of training and learning. And these trends are also found in the US in corporations which, despite being allowed by legislation to treat their workers badly, in fact treat them well. 'Mutual gains or human development enterprises are best able to achieve competitive advantage through their use of new forms of work organisation if they can avoid hire and fire flexibilities that provoke fear and insecurity', Taylor points out.[29] It looks as though there's no need for this underclass of fired and marginalised workers. Successful companies once again want to draw a loyal cohort of employees into their bosom and nurture them. But not enough (not enough companies and not enough workers). Which brings us back to the beginning: a new knowledge-based workforce . . . but only some of us?

This is underlined in another trend commentators are noting. However much the larger companies want to nurture us, there aren't enough of them to employ us all. Most enterprises are tiny compared with the relative handfuls of multi-nationals and other large employers. There are few in the middle. This hourglass effect, with organisations continuing to polarise between large and small with few in-between, looks set to continue. Jobs stuck in the middle are increasingly at risk too, whether we define 'middle' as those in medium-sized companies, or those in the middle of the work hierarchy. These latter are the most vulnerable to technological advances.[30] So if you consider yourself 'middle of the road' it might be time to rethink your skills. Commentators see continuing change as inevitable if we want our economies to continue to thrive, and economies and societies find change difficult, just as we often do personally and work-wise.

But Drucker's idea that a more wholesale workforce transformation is coming is now called into question by work from The Tomorrow Project.[31] This shows how, although commentators in the 1990s considered that a huge change in ways of working was inevitable, from today's standpoint there is less likelihood of this wholesale change. Permanent contracts still account for over 90 per cent of all employment contracts (in 2000, 94.1 per cent of working men and 91.6 per cent of working women were in permanent jobs). Most working people still only have one job (96 per cent in 2000), despite murmurings of the 'portfolio working' lifestyle that we heard in the 1990s. Average time spent in a job is increasing: in the 1992 Britain at Work Survey, only about a quarter of employees below the management/professional level thought it best to stay with their present employer; more than twice as many thought they would be best served by moving. Eight years later the position was reversed: in the 2000 Working in Britain Survey, most lower-level employees also saw their best chances in staying, not moving.[32] Over the same period, the length of time individuals spent with one employer increased from an average of six years and two months to seven years and four months.[33] Longer-term employees make it more realistic for organisations to invest in training; these employees then know more about the sector, organisation and partners/competitors. They're more confident, more optimistic and worth investing in. And because of anticipated skills shortages certain groups of workers will be paid more and treated better, though others won't be caught in this same silver net.

Family-friendly employers and what we think of our work

Having looked at Drucker's thoughts on population change, manufacturing and the information age's impact on workplace structure, along with recent evidence that this change isn't quite as predicted, let's look now at what employers are actually doing. This was touched on in terms of social policy in Chapter 2; here's a fuller account along with predictions of where it's going. We saw above how employees remain longer with their organisations; employers see the value in a stable workforce, so those in work benefit from increased training and sometimes better pay. In addition, employers are trying to help our work and life fit together better with a range of family-friendly policies. Employers' motives can be called into question here – as we saw earlier, the term 'flexibility' is itself pretty flexible in its meaning. In fact, researchers have found six different ways of defining it and some of them have benefits only for the employer, such as the hire-and-fire tactics noted above. So, which family-friendly policies really do work in our favour? As it became clear, from the 1960s onwards, that ordinary people's lives were changing, we began to notice our work–life balance. It's taken decades for changes to traditional working patterns (when men went out to work and women stayed at home) to be made. Those changes to working patterns that we find positive are motivated by the employer's need to attract, and then keep, the right workers. For instance, having a workplace crèche is a strong selling point if you're competing to attract top people, a proportion of whom will be parents of small children. Although, as reported earlier, take up is bafflingly low there's some evidence that where these family-friendly policies are well implemented they do help individual employees to reconcile work and family. A study by Thomas and Ganster shows how the flexible timetabling of work, along with supportive line management, can enhance employee's control over work and family demands which in turn reduces work–family conflict and stress.[34]

Researcher Nuria Chinchilla categorises the ways good employers provide what we need.[35] Firstly, they provide flexibility in both time and space. When there's a crisis, we can work fewer hours and work those hours from home in the short term. We also need social benefits and salary perks, such as medical insurance, pensions and life assurance, which help in times of crisis and make us and our families feel more secure all the time. Thirdly, we need professional support such as advice and training to balance work and family and to adapt work to new needs, as well as specific training to prepare employees, such as time management training. Lastly, we need service policies to help us to reduce the load outside work, such as childcare, cleaning, shopping, car parking and information. Commentator Robert Taylor underlines how this required mix of employer policies – and not solely the family-friendly ones – is seen in practice. He reports John Monks of the Trades Union Congress speaking: 'Family-friendly concerns are not the only consideration. Finding the time for learning or for taking part in the life of the community are equally powerful motivators when it comes to balance life at work with life outside.'[36] Taylor goes on to report other commentary on this issue. The Confederation of British Industry states that:

Achieving an appropriate balance between work and other aspects of life has advantages for society as a whole. Employers also recognise that people facing conflict between their roles as parents and their responsibilities as employees may be less productive at work. The removal of unnecessary obstacles that prevent parents from achieving their full potential within the labour market will help prevent skills shortages which continue to be a widespread problem. Demographic changes will maintain the momentum in favour of flexibility.

Yet the Institute of Directors is more sceptical:

People, on the whole, are not working unacceptable hours against their will; there is much employee satisfaction with work, and the stress 'epidemic' is grossly exaggerated; Britain already has more flexible working practices and the push for many more can be sentimentalist and unrealistic.[37]

This is backed up by research by Bloom, Kretschmer and Van Reenen showing no evidence that companies with good work–life balance policies such as shorter hours, flexible working and family-friendly policies have higher productivity once adjustments were made for better management in general.[38] However, in making these adjustments, might the research not also adjust-out the whole point of the exercise, to show whether employer/management approaches make a difference? The Institute of Directors is kidding itself and doing its members a disservice.

Researchers White and Hill are engaged in long-term research into how we feel about work.[39] They've compared attitudes to paid employment in 1992 with those in 2000 and found a decline in the level of work satisfaction among men and women over a wide range of aspects of their work. This includes size of workload, number of hours worked, training opportunities and job security. Twenty-one per cent of workers said in 1992 they found they had less time available to carry out their family responsibilities than they would have liked, compared with 27 per cent in 2000. This substantial change in employee perceptions has meant a 'marked apparent deterioration in people's experience of work.' What we liked least was the number of hours we worked and the amount of work that had to be done. Other aspects of our jobs, such as the variety it offered and the use it made of our abilities hadn't changed so much. The largest fall in job satisfaction in men was at the top and bottom of the work hierarchy, among professionals and managers as well as semi- and unskilled manual workers. The sharpest decline in job satisfaction among women was among those of us employed in semi- and unskilled manual work. This research on how we feel about our work (by

White and Hill) was carried out before work by the Tomorrow Project showing that people are staying longer in their jobs. More recent research underlines some of White and Hill's results. An annual survey from the Work Life Balance Centre found in 2006 that work-related ill-health and stress levels are still high, but so is job satisfaction.[40] We dislike missing family time or spending long hours at work but we also feel that our jobs are very rewarding and that our work is well planned and under control. They too note the low take up of certain flexible working arrangements and support services and the researchers suggest that this causes both employers and workers to miss out. Sometimes it takes a detailed look at what's on offer to discover why we might be shunning it.

One father interviewed for this book told us:

> There's an excellent crèche and then nursery available to the children of all staff, though there's a long waiting list; if you're new [to the organisation], you won't get your child in. And because of nursery lunch breaks they only take a few children right through the day. Most have to be collected at lunchtime then taken back later. It means if you've got a job that involves travelling to meetings or working over lunchtime, you can't use the crèche.

The authors of the Work Life Balance Centre report suggest that a limited knowledge of legal rights may create problems for employees trying to obtain an improved work–life balance. However, as the example above shows, it's not always about knowing our entitlements. Employers may be providing what they are required to in law, or more, but we may not be able to take this up even if we're aware of it. Old-fashioned employer or colleague attitudes, individual work or financial constraints and lack of support in the home are just some of the very good reasons we can't or won't always take up what's on offer.

Over time, as worker shortages kick in, the two-parent family package will gradually benefit so long as the family can afford to work less combined hours. This depends on how much money we've got, which depends partly on markets – commentators say that the pound will inevitably devalue over the next decade due to global markets. What will it cost to buy goods from China? Will 'the next China' be Africa? What will happen to the housing market? What will it cost to bring up a family? And to what extent will we continue our high standard of living or will we choose or be forced to compromise and downshift? Commentators vary from the doom-and-gloom brigade to those bullish enough to think our current relatively high stand of living will continue to rise. Matthew Slaughter, a US economic advisor, explains how standard of living is dependent on productivity, defined as the average value of output a country produces per worker.[41] In the US productivity grew between 1973–95 at 1.4 per cent per year, then from 1995–2000 productivity grew at an annual rate of 2.5 per cent. Since the end of 2000 productivity growth has accelerated to about 3.4 per cent per year. In this context it's easy to see how our standard of living is rising. Slaughter goes on to explain what this means: 'At the previous generation's growth rate of 1.4 per cent, average living standards required 50 years to double. At the current growth rate of 3.4 per cent, average living standards need just 20 years to double.' He puts this growth down to innovations and ever-greater economic output:

> Much of the initial acceleration after 1995 was related to infor-mation technology – both faster productivity growth by IT companies themselves and faster IT capital investment throughout the economy. More recently, productivity gains have been delivered by many other sectors including financial services and retail trade.

With other commentators looking positively at the future of many developed nations' productivity, it looks as though those frappuccinos might be safe for a while longer. Our leisure, on the increase, looks likely to remain high depending on the cost of living, income and preferred standard of living: knowing that our incomes will increase by 60 per cent by 2020 and double by 2030[42] is meaningless unless we know what the cost of living's going to be and economists are slower to predict that. Will we be able to cut our working hours? As well as this, the retirement age is set to increase in the longer term which will increase our lifetime working hours.

But how many of us will they help? The not-for-profit sector

This book's hinted that all of us are potentially part of an 'excluded' section of the workforce and society. Regarding the changing workplace, Suzan Lewis points out that:

> The proliferation of contracting-out, temporary contracts and other new forms of work, which increase flexibility from the employer's perspective, transferring risk and uncertainty from employers to employees, has created a growing peripheral or contingent workforce to whom family-oriented policies often do not apply.[43]

The workforce is polarising, not just between professional high-earners and grey economy, insecure, perhaps immigrant workers, but between those of us in 'proper employment' and those on the fringes. The not-for-profit sector, mentioned above, has a role here. Because this comprises a diverse sector, of local community groups right through to national, multi-branch organisations that are sometimes direct service providers and sometimes fund-raisers or grant givers, it's difficult to pigeonhole. It's not just about the smelly charity shop at the poorer end of the high street – it encompasses all sorts of groups which might be essential for our well-being in terms of feeling part of the community. When commentators talk about its increasing importance this is not only in relation to its growth as an employer of both paid and unpaid workers. It covers two other areas of emerging importance. The first is that voluntary work, which is readily available in this sector, can be used by each of us to practise and increase our skills. We all need to be involved in community work of some sort; it's essential to us as individuals to 'touch base' with people around us, even (or, especially) those with whom we don't have an immediate affinity. As we all need continually to improve our skills, we can do both within this sector. The other reason it's important is that it works for a 'common good', albeit that individual organisations, such as small charities, are each working to aid a discrete group of bene-ficiaries. Its work increasingly underpins society much as benefactors and religious groups did in the days before the welfare state. Government cannot afford the welfare provision it used to give; the not-for-profit sector is taking on this role. When Drucker talks about the future he outlines a 'new society' rather than a new economy. He talks of this new information society within which the not-for-profit sector is becoming increasingly important and which provides communities for us all and in particular the increasing number of knowledge workers.

How families are changing

Government commentary makes happy reading: former Trade and Industry Secretary Alan Johnson said in 2006: 'There has been a positive culture change in the home and workplace. Mothers are taking more time off when their child is born; the majority of fathers are taking up their new entitlement to paternity leave; and the number of new dads now working flexibly has tripled.'[44] This is followed by a list of the various changes reported in this chapter and earlier in the book, such as increases in flexible working and the take-up of paternity leave. I don't mean to be mean-spirited about it but the Department for Trade and Industry's assertion that there's been a positive cultural change in the family is a little over-strung, to say the least, when so many families are struggling and so many parents are nowhere near equally sharing the domestic burden. Is this your experience? 'Positive cultural change within the family' is certainly not mine, nor that of many of the women we've spoken with for this book. Even a decade ago in Sweden and other Nordic countries, where at the time 72 to 83 per cent of women were working all the way through from leaving full-time education until retirement, compared with 81 to 92 per cent of men,[45] commentators were noticing that men were taking a larger part in childcare. At that time, it was noticed that 'more and more young men . . . are trying to share parental leave – at least for one or two months. A new picture of fatherhood is emerging in which presence, closeness and care is combined with shared economic responsibility'.[46] I don't deny this is happening in Sweden and to a lesser extent elsewhere, nor the enormous good it does for the family when fathers do take a more active role. But it's not about ticking a box when a researcher asks whether the father took parental leave or works flexibly. That can mean almost anything and has nothing much to do with the family dynamic. Peter comments on this in Chapter 7, and I've know fathers who 'work flexibly' by taking time off work to play golf while their partners continue with childcare and domestic duties. This isn't flexible working in the way that researchers who interview respondents would accept it; mass response telephone surveys can pick up trends that simply aren't there, or not to the extent stated. And governments like to make as much as possible of positive figures and bury the negative.

We know that women aren't participating in the workforce within the UK to nearly the same extent as in Sweden. Indeed, most countries have poor participation rates compared to Sweden. Men are still doing much less in the house, as shown in Chapter 4. Here's another set of depressing statistics, this time from the European Social Survey as reported in 2006: 61 per cent of Portuguese men, 57 per cent of Greek men and 47 per cent of Spanish men told researchers they rarely, or never, do the housework. Twenty-two per cent of British men, by comparison, rarely did any housework, compared to only 8 per cent of Swedish men.[47] (With housework, though, it's worth noting that in Sweden there is virtually no bought-in domestic help: if you want the house clean, you have to do it yourself.) What men thought they ought to be doing was also interesting: over 75 per cent of Spanish and Portuguese men thought they ought to be doing half the housework, compared to 90 per cent of British men. The poor dears go on a guilt trip when the researchers' clipboards come out, but it doesn't last. To try to get around this problem, Spain's government passed a law in 2005 that obliges men marrying in civil ceremonies to pledge to 'share domestic responsibilities and the care and attention of children and elderly family members.' As one of the senators who backed the law said at the time, 'the idea of equality within marriage always stumbles over the problem of work in the house and caring for dependent people.'

'It all works out rather nicely for the middle-class male' says poet Kate Clanchy:

Just as the big promotions – senior consultant, producer, part-ner – are handed out, his female competitors conveniently go on maternity leave, only to reappear untidy, demoted, 'flexible', on the phone to the nursery about conjunctivitis, wondering, since women will always blame themselves, how all their hard work and brains and go-getting feminism got them here, exactly, and what on earth is the way out.[48]

As we've seen, Spain has to act (and is starting to legislate) if it's going to persuade its women to put up with the double burden of work and family. Because, as the female sociologist involved in the survey pointed out: 'Given that [children] take up so much time, we have decided not to have them.' I take my hat off to Spanish women. While we continue to have children (albeit at a slower rate, but essentially still churning them out) and struggle with the double load that gives most of us, in Spain they've simply said no.

Are we changing? Perhaps we're more aware. One happy snippet comes from research by the UK's Department of Trade and Industry in 2004.[49] This showed the low levels of satisfaction people have with their quality of life (looking specifically at workers in the IT industry). Examples include: half of the people asked don't get involved with their families as much as they'd like to; roughly the same proportion said it was difficult to get involved in school activities; and again, about half agreed that they miss out on their children's development. This probably isn't any great surprise – what's more interesting is that although women surveyed felt these things more strongly, there was still a strong feeling among fathers that they're missing out too. The survey report concludes that:

> These issues are no longer the sole preserve of women in the labour market and that a significant proportion of the male labour force in the (IT) sector are becoming uncomfortable with some of the costs of working long hours and without fully fledged flexibility.

Another report adds to this note of optimism. Recent research commissioned by the Equal Opportunities Commission shows that new fathers are spending more time with their babies but that there are still many barriers to prevent this happening, especially in low-income families.[50] The vast majority of fathers now take at least two weeks' leave from work around the birth of their child but this rate is higher in high-income families. Even so, learning that, of fathers with 'traditional attitudes', three quarters want to be more involved in caring for their children is worth a short round of applause. The facts remain, though: men (generally) simply don't take responsibility for children or domestic issues when there's a woman there to do it, and being more aware of it doesn't change it. If anything it makes us more frustrated – as they can now see the problem, why is it still there?

Families are these days defined as entities which don't necessarily even need a blood tie. Some stepparents end up as sole carers of their stepchildren, others in a mix of their own and their partner's children. Some families are headed solely by a man, or by men, or by women. Families don't have to include children. Yet we still generally see women at the core of the family as they have been for centuries. After all, don't women nurture, yearn, get broody; isn't it women who want the babies and are therefore the prime movers in creating the family to support them? The family is still at the heart of society. If there were no families there would be no society, at least, not as we know it. Yet families, in their old-fashioned format, hold women back in their careers. We're stuck right in the middle – the nuclear family is still, for most of us, the status quo. For better or worse, that's what we have and we need somehow to negotiate a path through the family's demands and the workplace's demands to find a balance. Going out to work has increased our economic independence. With cash in our pockets and the expectation that this will increase we have been able to make family choices that weren't open to us beforehand. This affects the shape of the family (it's viable to leave an abusive spouse, for instance, if you know you're able to feed the children you take with you, whereas in the past the options were often simply not there). It also changes the way in which we can negotiate our home

responsibilities. If the mother is earning she can afford to employ
a cleaner or a nanny. If she is earning and the father is not, he may
take over the domestic role and its responsibilities. It's that latter
word that niggles yet again – responsibilities.

As argued at the beginning of this book, it's only partly about
the doing of the day-to-day family work; the real burden is
being responsible for it. Hyman and other researchers say that
'whilst there is considerable rhetoric about the desirability of
achieving work–life balance, there are no definitions or standards
of work–life balance or family friendliness to draw upon.'[51] The
researchers point to increasing complexity of our lives outside
paid work as society goes through social change, reflected in the
dramatic growth in the proportion of lone-parent households as
well as the increase in the population of those aged 65 and over.
In the same vein, there are no laid-down rules for who should
do what in a family except in examples such as Spain's civil
marriages (as mentioned earlier in the chapter) which are
blatantly ignored. No one seems even to talk about this core
issue of responsibility.

Sandwich bars

Another issue that newspapers aren't talking much about but
which riddles many of my conversations is related to the ageing of
our populations. In olden days the family, still local, and belonging
to larger extended families, shared the looking after of older
people. Now, we're scattered to the four corners, there are fewer of
us, and the oldies last much longer. This latter is, hopefully, a great
joy. Yet when our parents and grandparents do age, and seem to
spend forever doing it with gradually declining health and fewer
and fewer friends of their own generation for company and
support, the burden rests on us. And we might live in Margate,
Manchester, Manchuria or Mars with children who need taking to
school and our own jobs and careers to pay attention to.

Those of us carers in the middle are sometimes called 'sandwich carers' or the sandwich generation, paper-thin slices of meat in-between two hefty chunks of bread. This generation always existed but there was enough time and support to make it workable. How can it possibly work now? And what does that mean for those lonely old souls and in our turn, for us? My own mother is poorly right now. I love her to bits and visit her as often as I can but the reality is that she moved to be near me when she became ill so has no local friends; my siblings live long distances away and I work full-time. As a parent I also have the home and the children to manage. There's not a lot of time left for my own life and I find myself resenting that. I deeply want my mother's final years (and hopefully, there'll be very many of these) to be happy and fulfilled yet the reality is that she's only happy when her family is there with her. Nursing homes, even the fantastic one my mother lives in, are all very well, but they're not home. Colleagues tell me of their own families' situations – being the only child of parents in their 90s who live hundreds of miles away, a mother physically ill who was previously caring for a father with dementia – how is my colleague to cope with her own family and her demanding job while also spending weekends driving to see her parents and feeling guilty that she's not there all the time? Just because there are nursing homes for our older people to live in doesn't mean that we have no responsibilities, or that we choose to abandon them there. We drive hundreds of miles, organise outings and visits, manage another set of paperwork, do battle with care agencies and fret. Do we simply endure these years as best we can, all of us in a stressful frenzy? What a great shame. And what a lesson for our own children: this, kids, is what to do when we ourselves become elderly. I'd rather pop the pill, thanks.

How we're changing

'We're screwing up our kids' lives and because of that we're screwing up our own lives and screwing up the future for everyone,' says journalist Joanna Moorhead about a book by Robert Shaw.[52] Shaw is an experienced senior US child and family psychiatrist. His book on parenting describes children who are emotionally damaged and indulged and are creating a generation that has lost the capacity to appreciate the feelings and needs of other people.[53] He puts this down to the way we now parent our children: that instead of spending time with them, we fob them off and frequently, feeling guilty about this, give them all the material possessions they ask for (whether or not they need or even want them) and so create selfish, lazy people who assume that everything is theirs by right. It's not a new message but it's pertinent to this discussion. Whether or not this emerging generation of youngsters, having experienced less direct parenting than earlier generations as more and more families have two working parents, are in reality any better or worse than previous generations is hard to gauge.

Research with younger children reported in Chapter 6 concludes that there's not much difference in those whose parents work more hours against those whose parents don't. Committed parents do try to return home to our children at a decent time each day. When we lavish good childcare on them, take them on trips where we can truly relax as a family and imbue the values of a more egalitarian generation, is it so bad? Shaw's take on all of this – underpinned as it is by the belief that mothers are innately better nurturers and carers and need to take on that role with their children – is a difficult one that cuts deep into the message that governmental and personal economics is giving us. Although care is okay, says Shaw, parenting is better. Will kids continue to change? Probably. Is this a bad thing? Possibly. Shaw's evidence – seen around us in the shopping malls and streets, he says – has surely always been there in that there have always been 'delinquents' and bad parents just as there always will be. The teenage children of the working parents that I know seem pretty well-adjusted. And do any of us honestly believe it's better simply to let our children do what they want all the time? Don't we come down hard on them when they're out of line, support their search for a way to be? We have to find a balanced way of operating within the many constraints that families have nowadays and if that means our children see less of us than earlier generations of children did – well, that's a cost, though whether this alone – or at all – has the consequence Shaw describes is debatable.

What about us adults – are we changing too? Commentators believe that we'll become less interested in material things – we'll take these for granted as we accrue more and more at lower cost – and we'll become more interested in new experiences. We can already see this in the boom of new trip destinations world-wide made possible by the cheap airlines. Aesthetics will become more important, though still rooted in the ongoing machinations of the old economy.[54] As we become increasingly dissatisfied with materialism we may return to religion or other spirituality; Patrick Dixon from the organisation Global Change predicts a rise in 'tribalism' alongside population ageing.[55] And this will all take place in the context of family and social fragmentation.[56]

Are these predictions happening already? Looking around, perhaps increased 'aesthetics' means throwing off the hard work of their mothers' generation to become celebrities or kept women, according to a recent poll of 3,000 women by *New Woman* magazine (which delivers its readers celebrity gossip and style, interviews and photos).[57] Less than a quarter of these women in their 20s aimed to have careers, and 70 per cent said they're not willing to work as hard as their mothers did. Once happily partnered, a quarter would be happy to rely on their partners and become homemakers. Only 31 per cent found their job fulfilling. The editor of *New Woman* magazine, Helen Johnston, says that:

> Young women think their mothers just ended up with two full-time jobs – work and home – while nagging their man to do more housework.[They] saw the blueprint their mothers and society had created for them and thought, 'We can do better'. They've watched their own mothers exhaust themselves and want a better work–life balance. If this means a young woman wants to restore her partner as the main breadwinner so she can achieve an easier life, so be it, why not. Modern feminism should be all about choice.

No wonder feminism gets such a bad press: do we now develop into generations of women who aspire to do as little work as possible, get on TV and be looked after by rich husbands? I know that things go in cycles (and that the women polled aren't necessarily representative of the population) but it makes depressing reading. On the other hand, at the ripe old age of 49 I do feel that I've worked so hard that really, I could do with a decent break. Retirement, maybe? And that's after three decades of enjoying work. So perhaps these young women are savvier than my generation – perhaps they've got it right, especially if less than a third find their work fulfilling. Yet if they follow their dreams into dependence, not only do they put themselves at risk financially in having no fallback should things go wrong, but there will be even less workers in the population. Government won't be happy about that. It's unlikely, though, that many will find their dream lives. There are only so many 'Mr Right's to go around. And these are only aspirations; how many of us, in our time, wanted to be showjumpers, astronauts or chief executives? And how many of us made it? So although some of us may be screaming at the thought of going backwards to more generations of women running home and children without their own power or independence, surely society won't allow it. These young women will, in the main, have to work if they're to enjoy the benefits of being in the top half of our hourglass society. So instead, we can feel sorry for them as, without the aspirations to have fully-fledged careers of their own and the hard work behind them (in education and early work experience) to get them on the career ladder, there are going to be more that two thirds who don't find fulfilment in their work – or in the poor rewards that level of work brings.

A revised social structure

It's easy to forget how fast society is changing and how the time-bubble we live in and take for granted comprises only one second in a very long hour or more. It's not so long since people's perceptions and expectations were, mostly, completely different to ours

Sue from Devon remembers:

> When I was young, 30-odd years ago, my best friend went off to become a teacher. At the time I thought, 'Oh gosh, well, that's bad, she should be at home with her children. You shouldn't leave them and go off to work; you shouldn't leave them with a carer.' I genuinely believed that the best benefit to your children was to bring them up and get to know them and not shove them off onto someone else.

Parents or grandparents may recognise this from Nadia Sitas as a description of their early parenting lifestyle in the 1970s onwards . . . though there's something not quite right:

> Some women just never really have a job; they get married and then their role is wife and mother. Men carry on working throughout, doing exactly the same; it's up to the women [who do work] to take off time to be a mother. You reach a certain age,

say mid-20s, when there's a lot of pressure to have kids. You take some time from work to look after the child, and then go back on a part-time basis; you have a domestic helper who does most of the childcare until they go to school.

[For career women, the maid takes over] from the morning, when the mother goes to work to when she comes home so it could be anything from 7.00 in the morning until 6.00 at night. A lot of domestic workers are live-in ... They look after the child and do housework too and, more often than not, are the child's parent for a while. Because when the mum comes home it's pretty much bedtime for the child, so for a good part of the child's life they don't really know their parents well. More than 50 per cent of women opt for that.

Nadia is describing the middle-class norm in South Africa. To many, it reads like a time-warp movie with unsettling differences:

There's no [government] childcare support, there's no educational support. You have to pay for everything. Whether your kid goes to nursery school, whether you have a domestic helper, whether they go to school, you don't get anything, even if you're unemployed and single. If you're with a good company they may allow you a bit of flexibility but more often than not they don't. If you stop working there's no guarantee to you'll be allowed back into your position. People will employ men over women for that reason, so they don't have to pay maternity leave. They'd much rather have a man who will be consistent throughout the whole time. [Men earn more than women], it's not legal but it happens the whole time.

These differences are made possible by the economic and social structure:

Unemployment is so rife you can grossly underpay domestic workers and you can be guaranteed to find someone to look after your child. The domestic help is so desperate to work that they'll do it for next to nothing, so it's not really such a financial drain at all. Whereas, if they were maybe working [in the UK it would] be a different story. But there, they know there aren't any rights for workers so they'll take what they can.

South Africa has undergone enormous change since the days of Smith's apartheid yet there's still a huge underclass of people, supporting the middle classes, who work hard for low wages and a poor standard of living. Our 'more developed' society delivers greater equality and with this we lose something that middle-class parents from the past and South African parents now rely on: domestic support at affordable cost. With our reducing birth rates will this loss of an underpaid underclass increase until we can't afford childcare any longer?

We welcome migrants from Eastern Europe and elsewhere into our UK, US and Australian care homes, nurseries and homes: we pay them less and they perform tasks that local people aren't prepared to do. There's an advantage for them as many feel a need to learn English, make contacts, make money to send home and perhaps enjoy their new and different life a little before returning home. And many of them do – the average expected time for Eastern European migrant workers to stay in the UK, for instance, is two years, and the average length of stay for unauthorised Mexican immigrants into the US is around one year and five months.[58]

What will we do once they get fed up slaving for us and their own economy is strong enough – will we be travelling to work for them again, as we did in the 16th and 17th centuries?[59] And if so, what will this mean for parents and work?

In South Africa, for the working classes (forced to work but unable to afford domestic help) as Sitas says: 'A lot of the time the burden falls on the family so aunts and uncles will take part in the childcare. People can't afford to hire childcare so either they just don't work or family and friends help out.' Is this where we're heading, back to the days when we live near our families and develop strong communities simply because, if we want to have children, we'll have no choice?

With salaries for the skilled expected to rise and increasing numbers of workers unattached to the major employing organisations that provide the healthcare, pensions and paid vacations that most of us now take for granted, might we become more socially polarised too, with increasing numbers of a poor working class who, depending on the performance of the economy, might be the workless class? Would these people make good nannies for our children or would there be too many tensions? Do we move further and further to a 'black economy' and restless society with its intrinsic dangers? The US model of this type of polarisation, where 24 per cent of working women have no paid vacations, 29 per cent no paid sick leave and 34 per cent no pension benefits,[60] leads to comments such as this from Brennan, an American working woman:

> I want to have children some day, but I'm afraid of what their future might look like. The middle and lower classes are all struggling to get by, while the super-rich get rewarded with things like the estate tax repeal and outrageous tax breaks.[61]

The future

So where are we heading and what will it look and feel like? Here's a summary of what some of the commentators writing now are saying, and how they think the future will pan out. Some of this has been discussed above; where the thoughts are new they're from Duncan Neish of Scottish Enterprise:

The skills that employers will need and the skills that are available will continue to change and companies will need to adapt in order to attract those fewer people who have the required skills. At the same time our economy will continue to boom and our standard of living will continue to improve. We'll carry on spoiling our kids so that the next generations are spoiled and lazy and won't want to work as hard as we do. With more single-person units of housing, more of us will be raising our families alone. We'll have more choices because our work and personal situations will be more mobile. This will suit some of us, but others will find ourselves lost.[62]

We'll spend more time with the people we like and grow less sensitive to people we don't know; as we spend less time getting to know new people, so it will dull our sensitivity to the needs of strangers on the edge of society.[63] So the hourglass labour force's promotion of enduring and new social inequalities won't matter to us so much. We'll see a greater ethnic and cultural mix and a – slow – narrowing of sexual inequality. More of us will understand the difference between standard of life and standard of living. And we may even find God. Just as real family (in any of its definitions) is the place to find unconditional love and support so real employment is the only place we'll find the full gamut of family-friendly policies but more than that, the full range of pension, sick leave and other benefits that will become increasingly essential. We'll (in the main) be jolly pleased we're so special as to be sought after and fought over . . . but it might not feel like that when we don't have the freedom to go for the opportunities offered.

Are these commentators right? Remember that a decade or so ago they were telling us that the future would bring increased leisure for everyone, which is certainly not what we have now. They're simply extrapolating from their experiences and findings and who really knows what's going to come next? Yet the act of looking ahead – of walking into the future forwards rather than backwards – prepares us for whatever does come. It's something we can do for ourselves: instead of constantly having our heads down against the onslaught of the daily and weekly grind, if we can free up even half an hour now and again, we can start to think through some of our own 'expert truths' for our futures (as the final chapter explains). We each have our own little research project, after all, in our own life, family and career.

9

CHANGING THE WORLD

The last chapter sent us to work in the community in our spare time. Good idea, though impractical for many working parents. Chapter 4 hinted that we could being taking a greater part in local or national politics. Fantastic when we retire and the kids are looking after us; not so sensible now (even if we're interested, which most of us aren't). The priority is often about getting through the day, week, year of juggling with enough grace and energy left to enjoy our families. Some of us do find the time and objectivity to do more – perhaps we have stronger support at home, or our children sleep better, or our jobs are less demanding, or perhaps the opposite: maybe our lives and jobs demand that we make steps towards change.

Here's a horror story from American divorcee Terry Martin Hekker:

> The judge had awarded me alimony that was less than I was used to getting for household expenses, and now I had to use that money to pay bills I'd never seen before: mortgage, taxes, insurance and car payments. And that princely sum was

awarded for only four years, the judge suggesting that I go for job training when I turned 67.[1]

As an older woman from an earlier generation, Hekker was completely unprepared when her life's structure and safety net – her marriage – was taken away.

Diane Baker explains how it felt for her:

> Suddenly one day he turned round and said he was leaving and that was it. To say I couldn't even think about what to eat for dinner was an understatement; I was completely and utterly shattered. I can remember thinking that I really wasn't myself and if I could just get back to being myself I'd be all right. It took me a long time and what brought me back was that I applied for a job that I didn't think I'd get because I hadn't worked in conventional paid employment for a long, long time.

The initial change that Diane describes wasn't her choice. But our lives are continually changing, whether or not we like it: simply deciding to try for a baby changes us, let alone having a child with all the repercussions being a parent brings.

Gillian, in her late 20s, describes what happened to her:

> People [at work] said things would be fine and stay the same, just that I wouldn't be there so long each day. It wasn't like that. The moment I got back in I could feel it was different. People just treated me differently and at the time I thought it was them. Looking back, it was them but it was also me. Having [my daughter] changed me. It made me better in lots of ways, but I wasn't the person they'd worked with for six years. They reacted to that and I reacted to them.

Gillian now runs her own business, as many women do. The older mothers, above, get by as best they can. For these earlier generations the goalposts have been moving while they were still playing their football match. Today's young women have the huge advantage of knowing how things stand from the outset – or at least, that things are changing even when we don't know quite how and where. How many of us can be sure that we'll be able to continue with our careers? One of the larger poverty groups is older divorced women: how can we be sure that our marriages will succeed? Or that no other calamity will hit, requiring us to be the sole breadwinner? Or that our pension plans will pay out? So we need to ensure that whatever happens we have a job, or can get work, that pays enough to give us a reasonable standard of living and that if we take a break from this, to know that we have a route back in. Or that if we can't work, we're protected financially. To do less is plain stupid. We can do it by knocking everyone off the ladder as we ascend, or we can use gentler, equally dogged tactics and while we're at it, change the environment we work in so that we all have a chance of avoiding frostbitten toes in old age.

And there's another reason to make change: society is asking it of us. We're the focus of a quiet but gathering revolution. Our country needs us and our family needs us. We've gone from times when a woman's place was severely constrained and yet, in its own way, was held in a certain esteem, to being 'one of the boys' but a less useful one because we get monthly cramps then take maternity leave. They're expecting us to slog our uteruses out in paid work, to continue to populate the world, bring up useful and socially balanced youngsters (in our spare time) and to balance the whole caboodle while also keeping a sense of society, community, family and humour. Are we already at a point where the only useful woman is one who does all of this successfully and uncomplainingly? That's why we've not only got to change the world from the way it was and is (as described in this book) but we've got to change it towards what we want and need, not towards what they insist. Career woman? If that's what you want. Part-time worker and part-time parent while retaining the status and pay you've worked so hard for? If that suits you. Full-time mother? If that's the right thing. Whatever the formula that allows us to work, play, be rewarded and have choice to make change, then that's what we need to be working towards for ourselves, as well as for our kids when it's their turn. To do that, we need a strong sense of 'where we are'. Which is where extraterrestrials come in . . .

A spy from Mars, landing on our moon and pointing its huge telescope towards Earth, might describe this:

Women are legally equal; they feel able and want to participate fully; they're permitted to do so until they have children then obstacles arise that prevent them using their skills fully either at work or at home; the obstacles perpetuate inequalities and bitterness; these destabilise the workplace and the family there- fore also society; stresses rise; struggling women see that they can't afford the time, energy or cash to have so many children; the birth rate falls; the developed world becomes unsustainable; women are told they must work harder; their dreams and ambi- tions are shattered; they slog their whole lives through – longer as retirement ages extend – and are exhausted; they teach their kids that they can have it all; a new generation grows up feeling able to and wanting to participate fully; they perform the whole charade over and over again. They are exhausted and unable to resist. Time is ripe for invasion. Message out.

When this same Martian lands in the middle of the UK and sees the scenario from ground level by chatting to a succession of (rather bemused) women it might report these grass-roots grumbles: the old contract where women, when they had children, were cared for by men and their extended families has been blown away; women now have to do everything and are at any moment vulnerable to desertion often with no redress; women's intrinsic sociability is disallowed by the nuclear family; rigid single-layer communities of peers (with fewer older and younger people or people from different walks of life interwoven, as they would have been old-style), living in towns and cities with no time to access these life saving sociable needs nor pass them on to the children; work–life imbalance; a rigid workplace; doing two jobs; finding the required domestic help; finding enough support at home; different networks for men and women; the pay gap; not enough time; spending less time with the kids leading to behavioural problems (of parents as well as kids); unable to relocate for promotions; organisational structure: the glass ceiling, the concrete ceiling; the different ways that men and women think and work . . . stress!!!!!

This Martian will find it interesting. It might carry out some anthropological research. It would certainly see it as crazy.

Add what the Martian might glean to the views of the women who speak through this book. Here are a few more to show what different 'stages' of women are seeing and feeling.

Investment banker 'Ms Starling', in her 20s, who doesn't yet have children, sets the scene:

It's going to change [in banking] because more and more girls are starting to work here; you have more females doing the front office trading jobs, the sales jobs. Female attitudes are changing, it's like: I can do it all. Maybe when you hit the real world, after a while and you hit 28 and 29 and you are trying to do it all and it's difficult, then you don't succeed. But in the next generation that are coming out, the graduates I see, it's normal for them to want it all; it's that sort of mentality that they have.

Yes, and women have had that mentality since I was a young woman (if not before) but the reality is still here: women's careers collapse once we have children. Anna Canty, pregnant with her first child, sees a joint way forward: both parents playing equal roles in childcare, in the early months at least. Some of what she talks about is already changing with legislation increasing the length of leave for both mothers and fathers (see the Appendix for the current situation in the UK), yet legislation is one thing and the practical situation another:

> I think it's the most important time of your life, having a baby; you bring it home and you really need that help and support. I don't think two weeks [paternity leave] is enough. It should be a joint thing; mother and father are both important . . . if the mother gets six months and the father only gets two weeks it just doesn't seem right. Speak out when you're not happy and don't just say: 'there's nothing I can do about it'. Until people start voicing their concerns then nothing's going to change. You've got to be forceful about these things.

Easily said, but how easily done? Perhaps our own understanding and initiative, hard graft and compassion may be able to lift us out. Jenny Bell, not yet a mother, sees this as the way forward:

> Making sure that equal opportunities are present in employer's policies, which they are mostly, and that they are actually adhered to. And that you have the same opportunities as men and if you feel like you're being discriminated against then speaking out about it. Think about what you want from life and what your priorities are and how you can possibly fit them together and have a balanced lifestyle.

We need this verve and energy and optimism if we're going to move forward. Yet we're still caught in the cycle that the Martian saw from the moon: as we have our children our lives change and we start to see what was there all the time but our optimism kept us blind from. Few of the older women in this book speak in the same tones as the younger, childless ones – naturally enough, and that's fine except if each generation loops back to find that we've barely moved on and a new generation of women are thwarted in their careers and ambitions.

Sue, an older mother from Devon, has a longer view of it:

I don't think things have changed that much. It's always the mother they ring. Somebody's got to be the main carer. If the couple were sensible they could draw up a plan of action before the child was born so it could fall on the father, not the mother. But one of them, no matter how good their job is or how skilled or trained they are, has to be able to drop everything and say 'my child's the most important, it's got to go to hospital,' or whatever. Nobody else can take care of that for you. Employers know that, and it's going to be difficult if you know that your employee is liable to walk out in the middle of a meeting. And there are the school holidays, what happens then? So it is all a downward spiral, there's not much optimism one can give. It's a never-ending problem and there aren't easy answers for it.

You may think that things have changed for women and that when you have children it'll all be plain sailing. Believe me, and the evidence in this book: they haven't changed as much as you'd like to think.

What they want for us

We elect politicians so they can sort stuff. Former US President Bill Clinton said in 1997: 'By investing in women, we enable them to reach their fullest potential as individuals and as members of our society. When women thrive, their families thrive. When families thrive, communities flourish and our nation reaps the benefits.'[2] Fantastic, though not overly specific. How are they going about it? Former British Prime Minister Tony Blair tells us what he thinks:

> It is only through investment and expanding childcare services in a costed and worked through way that we can provide genuine choice.

Well said, PM. Then he tells us what *we* think:

> Paying cash to all mothers to stay at home could be a £5/US$10 billion bill that is completely unaffordable. The families of this country want real choices not false choices. They want their Government to live in the real world not a fantasy world.[3]

Perhaps they want their government to spend on what the electorate wants, not on what the Blair/Bush alliance decrees (an estimated UK £3.3/US$6.5 billion so far on the Second Iraq War,[4] for instance)? No one's suggesting that the government should spend £5/US$10 billion-a-year for all mothers to remain at home with their children: most of us don't want this and wouldn't take it up. And anyway, do you believe that figure? We know our future earnings and our sanity are on the line if we hang about playing tennis and drinking daiquiris all day (do people really do this?). We know that the mortgage needs paying. Yet we know that our children need to spend time with us as much as we need to spend time with them.

As Laine says:

> Children do suffer when both parents are career-minded, when career takes priority. I think one parent should be prepared to make their children their work for one or two years; it's nothing in terms of a lifetime, it is not much. But the

attitude towards this form of parenting needs to change; parent-work should be paid work. Stay at home parents should be paid for the work they do.

You may not think this way: your family may be happy with two parents in full-time work and that's fantastic too, though it still doesn't get over the fact that it rarely works in the medium term without oodles of family support or one parent taking a step back. But whatever we choose, what we want is a halfway decent chance of making our chosen equation work. Lobbying groups have come up with a number of ideas, such as Blair's, that Laine, from a pragmatic mother's viewpoint, sees as essential.

The Network for European Women's Rights says:

Women across Europe experience a growing pressure due to their double status: they have to engage in paid and unpaid work. In the context of the ever-growing withdrawal of the state from social and family matters, some have suggested ways of revaluing the unpaid work assumed by women offering at the same time, alternatives to formal employment.[5]

The Network goes on to list five alternative models put forward by researcher Robeyns: low wage employment subsidies (where lower-paid work would be subsidised, as happens already in many countries through family benefits and the minimum wage, aid that helps many families but by no means all and that anyway doesn't directly subsidise lower paid work); basic stock or stake holding (using cooperative, collective and partnership models for ownership of employing organisations, for instance. Again, this does happen, commonly in rural European economies though rarely in the more profit-driven wider economy); sabbatical accounts (providing workers with a certain amount of time off followed by the right to subsequent subsistence income); basic income (a minimum income paid to individuals rather than households irrespective of income from other sources and without requiring the performance of any work or the willingness to accept an offered job); and wages for housework (which, the report points out, wouldn't help to bring men further into domestic responsibilities and might instead prevent women from finding paid work – and a career – outside the home).[6] How do these sound to working women?

Diane Baker says:

I think that there should be wages for housework. Every woman who stays at home and brings up children is contributing to the future of the world and their society and their country. Without those children being born we don't have anything to work for. I know how it sounds but the thing is, if women were paid for the work they do in bringing up children, then the way they are viewed would be completely different because people respect and understand a person with a wage packet in their hand. This is what it's about. It's purely money.

A woman who's been working at home caring for children has been working very hard indeed and has the products and skills to show for it. What she doesn't currently have is status which, as Baker points out, is synonymous with income. If we increase our income (via paid-caring or other plans – we don't care how it's done) then we continue to carry worth with us, we feel equal and we are perceived as equal.

The models outlined are all good ideas though all have flaws. The same could be said of the work being done by governments to redress imbalance – they are (often) good ideas though when put into practice, many of them don't work as expected. But neither did the first attempts at flight, or using half lemon skins as contraceptive caps. Great in their time, well worth exploring but essentially waiting for some new thinking, more research, new technology and the will to invest. Good work, chaps (and chapesses) – but more sustained effort, please.

And while we're waiting for improvements on the first flight, or for contraception that doesn't smell of lemonade, do we sit around and expect it to be handed to us on a plate? Our prime skills may not be in designing flying machines nor in sperm-zapping but we can all think. Modern mothers feel we have to do everything. We're taught to be ambitious and reach our potential, and we see that we should do well in both paid and unpaid roles. What if we came around to thinking that this isn't the best way forward? What if we reverted to seeing the norm where we choose either career, or children, and that if we want to have children as well as work, accept that this work would be part-time and/or that we wouldn't reach the top? Maybe this is why some older mothers pack in the idea of 'career' and see that it's not the most important thing – because they earn enough, and they're mature enough not to mind about a little matter of kudos. Would we ever earn enough? Would feminists be incensed? Could we cope with the lack of esteem? But mightn't it be better to have a planned 'secondary' route rather than the almost inevitable disappointment we have now?

As commentator Catherine Hakim says: 'Men have always recognised that you really have to make choices. Women have deluded themselves into thinking that you don't.'[7] She goes on to show how women working part-time in professional jobs are mostly happier than those who stay at home to care for the kids full-time or have tedious full-time jobs. But she concludes that these part-time people probably aren't going to make it to the top of the career ladder. Could we (should we) make that our choice? At least for now: Hakim reminds us that many parents will start new careers after their children are more independent – a two-tier career – and that there's worth in this. Though with the UK government going some way towards enabling women to have more choice and starting to allow the work–life balance to work for us – assuming everything else is in our favour – then accepting Hakim's view that mothers won't make it to the top cuts many potential women MPs out of the legislature; and without them, who in government will continue pushing for what we really need?

This book has been asking whether and how children ruin our careers. Having trawled through the research and spoken to dozens of people it's fair to say that yes, having children ruins your career if you're the main carer, however much you farm them out to other people. This applies to all the loving and well-meaning parents we've spoken to and read about. I'd guess it also applies to those few parents who aren't so interested in their kids – even then, who's going to be that 'default parent' when things go wrong at home and school? Being motivated as a good parent, or trying to ignore parenting, don't make the bare facts go away. So what are we going to do about it?

Chapter 7 looked at options such as not having kids, having only one, choosing a partner who will take on that 'default parent' role. These are all about 'us', and are short- to medium-term. For many of us these decisions were already made a while back and we're now stuck with the repercussions (good and bad). What about everyone else, and what about the longer term? Perhaps we don't care. But most of us at some stage think about the legacy we're leaving our children – sons as well as daughters. We try to recycle more, use less carbon, many of us are involved in charities or community work to support people less fortunate . . . these are all building a better society for our kids. But we tend to forget the workplace and that massive, overriding part of our lives becomes invisible yet again. This is where we could be making strong and irrevocable change in order to pass down some sort of parity for all, where they'll stand a decent chance whatever their sex or background. Many of the women we've spoken with have talked about the future and looked ahead from their own perspectives. There's been a range of different thoughts and views and many of these involve action. Action involves planning (something parents become fantastic at). If society has already given us Plan A and governments Plan B, why not create our own Plan C?

Peter Childs, a researcher into creative thinking, describes how, by concentrating on one specific thing, we push chemicals into our brains which then, overall, operate at a lower level.[8] The part that's working at the task we're concentrating on does well but overall brain function reduces. Most creative and innovative thinking is quashed during that time. To allow our brains to operate creatively – to come up with novel approaches, new ways of thinking and ways out of the box – generally we need to let our minds wander a little and not focus too hard on the issue in hand. Reading this book will have whooshed the adrenalin and made us think in a certain pattern, which is useful. To go beyond that and find creative ways forward it helps to sit back for a while, daydream; dig the garden, gaze at the view from the train. Then some of the following pointers, which after reading will settle unobtrusively in the unconscious, will help these creative ideas come through for what we need to do next.

Creating a personal 'Plan C' – the way our minds work

Get a personal philosophy. If you haven't got one, plagiarise. This is UK MP Tessa Jowell's:

> I think you have to start by accepting the basic rule, which I always did, which is: 'I'm only irreplaceable to my children. In almost every other circumstance, I'm replaceable' . . . it . . . separates the really difficult decisions from those which are a matter of course, and most of them are just a matter of course.[9]

Creating new lives changes us. Laine talks about the process:

> This is how having children has impacted on me: now there is
> someone outside of myself for whom I will give up my life in an
> instant in order for him/her to live better/longer/more and this
> feels like an instinctual dictum, way outside my sphere of
> control. From pregnancy the body is taken over, there is a
> period of fear and even resentment, and the body is never the
> same; there is a looseness. I think this is the same in the psyche,
> but not acknowledged.

Though the giving can seem never-ending the whole mothering
package sets us aside from other people and allows us to see life,
and to prioritise, differently – if we can keep perspective and if
this 'looseness' is used as an advantage, not a disability. We can
each draw up a way of approaching this, and the world, in order to
be able to move forward. A part of that subtle change of thinking
involves removing our own preconceptions and prejudices. If
we expect men to stop being prejudiced perhaps we can show
them how. If we're looking at whether cultural attitudes will
change how men will take an equal share at home, we ourselves
can accept that men are equally good at running a home and let
them do it. So what if white shirts are slightly less bright white?
What does it really matter?

Researcher Robert Taylor sees a need to look at how the shape
of the workplace is changing in terms of increasing the numbers
of women participating in it and to look at the effects this is
having on men (something there's not been much research on).[10]
If men feel emasculated when work fails them and then feel
worthless in their own homes, it's not much fun for anyone.
Mothers can negotiate a new form of family unit that includes
men and doesn't alienate them. Mothers have a 'new order' to
offer – if we're big enough to do it.

Diane Baker says:

Why do men earn more than women? Because it's always
considered that a man has a greater economic burden. Nobody
thinks about a woman: 'oh dear, I better make sure she gets a
square meal otherwise she won't be able to do her job'. But
that's what people think about men. Basically a change in the
way people think [is needed], which is why the independence
and strength of women has to be given to them by other women.
We need to support and show that faithfulness towards each
other to keep us economically strong and sound so that we can
have parity.

And finally on the way we think . . . can we increase our flexibility
of thought and action at home and family? For example, in any
family there are sometimes conflicts over who does what, how and
when. These elements are changing continuously as children's
needs change and our needs change too. If we expect our partners
and employers to change to help us, perhaps we too need to be
prepared to change to help them. Not giving by ourselves away but
by being prepared to be flexible in a wider sense.

The way we act at home

If things are going to change for us and our children then men
must be as practically able and self-sufficient as women; we're the
ones who can allow that happen. If they don't, or won't, take on
equal responsibility and we refuse to tolerate that, then they
would change. Chapter 7 has already talked about how we can give
our children the life skills and attitudes they'll need. A good
friend of mine works advising young people who find themselves
in difficulty. She comes out with tales like this: 'She's 18 and
starving and dirty. Her mother wouldn't let her in the kitchen at
home and now she's left home she has no idea how to make toast.

TOAST!!!' This young woman didn't know, either, how to go to a launderette to wash and dry her clothes, nor that her poor diet of crisps and chocolate would affect her ability to think straight, as well as changing her body. I was shocked that this was happening to a young woman and later asked myself: would I be equally shocked if this story was about a young man? These patterns are deeply set. Can we address the way we raise our children, whatever their sex, and not make assumptions that our sons will be cared for in later life or give our daughters the mindset that they'll take on that role?

Diane Baker puts it this way:

[With] women who don't expect their husbands or boys to cook: you disable them emotionally. Female power at home is paramount, it's amazing how powerful we are . . . and in lots of ways we make the mistake of undermining our own position by allowing men to behave badly.

She goes on to describe how it becomes when there's a partnership without these preconceptions of equal skills and sharing:

If there are partners together, and they're working and they have children, if equal responsibility is dished to them then they both have to take it on and, when problems arise, they both have to think 'what about the children?' Not 'oh well I'm off, she can stay at home and look after them', which is usually the case.

Baker also sees how this approach impacts on children's understanding and emotional development. She says of her adult son:

He's still a real 'bloke's bloke' but he has a different attitude to how much he shares at home with his woman and his daughter. He decided to follow a career that meant he had some space for him to spend time with his family. He came to me and said 'I might not be a high-flier, Mum, but I want quality not quantity.'

We can also train our daughters to be more than nannies and our sons to be more than builders. I'd hope that the message has got through to careers advisors and they now understand how important it is for girls to be encouraged to make the most of their potential by going into a career that has promotion and earning potential. And also, as Baker says: 'they should be advised very carefully about the way they go in order that they can pick up on their career later if they wish to, without it being too traumatic and daunting that it makes it hard.' It's not just a job for careers advisers — we too can underline to our children the importance of having work that earns enough.

Diane Baker continues:

I would like to be sure that my daughter has independence enough to have her own money, to always have her own place, and that's why I despair when I see women today letting their lives drift, and not making for themselves and as soon as they find a man they think 'well that's alright, I don't have to do anything'; they don't hold on to what's theirs, they give it all away. There were always reasons why women shouldn't have the vote; there were always reasons for why women couldn't be in parliament (and the main reason for that was because women didn't have the right facilities, which meant lavatories!). There will always be these spurious reasons which will be given for why women can't do these things; you still occasionally get these ridiculous things. But it is power and it's making sure our daughters have that power, somewhere to live that's always theirs, that gives them power and it's power in the end and that comes from money.

And finally on the subject of making change within the home, perhaps we need to engage in some subtle sabotage. Think about this from Chapter 8: 'While we continue to have children (albeit at a slower rate, but essentially still churning them out) and struggle with the double load that gives most of us, in Spain they've simply said no.' Hmm. Shall we vote with our Inter Uterine Devices?

The way we act at work

As reader of this book you're likely to be a person who agrees that legislative change needs to continue.

However, commentator Robert Taylor says;

> Evidence shows that it is . . . poorly enforced, meaning for example that new and expectant mothers continue to lose their jobs despite legislation to protect them. It is generally accepted that the existing legislation is patchy, complex and ineffective for both individuals and business. It focuses on cure rather than prevention and fails to deal with the complex and deep rooted causes of discrimination.[11]

This isn't the case in Europe. Taylor continues:

> It is true that [in the UK] minimum regulations have protected women and children from excessive exploitation in the workplace since the early industrial revolution. Negotiated voluntary agreements between employers, trade unions and employees have also played an important part in ensuring workers are not compelled to work excessively long hours and enjoy limited holiday breaks and do secure at least some mutually acceptable control over the pace and content of their work. But by the standards of continental Europe this approach has been neither universal nor comprehensive.

In Europe, a culture of acceptance underpins both legislation and enforcement; in the UK we legislate but no one takes it seriously. Which is bizarre given that 'in the Nordic countries in particular it is widely acknowledged that such an approach has actually proved beneficial for corporate performance.'[12] This non-compliance culture is contagious: we ourselves sometimes assume that the law doesn't apply to our situation.

Take the pay gap outlined in Chapter 2. It's easy to think that 'equal pay' means that a man and woman doing exactly the same job get the same pay for it. But it goes beyond this – it entails people with equal skills and responsibilities earning the same pay. Where the majority of workers in one sector of an organisation are women and their skills and abilities are on a par with a majority of men doing parallel work in another part of the organisation, are both groups being paid the same? If the answer's 'no' then it flouts equal pay legislation and we need to do something about it. There are many examples of where unions and workers together have used the law to improve matters for working women. For instance, cleaners of the walls in an NHS hospital, who were mostly men, were earning more than floor cleaners, mostly women. In the school meals service, women had their pay cut when the service was privatised whereas the (mainly male) maintenance staff didn't. They won their equal pay case. In Canada, the public sector union won a substantial pay award for women in the low-paid sector and in New Zealand primary school teachers (predominantly women) now earn the same rates of pay as secondary school teachers (mainly men).[13] If we understand this type of inbuilt inequality for what it is, when we come across it (or, when it comes across us) then we can do something about it.

The way we're supported

Parents need support and many of us live a long way from families who might supply that. Communities are there to support us but this will only happen if we engage: give to it, take from it and become unafraid to ask. As Laine says, 'Mothers spend the first year loving their babies, welcoming them, securing them in the world: a community is imperative.' Chapter 7 looked at this in more detail; it's here again as a reminder: next time you run out of eggs, pop next door rather than the corner shop; that comes later, when it's time to return the borrowed eggs at a less-harried time.

Emotional postscripts

Firstly, women are brilliant at emotion: why not use it rather than let it (sometimes) use us? 'We must get angry', says commentator Mariella Frostrup: 'I'm starting to think that the only answer for women is to start kicking up a fuss all over again. We need to make the issues that make our lives impossible political.'[14]

Yet at the same time she's saying that we need to chill, because being angry is self-defeating:

> The longer you're angry, the less likely you are to be happy, and the longer you're unhappy the greater the increase in your rage.

Tough one to figure out but it makes some sense. Enacting a controlled rebellion — a refusal to let things lie — with a calm that allows us to think clearly (without the adrenalin focusing our minds too strongly) allows us to have the most from what's on offer while also keeping a clear head to plan for ourselves and others.

And secondly: don't feel guilty. As Diane says of returning-to-work mothers:

> They [need] to be relieved of the guilt of going to work and trying to have a better life for their family. There was a time years ago, in the '50s and '60s, where [people said] 'she only works for "pin money"', and some of them did. But some did it

simply because they couldn't stand being at home all the time, and that doesn't necessarily make you a bad mother.

UK MP Julia Drown stepped down from her parliamentary role because of family commitments, stating:

> I will miss it but you can't be in two places at once and, you know, so many of my constituents tell me quite rightly, 'You only have the children once.' I love them and my family to bits, and I want to have more time with them.[15]

That doesn't mean that she's stopped playing her part in politics and in making change she feels the country needs; she can continue to do that in the way she approaches her life and work, in the small things she thinks and says and does. And when her children are grown perhaps she'll pick up her political career again.

A few of us will become household names. Many of us will be active in some way, perhaps known for our views locally or within our organisations. All of us have a role to play in the everyday way we approach our lives and our gender.

The 'F'-word

Most of us don't have mothers who were active feminists and haven't spent our lives campaigning. Some of us shudder at the term: I certainly don't want to be tainted by the 'F'-word. It's not about labelling people; it's about working slowly, gradually, positively and doggedly to change something that's fundamentally wrong. It's about making it 'situation impossible' for women to get to the state, as I did, of being unable to get out of bed in the morning and wishing, so wishing, that the men in white coats would come to take us away. Not certifiable. Not irrational. In fact, incredibly strong. Just incapable, in this mad set-up, of doing everything so well for so long.

Diane Baker says:

I campaigned for women's rights and I was a fighter and still am
and will do that until I die because I think it's my duty. And it's
not for me; it's for my daughter and her daughter and her daughter and hers. My mother said to me, 'it doesn't matter how much
you get, you have to still keep fighting, you never get it all at once,
you won't get it all in your lifetime and if you think you're going
to and you give up because of that, you're wrong, morally wrong.'
I know it sounds a bit serious but it is serious . . . Saying it's
'women's' rights' is all very well but it is actually a human right.

Get to the top? Be a career star? Be a nurturer and homemaker?
Do both? Earn pin money? Rely on our man? They're questions
all of us, on having children, are faced with. Our circumstances
vary so widely that there can't be a stock answer. At the risk, as has
happened to the author and philosopher Brenda Almond, of being
branded a Conservative, consider whether there's truth in her
thought that 'variety and choice may be less accommodated to
human nature than many people today have chosen to believe'.[16]
She's writing about whether we're suited to polygamous relationships so I'm taking her out of context but perhaps it stands as a
more universal question – maybe we're simply not like that. We're
brought up to expect every variety, every choice. When our families and careers collapse, suddenly we lose those. Of course, we
can work, always, towards fairness, a deep-seated equality of
thought and assumption within our family, for our family, and for
many of us we extend that to society too. Yet do we fundamentally
need all this choice if our situations are far from equal: if our
path, like our partner's, is towards a family compromise that
makes us all happy, perhaps our upbringing's promise of never-
ending choice is not only misleading us but also unnecessary?
And perhaps above all we need love, security and stability?

Once each of us has found answers let's tell governments what they need to do to underpin and lead society during this burgeoning century — how they can give us a system that addresses barriers such as childcare and the cost of getting back to work. Isn't that the best legacy we could ever hope to leave our children? There's lots here to get the 'F'-people grinding their teeth. Over to you.

Appendix

By Sophie Tanner

Legislative and support structure for parents in the UK, February 2007

This section is for guidance only. It does not provide an authoritative guide to the issues covered and you should do your own research and, if necessary, take legal advice before acting on any of these matters.

1. Statutory Maternity and Paternity Pay

1.1 Statutory Maternity Pay
This is the payment a woman receives from her employers when she gives birth to, or adopts, a baby.
Eligibility:
- You must be the biological mother or adopter of the child.
- You must have been employed by the same employer without a break for at least 26 weeks into the 15th week before the week your baby is due.
- You must earn an average of at least £84 a week (before tax).
How much you get:
- 90 per cent of your average weekly earnings for the first six weeks of your maternity leave.
- Either £108.85, or 90 per cent of your average earnings if this is less than £108.85, for the remaining 20 weeks.

- You pay tax and National Insurance in the same way as on your regular wages. Your employer reclaims the majority of Statutory Maternity Pay from their National Insurance contributions and other payments.

http://www.direct.gov.uk/en/Bfsl1/BenefitsAndFinancialSupport/DG_100 18741 accessed 22 January 2007

1.2 Statutory Paternity Pay

This is the payment a man receives from his employers when he becomes a father, or adopts a child.

Eligibility:

- You must be the biological father or adopter of the child or be the mother's (or adopter's) husband, partner or civil partner or have or expect to have responsibility for the child's upbringing.
- You must have continued to work for the same employer without a break for at least 26 weeks by the 15th week before the baby is due, or employed up to and including the week your wife, partner or civil partner was matched with a child.
- You must continue to work for that employer without a break up to the date the child is born or placed for adoption.
- You must be earning an average of at least £84 a week (before tax).

How much you get:

- If your average weekly earnings are £84 or more (before tax), Statutory Paternity Pay is paid for one or two consecutive weeks at £108.85, or 90 per cent of your average earnings, if this is less.

http://www.direct.gov.uk/en/Bfsl1/BenefitsAndFinancialSupport/DG_100 18741 accessed 22 January 2007

2. Alternative support for the unemployed or self-employed

2.1 Maternity Allowance

If you're pregnant or have a new baby but don't qualify for Statutory Maternity Pay, you may be able to claim Maternity Allowance. This will be paid by Social Security.

Eligibility:

- You're employed, but not eligible for Statutory Maternity Pay.
- You're registered self-employed and paying Class 2 National Insurance contributions, or hold a Small Earnings Exception Certificate.
- You've been at work for at least 26 weeks of the 'test period' (66 weeks up to and including the week before your baby is due). Part weeks count as full weeks.
- You earned an average of £30 in any 13 of the weeks in the test period.

How much you get:
- Maternity Allowance pays a standard weekly rate of £108.85, or 90 per cent of your average weekly earnings (before tax), whichever is the smaller.
- From a baby's due date of 1 April 2007, Maternity Allowance is paid for a maximum of 39 weeks (prior to this due date it was paid for a maximum of 26 weeks).

http://www.direct.gov.uk/en/Bfsl1/BenefitsAndFinancialSupport/DG_100 18869 accessed 30 January 2007

2.2 Incapacity Benefit

If you can't work because of illness or disability you may be able to get Incapacity Benefit, a weekly payment for people under State Pension age – currently 60 for women and 65 for men.

Eligibility:
- Your Statutory Sick Pay has ended, or you can't get it.
- You are self-employed or unemployed.
- You have been getting Statutory Maternity Pay and have not gone back to work for your employer because you are incapable of work.
- You were under State Pension age when you became sick.

You must also have been:
- Paying National Insurance Contributions.
- Unable to work due to sickness or disability for at least four days in a row (including weekends and public holidays).
- Getting special medical treatment and unable to work for two or more days out of seven consecutive days.

How much you get:
- Short-term (lower rate) – £59.20
(higher rate) – £70.05
- Long-term (basic rate) – £78.50

http://www.direct.gov.uk/en/Bfsl1/BenefitsAndFinancialSupport/DG_100 18913 accessed 30 January 2007

2.3 Sure Start Maternity Grant

This is a one-off payment to help towards costs of a new baby for people on low incomes. The grant comes from the Social Fund and you don't have to repay it.

Eligibility:

You can get Sure Start Maternity Grant if you or your partner or your civil partner receive any of the following:
- Income Support
- Income-based Jobseeker's Allowance

- Pension Credit
- Child Tax Credit at a rate higher than the family element
- Working Tax Credit where a disability element is included in the award

And if one of the following applies to you:

- You or your partner or civil partner are pregnant or have given birth within the last three months
- You or your partner or civil partner have adopted a child within the last three months and the child is under one year old
- You and your husband or wife have been granted a parental order for a surrogate birth within the last three months
- You're getting benefit for a dependant under the age of 20 who is pregnant or has given birth within the last three months

How much you get:

- £500 for each baby. Your savings won't affect the grant.

http://www.direct.gov.uk/en/Bfsl1/BenefitsAndFinancialSupport/DG_100 18854 accessed 30 January 2007

3. Parental Leave

As long as you meet certain conditions, if you're a parent, or adopter, of children under five, or disabled children under 18, you have a statutory right to take unpaid time off work to care for them.
Eligibility:

- You have been employed by the same company for a year or more and are an 'employee' with a contract of employment
- You are a parent named on the child's birth certificate
- You have legal parental responsibility for a child under five (or a disabled child under 18)

How much you get:

- If you've worked for the same employer for a year you can take:
- 13 weeks unpaid off work (in total, not per year) for each child, up to their fifth birthday.
- 18 weeks unpaid for each disabled child, up to the child's 18th birthday
- Either parent has the right to parental leave. If you're separated and your ex-partner looks after the children, you have the right to parental leave if you keep formal parental responsibility for the children. Foster parents do not have rights to parental leave. Parental leave is usually unpaid. It's different from maternity or paternity pay (see 1), which is related to the birth of a new baby.

3.1 Maternity Leave
Eligibility:
· You must be an 'employee', ie working under a contract of
  employment.
How much you get:
· Statutory maternity leave is for 52 weeks.
· If the week your baby was expected to be born starts before 1 April
  2007, it was for 26 weeks, with an extra 26 weeks if you met certain
  conditions.
You may be entitled to receive Statutory Maternity Pay for up to 39
weeks of the leave (see 1.1).

3.2 Paternity Leave
Eligibility:
· You have been continuously employed by your current employer for
  26 weeks or more by the 15th week before the baby is due.
How much you get:
· You are entitled to take either one week or two consecutive weeks'
  paternity leave. The period in which you must take your leave will
  begin on the day the child is born and finish 56 days after the day the
  child is born. Paternity leave applies to people in same-sex
  partnerships as well as heterosexual partnerships.
You may be entitled to paid paternity leave (see 1.2).
http://www.worksmart.org.uk/rights/viewsubsection.php?sun=53
accessed 15 February 2007
http://www.direct.gov.uk/en/Parents/Workingparents/DG_10029285
accessed 15 February 2007

3.3 Adoption Leave
If you adopt a child the rights you have are similar to those of natural
parents.
· Statutory Adoption Leave is for 52 weeks. Statutory Adoption Pay is
  for up to 39 weeks at up to £108.85 per week.
Paid adoption leave is available to employed people who are adopting a
child on their own, or for one member of a couple who are adopting
together. The couple can decide who can take the paid leave. The other
member of the couple, or the partner of the adopter, may be able to
take paid Paternity Leave (see 3.2).
http://www.direct.gov.uk/en/Parents/Workingparents/DG_10029406
accessed 16 February 2007

4. Ongoing Financial Support

4.1 Child Benefit

Child Benefit is a tax-free monthly payment to any individual bringing up a child or young person. It is not affected by income or savings so most people who are bringing up a child or young person qualify for it. Although Child Benefit isn't 'means tested', it can affect the amount of other benefits you may be getting that are means tested.

Eligibility:

You'll be able to get child benefit if you're bringing up:

- A child aged under 16.
- A young person under 19 who is either studying in full-time non-advanced education (A level or equivalent) or on an approved training programme.
- A 16- or 17-year-old who recently left school or training and registered for work or training with the Careers or Connexions Service or similar.

How much you get:

- £17.45 a week for the eldest child
- £11.70 a week for each additional child

http://www.hmrc.gov.uk/childbenefit/index.htm
http://www.ukbenefits.org/child_benefit.html
http://www.direct.gov.uk/en/Parents/YourMoney/DG_10016699
accessed 16 February 2007

4.2 Child Tax Credits

If you're responsible for a child or young person who normally lives with you, you'll probably be eligible to get Child Tax Credits, a means-based benefit.

Eligibility:

- The family income must be no more than £58,175 a year (up to £66,350 if you have a child under one).
- You must be responsible for at least one child under the age of 16, or a young person under 19 who is either studying in full-time non-advanced education (A level or equivalent) or on an approved training programme.

How much you get:

- Credits are based on each individual's circumstance so you must provide HM Revenue & Customs with required information on your: annual income, partner or civil partner's annual income, number of children.

The payment is made up of several elements:
- A family element paid to any family with at least one child and worth up to £545 (2006–07 tax year).
- A child element paid to each child in the family and worth up to £1,765 (2006–07 tax year).
- A disabled child element paid to each disabled child and worth up to £2,350 (2006–07 tax year).
- A severely disabled child element which is the highest rate care component and you can claim this as well as the child and disabled child elements. This is currently £945 (2006–07 tax year).

http://www.direct.gov.uk/en/MoneyTaxAndBenefits/BenefitsTaxCredit-sAndOtherSupport/TaxCredits/DG_10039727
http://www.ukbenefits.org/child_tax_credits.html
http://www.workingfamilies.org.uk/asp/family_zone/fs_ben1_taxcred-its.asp accessed 17 February 2007

4.3 Child Maintenance
Child Maintenance is paid for children who live away from one or both of their parents. It is an amount of money paid regularly by the natural, non-residential parent to the parent with care.
Eligibility:
- Child Maintenance covers natural children up to the age of 17 or 19 if they are in certain types of full-time education.
- Other persons, such as grandparents with care of the children, may apply to the Child Support Agency for assessment for child maintenance.

How much you get:
- The Child Support Legislation sets out a complicated formula to calculate the level of Child Maintenance payable by the non-residential parent. This is based on each parent's income and certain limited outgoings, including housing costs. Currently there is a general rule that an absent parent should not pay more than 30 per cent of net income in maintenance.

http://www.csa.gov.uk/new/apply/#Q2
http://www.divorce-online.co.uk/redirect.asp?goto=/help/childsupport/maintenance.htm
http://www.direct.gov.uk/en/Bfsl1/BenefitsAndFinancialSupport/DG_100 18808 accessed 17 February 2007

4.4 Disability Living Allowance

This is a tax-free benefit for children and adults who need help with personal care or have walking difficulties because they are physically or mentally disabled. It is not normally means-tested.

Eligibility:

You can get Disability Living Allowance if:

- You have a physical or mental disability, or both.
- Your disability is severe enough for you to need help caring for yourself or you have walking difficulties, or both.
- You are under 65 when you claim

How much you get:

Disability Living Allowance has two components:

- A care component – if you need help looking after yourself or supervision to keep you safe.
- A mobility component – if you can't walk or need help getting around

The care component and mobility component are paid at different rates depending on how your disability affects you.

http://www.direct.gov.uk/en/DisabledPeople/FinancialSupport/DG_10011 731 accessed 17 February 2007

5. Working Parents

5.1 Working Tax Credit

This is for people on low incomes working 16 or more hours a week, whether they are employed or self-employed, and can include support for childcare.

Eligibility:

- Being eligible for Tax Credits isn't the same as being entitled to them. Your tax credit award is worked out by calculating a 'maximum award', made up of all the elements you are eligible for, including a childcare element. Your income is then worked out and the maximum award is reduced to give the amount you are actually entitled to.

How much you get:

- This is a complex calculation; go to the appropriate web pages, your Citizens Advice Bureau or direct to HM Revenue and Customs.

http://www.adviceguide.org.uk/index/life/benefits/benefits_and_tax_cre dits_for_people_in_work.htm#working_tax_credit

http://www.workingfamilies.org.uk/asp/family_zone/fs_ben1_taxcred its.asp

http://www.direct.gov.uk/en/MoneyTaxAndBenefits/BenefitsTaxCredit sAndOtherSupport/TaxCredits/DG_4015483 accessed 17 February 2007

5.2 Rights while absent from work

The Sex Discrimination Act 1975 states that it's unlawful to discriminate against a woman 'by dismissing her or subjecting her to any other detriment'. No male comparator is required because pregnancy is a condition unique to women. There can be no question of comparing a woman's pregnancy with a man's illness.

http://www.emplaw.co.uk/researchfreeredirector.aspx?StartPage=data%2f972u5.htm accessed 17 February 2007

5.2.1 Pay

· You should be paid for time at antenatal classes.
· You should continue to receive pay rises and most bonuses during ordinary maternity leave. Pension contributions will continue during this time.
· During maternity leave you will either be entitled to maternity pay – paid by your employer – or, depending on your earnings, to maternity allowance – paid by Social Security (see 2.1).

5.3 Keeping Your Job

· You cannot be (legally) dismissed because you are pregnant or for reasons connected with your pregnancy or maternity leave.
· You should be offered the same training and promotion opportunities as other staff while pregnant.
· You should be allowed to keep the same duties and responsibilities while pregnant.
· You must be allowed to return to your own job unless this is genuinely not possible (eg redundancy situation) when you should be offered a suitable alternative.

5.4 A Safe Pregnancy

· You and your baby must be protected from risks to your health at work.
· Your employer needs to carry out a health and safety risk assessment.
· Possible risks include:
    Unduly stressful work.
    Working alone.
    Working in awkward work positions.
    Unnecessary travelling.
· You should have a suitable place where you can rest and later breast-feed.
· You are entitled to 26 weeks ordinary maternity leave.

- For women whose expected week of childbirth is on or after 1 April 2007, all women will be entitled to additional maternity leave of 26 weeks, which starts from the end of ordinary maternity leave. (See 3.1)

The two main acts that give you rights during pregnancy and maternity are the Employment Rights Act 1996 (as amended by the Employment Act 2002) and the Sex Discrimination Act 1975.
http://www.eoc.org.uk/Default.aspx?page=15659 accessed 17 January 2007

5.5 Rights when returning to work
You have the right to return to your old job after having a baby on your old terms and conditions unless it is 'not reasonably practicable'; then, your employer must offer you a suitable alternative job with similar terms and conditions. If you're dismissed this will normally count as unfair dismissal if it is for a 'prescribed reason' connected with pregnancy, maternity or taking maternity leave (or parental leave). You must normally have completed at least one years' continuous employment with the same employer before the date of your dismissal. Then you have the right to require the employer to provide a written statement of reasons for dismissal. There are exemptions and exceptions.
http://www.emplaw.co.uk/researchfreeredirector.aspx?StartPage=data%2f972u5.htm accessed 17 February 2007

5.5 Flexible Working
The Employment Rights Act 2002 introduced the right to request flexible working. You can ask your employer to work flexibly and they have a duty to consider this seriously. This is available to both men and women, and covers the hours an employee works, the times s/he is required to work and the place of work. Any change is permanent. If you want a temporary change this must be specifically negotiated with your employer. The Sex Discrimination Act 1975 prohibits direct and indirect sex discrimination. Women have successfully argued that being made to work full-time without justification is indirect sex discrimination because we're more likely to have childcare responsibilities.

5.5.1 Rights to Request
To qualify for the right to flexible working you must:
- Have a child under 6 years old, or under 18 years old if the child receives Disability Living Allowance.
- Make the request no later than two weeks before the child's 6th (or 18th) birthday.

- Be responsible for the child and the reason for the request must be for you to care for the child.
- Have worked for your employer for at least 26 weeks when you make the request.
- Not be an agency worker or a member of the armed forces.
- Not have made another application under the same right during the previous year.

Your request must be in writing (this includes emails and faxes) and dated and include the following:

- Indicate that it's an application under the statutory right to request flexible working.
- Confirm that you have responsibility for the upbringing of the child and state your relationship to the child.
- Explain what, if any, effect the change would have on your employer and how this could be dealt with.
- State what working pattern you're applying for.
- State what date you want the change to start.
- State whether you have made an application before and if so when (you can only make one application a year).

http://www.emplaw.co.uk/researchfreeredirector.aspx?StartPage=data%2f972u5.htm

http://www.workingfamilies.org.uk/asp/family_zone/fs_pr5_after_maternity.asp

http://www.eoc.org.uk/Default.aspx?page=15659 accessed 18 February 2007

6 Equal Opportunity Legislation

6.1 The Sex Discrimination Act 1975

- Prohibits sex discrimination against individuals in the areas of employment, education and the provision of goods, facilities and services and in the disposal or management of premises.
- Prohibits discrimination in employment against married people. Since the Civil Partnership Act 2004 came into force the same protection is afforded to those in a civil partnership as those who are married.
- Prohibits victimisation because someone has tried to exercise their rights under the Sex Discrimination Act or Equal Pay Act.
- Applies to women and men of any age, including children.
- States that discriminatory advertisements are unlawful but only the Equal Opportunities Commission can take action against advertisers.

• Applies in England, Wales and Scotland.

6.1.2 Discrimination on the grounds of pregnancy or maternity
There are special provisions in the Sex Discrimination Act prohibiting
discrimination on the grounds of pregnancy or maternity leave in
employment. If a woman can show that 'but for' her pregnancy or
maternity leave she would not have suffered less favourable treatment,
this is sex discrimination. She does not have to compare herself to how
a man was or would be treated.
http://www.emplaw.co.uk/emplaw/employee/research-employee.aspx
http://www.eoc.org.uk/Default.aspx?page=15296 accessed 18 February
2007

6.2 Equal Pay Act 1970
This gives an individual a right to the same contractual pay and bene-
fits as a person of the opposite sex in the same employment where the
man and the woman are doing:
• Like work.
• Work rated as equivalent under an analytical job evaluation study.
• Work that is proved to be of equal value.
Your employer isn't required to provide the same pay and benefits if
they can prove that the difference in pay or benefits is genuinely due
to a reason that isn't related to sex.

http://www.emplaw.co.uk/emplaw/employee/research-employee.aspx
accessed 18 February 2007

6.3 Work of Equal Value
Men and women employed by the same employer are entitled to the
same terms if they are employed in different work which is 'of equal
value'. There are exceptions to this. To succeed with a 'work of equal
value' claim you must show that there's someone of the opposite sex
doing work of equal value for higher reward. This person doesn't have
to be doing identical or the same work, but it must be sufficiently
similar for a reasonable comparison to be made.
http://www.emplaw.co.uk/emplaw/employee/research-employee.aspx
accessed on 18 February 2007

6.4 Gender Equality Duty 2007
This requires public authorities to promote gender equality and elimi-
nate sex discrimination. Instead of depending on individuals making
complaints about sex discrimination, it places legal responsibility on

public authorities to demonstrate that they treat men and women fairly. This covers policy making, public services such as transport and employment practices such as recruitment and flexible working. http://www.eoc.org.uk/Default.aspx?page=15016 accessed 18 February 2007

7. Women and Pensions

Women's pension entitlement is generally lower than men's:
- Women's average income in retirement is just 57 per cent of men's.
- Only 16 per cent of retired women are entitled to a full basic pension in their own right.
- One in five single women pensioners face poverty in retirement.

This is because women are more likely to undertake unpaid parenting and caring commitment throughout their lives, with consequent lower pay when in work. Home Responsibilities Protection for parents and credits for carers give certain recognition of parenting and caring contributions.
http://www.eoc.org.uk/pdf/women_and%20pensions.pdf accessed 18 February 2007

Legislative and support structure for parents in the US, April 2007

This section is for guidance only. It does not provide an authoritative guide to the issues covered and you should do your own research and, if necessary, take legal advice before acting on any of these matters.

Conversion rate: US$1.9918 (US) to £1 (GB) as at 1 April 2007

Structure of US Government

The US has a federal government (ie the various states in America) unite under a central authority but are independent in internal affairs. Each state has its own written constitution, government and code of law which can vary greatly. The following information is based on central government funding schemes and grants but it is recommended that you research your own state's benefit program.
Website: www.GovBenefits.gov

1. Maternity leave

The time a mother takes off from work, paid or unpaid, due to pregnancy and childbirth is known as maternity leave. Because paid
maternity leave is not readily available from most employers in the US,
women usually use a combination of short-term disability, sick leave,
vacation and personal days in order to have some portion of their
maternity leave paid.

The Family and Medical Leave Act (FMLA) guarantees women who are
on maternity leave that their job will be protected for up to a maximum
of 12 weeks in any 12-month period.

Website:

http://www.nationalpartnership.org/site/Search?query=FMLA&inc=10
accessed 21 April 2007

2. Paid Parental Leave

California leads the US with its paid parental leave policy and law. It
provides partial income replacement (around 50–60 per cent) for up
to six weeks per year to care for a new baby. However states such as
New York, Rhode Island, Hawaii and New Jersey have short-term
disability insurance funds that can be used to fund maternity leave. In
these states, pregnancy and childbirth are considered disabilities;
mothers can generally take time off with income replacement of six to
eight weeks. Fathers, adoptive or foster parents are not eligible to
receive paid family leave under a short-term disability insurance plan.

Website: http://nccic.acf.hhs.gov/itcc/PDFdocs/B2Three_AAGFinancing.pdf
accessed 21 April 2007

3. Child Care and Development Fund

The Child Care and Development Fund provides assistance to low-
income families who need child care due to work or work-related
training and education.

Eligibility:

· You must be a parent or primary caregiver responsible for children
  under the age of 13 years of age, or under 19 if incapable of self-care.
· Your financial situation must be low income or very low income.
· You must also be either employed or, in some States, enrolled in a
  training or education program.

Website: http://nccic.acf.hhs.gov/statedata/index.html accessed 21 April
2007

4. Child Care Resource and Referral Services

These services help parents locate and choose quality childcare by providing referrals to local childcare providers, information on state licensing requirements, availability of childcare subsidies and other information.
Eligibility:
· You must be a parent or primary caregiver responsible for children under the age of 19 years or responsible for a child(ren) with a disability.
Website: http://childcareaware.org/en/findcare/index.html?state=AL accessed 22 April 2007

5. Child Support Enforcement

This programme provides services to locate absent parents or establish paternity and enforce support obligations. Services are available if you have custody of a child who has a parent living outside of the home.
Eligibility:
· You must be a parent or primary caregiver who needs help establishing paternity, a child support order or collecting child support.
Website: http://www.acf.hhs.gov/programs/cse/index.html accessed 22 April 2007

6. Child Tax Credit

Depending on your income, this program can reduce the Federal Tax you owe by US$1000 for each qualifying child under the age of 17.
Eligibility:
· You must be a parent or primary caregiver responsible for a child who attends school (high school or under).
Website: http://www.irs.gov/newsroom/article/0,,id=106182,00.html accessed 22 April 2007

7. Child and Dependent Care Credit

This programme can reduce your tax by claiming the credit for child and dependent care expenses on your Federal income tax return.
Eligibility:
· You must be responsible for a school-age child and you must be a taxpayer who is interested in receiving tax information and tax preparation assistance.
Website: http://www.irs.gov/newsroom/article/0,,id=106189,00.html accessed 22 April 2007

8. Tax Benefits for Adoption

This programme enables you to take a tax credit of up to US$10,000 for qualifying expenses paid to adopt an eligible child. Qualifying expenses include reasonable and necessary adoption fees, court costs, attorney fees, travelling expenses and other expenses directly related to the legal adoption of an eligible child.
Eligibility:
· An eligible child must be under 18 years old, or be physically or mentally incapable of caring for him or herself.
· The adoption credit can't be taken for a child who is not a United States citizen or resident unless the adoption becomes final.
Website: **http://www.irs.gov/taxtopics/tc600.html** or **http://www.usa.gov/ Citizen/Topics/Benefits.shtml** accessed 22 April 2007

9. Foster Care

This programme provides Federal financial assistance to states to assist with:
· Costs of foster care maintenance for eligible children
· Administrative costs to manage the programme
· Training for staff, foster parents and private agency staff

The implementation of the program may differ by state.
Eligibility:
· In order to qualify for this benefit programme, you must be certified to provide 24-hour, substitute care in your home for a child who is under the supervision of a state child welfare agency and who is under age of 18 years.
Website: **http://www.acf.hhs.gov/programs/cb/programs/4efc.htm** accessed 22 April 2007

10. Immunization grants

The Vaccines for Children (VFC) programme purchases vaccines for children in certain eligibility groups who can't afford to buy vaccines. Doctors can get these vaccines for their patients who qualify by joining the VFC program in their state.
Eligibility:
· In order to qualify for this benefit program, you must be under the age of 19 years.

- You must need financial assistance for health care/insurance costs or receive or be eligible to receive Medicare.

or

- You must be Native American/American Indian and you or a family member must be enrolled in a federally recognized American Indian tribe or Alaskan Native village.

Website: http://www.cdc.gov/nip/ accessed 22 April 2007

11. Other grants are available to include:

Indian Child Welfare Act Title II Grants, Medical Dental Expenses Tax Credit, Social Services Block Grant, Special Improvement Project, Tax Benefits for Education. As well as many other programmes and grants that may be available in your area.

Website: http://www.govbenefits.gov

Useful Websites

http://www.govbenefits.gov
http://www.hhs.gov/children/index.shtml#income
http://www.cdc.gov/nip/
http://www.acf.hhs.gov/programs/cb/programs/4efc.htm
http://www.irs.gov/taxtopics/tc600.html
http://www.usa.gov/Citizen/Topics/Benefits.shtml
http://childcareaware.org/en/findcare/index.html?state=AL
http://www.nationalpartnership.org/site/Search?query=FMLA&inc=10
http://mchb.hrsa.gov/whusa_05/pages/0304ml.htm
http://www.census.gov/prod/2001pubs/p70-79.pdf

Legislative and support structure for parents in Australia, April 2007

This section is for guidance only. It does not provide an authoritative guide to the issues covered and you should do your own research and, if necessary, take legal advice before acting on any of these matters.

Conversion rate: US$2.4 (Australia) to £1 (GB) as at 1 April 2007

Structure of Australian Government

Australia is divided into six states and two main territories; under its federal system of government these play a major role in providing government information and services to the public. There are three levels of government: commonwealth (also know as 'federal government'), state and local. The commonwealth government passes laws which affect the whole country as a whole. The following information is based on commonwealth legislation that applies to all eligible people in Australia, although it is worth checking with your local government, in case the law varies in your area.

Website: **http://www.australia.gov.au/govt-in-aust** accessed 10 April 2007

1. Maternity or Parenting Payment

1.1 Maternity Payment
This is the payment a family receives from their local government Family Assistance Office following the birth (including stillborn babies) or adoption of a baby. It recognises the extra costs incurred at the time of a new birth or adoption of a baby and is not income tested. This payment replaced the Maternity Allowance and Baby Bonus from 1 July 2004.

Eligibility:
· You must meet the residency requirements.
· You must have a dependent child, except in cases of stillbirth.
· You must have care of a newborn child within 13 weeks after the birth if you are a non-parent carer.
· From 1 July 2005, the age limit for adopted children to be eligible for Maternity Payment was extended from 26 weeks to under two years of age.

How much you get:
· Maternity Payment is a one-off payment of US$4,,133 for each child and is usually paid as a lump sum. It is payable for each child in a multiple birth. If there is a change in care during the 13 weeks eligibility period, the payment may be apportioned between two carers.

Website: **http://www.familyassist.gov.au/internet/fao/fao1.nsf/content/ payments-maternity_payment** accessed 1 April 2007

1.2 Apportioning Maternity or Parenting Payment
Maternity or Parenting Payment is mainly payable to one eligible claimant, with the default payee usually being the mother. However, in some cases (mainly if there is a change of care) the payment can be split between two or more eligible people by arranging a percentage for each person. Maternity Payment cannot be apportioned between two members of the same couple.

Website: **http://www.familyassist.gov.au/internet/fao/fao1.nsf/content/ publica tions-factsheets-maternity_payment_eligibility.htm#2** accessed 19 March 2007

2. Maternity Immunisation Allowance

Maternity Immunisation Allowance is a payment for children aged 18 to 24 months who are fully immunised or who are exempt from immunisation. It is not income tested and can also be paid for stillborn babies and children who die shortly after birth.
Eligibility:
· There are broad eligibility criteria and only one person can be eligible unless the care of the child is shared between two or more carers.
How much you get:
· The Maternity Immunisation Allowance is a one-off payment of US$229.70.

3. Family Tax Benefit (A)

This helps families with the cost of raising children. It is worked out from your family's annual income, how many children you have and how old your children are.
Eligibility:
· You must have more than 10 per cent care of a dependent child who is: under 21, or a full-time student aged 21 to 24.
· You must be an Australian resident, or a special category visa holder.

How much you get:
· This varies on your income and there is a limit at which Family Tax Benefit is no longer paid.
· Your benefit can vary from US$1,828.65 to US$5,332.65 per child, per year.

4. Family Tax Benefit B

This gives extra assistance to families with one main income, including single parent families and families with one main income where one parent chooses to stay at home to care for their children.
Eligibility:
· You have a dependent child who is under 16 years or 16 to 18 year and a full-time student.

- You and your child are Australian residents or are a special category visa holder residing in Australia.

How much you get:
- For two parent families with one main income, the partner earning the higher amount is not taken into account, only the partner earning the lesser amount is subject to the income test, they can earn up to US$4,234 for the financial year before it affects their benefit. The maximum benefit they can receive is from US$2,197.30 to US$3,153.60, depending on the age of the child.
- For single parent families: Your income is not taken into account. Single parents receive the maximum rate of Family Tax Benefit Part B, regardless of income. This is US$2,197.30 to £3,153.60, depending on the age of the child.

Website: **http://www.familyassist.gov.au/Internet/FAO/fao1.nsf/content/ payments** accessed 1 April 2007

5. Child Care Benefit

This is a payment that helps families who use approved and registered childcare. Your child care service can tell you if they are an approved provider and if they receive Child Care Benefit payments from the government on behalf of eligible families.

Eligibility:
- Your children must meet the immunisation requirements if they are under the age of seven.
- You or your child meet residency requirements.
- Your child attends approved or registered care and you have the liability to pay for the cost of your childcare.

Please note: If your employer contributes towards the cost of your childcare through salary sacrificing or salary packaging, you will need to determine who has the liability for the costs. The issue of liability depends on who is obligated to pay for the childcare fees. You will need to contact your employer if you are unsure who is liable.

How much you get:
- There are various eligibility criteria that depend on your income; if you qualify you'll get between US$148 and US$482.84, depending on your number of children.

6. Other Types of Government Assistance

This includes the Large Family Supplement, Multiple Birth Allowance, Rent Assistance, Health Care Cards, Double Orphan Pension, Jobs Education and Training (JET), Child Care Fee Assistance.
Website: http://www.familyassist.gov.au/Internet/FAO/fao1.nsf/content/payments accessed 1 April 2007.

7. Welfare to Work Package

The Australian Government announced a package of reforms in the 2005–06 Budget which aim to make Australia's welfare system more sustainable. The Welfare to Work reforms focus on four priority groups: people with disabilities, principal carer parents, mature age job seekers (50 or over) and people who have been unemployed for a long time.
Key elements in the package are:
· A new wage subsidy programme for employers called Wage Assistance.
· Additional uncapped places for outside school hours care and Family Day Care.
· Extra training and skills development services.
· A new Employment Preparation service for parents, carers and the mature aged.
Website: http://www.movingintowork.gov.au/moving intowork/Overview/ accessed 1 April 2007.

Useful Websites
http://www.familyassist.gov.au/
http://www.australia.gov.au
http://www.ag.gov.au
http://www.australia.gov.au/front/subjects
http://www.facsia.gov.au
www.movingintowork.gov.au
www.oecd.org
www.sprc.unsw.edu.au

Summary of good web pages

These are useful websites for an overview of all aspects of childcare including: Maternity and Paternity pay, Parental Leave and other allowances:
http://www.direct.gov.uk/en/index.htm –
http://www.worksmart.org.uk/rights/viewsubsection.php?sun=53

These are great websites for finding local childcare help and provision:
http://www.childcarelink.gov.uk/index.asp
http://www.nacis.org.uk/
http://www.hmrc.gov.uk/childbenefit/index.htm
http://www.ukbenefits.org/child_benefit.html

These are good websites for advice on tax credits, child maintenance and for single parents:
http://www.csa.gov.uk/new/apply/#Q2
http://www.divorceonline.co.uk/redirect.asp?goto=/help/childsupport/maintenance.htm
http://www.adviceguide.org.uk/index/life/benefits/benefits_and_tax_credits_for_people_in_work.htm#working_tax_credit
http://www.workingfamilies.org.uk/asp/family_zone/fs_ben1_taxcred its.asp

These websites provide a comprehensive overview of Equal Opportunities:
www.nacab.org.uk
www.eoc.org.uk

These websites provide up to date legal advice:
http://www.emplaw.co.uk/researchfreeredirector.aspx?StartPage=data%2f972u5.htm
www.acas.org.uk
www.lawcentres.org.uk
www.ets.gov.uk
www.justask.org.uk

Endnotes

Introduction

1. Equal Opportunities Commission Pregnant and Productive campaign. Summary at **http://www.eoc.org.uk/Default.aspx?page=15524**, accessed 3 November 2006
2. **http://www.lhmu.org.au/childcare/news/2005/1119663006_15898.html**, accessed 1 June 2007

1. How Jobs Happened

1. Equal Opportunities Commission, Press release, 26 October 2006, at **http://www.eoc.org.uk/Default.aspx?page=19724**, accessed 3 November 2006
2. Harrison, C (1997) 'The Changing Role of Women in American Society' in *US Society and Values*, **http://usinfo.state.gov/ journals/itsv/0597/ijse/ijse0597.pdf,** accessed 26 May 2006, p 11
3. Blackwelder, J K (1997) *Now Hiring: The feminization of work in the United States, 1900–1995*, Texas A&M University Press, Texas, p 224
4. Moore, D P (2002) 'Boundaryless Transitions: global entrepreneurial women challenge career concepts', in Burke, R J and Nelson, D L (Eds), D L *Boundaryless Transitions: Global Entrepreneurial Women Challenge Career Concepts*, Blackwell Publishers, Oxford, p 245
5. Chinchilla, N and Leon, C (2005) *Female Ambition: How to reconcile work and family*, Palgrave Macmillan, New York, p 8
6. Paul Adams, Vice President, Pratt Witney, at the American Society of Mechanical Engineers annual conference, Barcelona, 10 May 2006
7. Wichterich, C (2000), The *Globalized Woman: Reports from a future of inequality*, Spinifex Press, Victoria, p 36

8. Murphy, E with Graff, E (2005) *Getting Even, Why women don't get paid like men – and what to do about it,* Touchstone, New York
9. Wichterich, C (2000) as above, p 168
10. Wichterich, C (2000) as above, p 167
11. Chinchilla and Leon (2005) as above, p 7

2. WELCOME TO WORK

1. Steven Landsburg, Forbes Online, 2006, at http://www.forbes.com/2006/ 05/20/steven-landsburg-labor_cx_sl_06work_0523landsburg.html, accessed 2 November 2006
2. 2004 figures taken from Gaber, I (2006) 'The Work-Life Balance – have we got it right, or do we all work too long?' by Ivor Gaber in *Society Today,* Pub ESRC http://www.esrc.ac.uk/ESRCInfoCentre/about/CI/CP/ Our_Society_Today/Spotlights_2006/long_hours.aspx?ComponentId=1401 1&SourcePageId=14015, accessed 5 January 2007
3. Carnell, B (2001) 'Sri Lankan Prime Minister: Please Have More Children', 20 June 2001, at http://www.overpopulation.com/articles/2001/000067 .html, accessed 17 November 2006
4. When a country's birth rate is around 2.1 children per woman, each couple is having the number of children needed to replace those that have died within the population. This 'replacement level' will lead to a country's population remaining constant. The rate is higher than two children per couple because there are about 5 per cent more boys born than girls, and because some girls will die before they reach the end of their childbearing years. Countries with higher mortality rates need a higher birth rate to maintain the population. Source: http://www.prb.org/pdf05/ FreqAskdQuestnsWPDS_Eng.pdf, accessed 2 June 2006
5. 2002 figure, at http://www.eu-cu.com/uk.htm, accessed 1 September 2006
6. 'Women's Earnings, Work Patterns Partially Explain Difference between Men's and Women's Earnings, United States General Accounting Office', Report to Congressional Requesters, October 2003, at http://www.gao.gov/new.items/d0435.pdf, accessed 24 March 2006
7. Hinsliff, G, 'Why the pay gap never went away', *The Observer,* 26 February 2006, at http://www.guardian.co.uk/gender/story/0,,1718304,00.html, accessed 2 June 2006
8. Frost, V, 'Hanging on for Help', *The Guardian,* 27 January 2007, at http://money.guardian.co.uk/workweekly/story/0,,1999344,00.html, accessed 2 February 2007 discussing recommendations from the Women and Work Commission at http://www.womenandequalityunit.gov.uk/pub lications/wwc_govtactionplan_sept06.pdf, accessed 2 February 2007
9. Hinsliff, G (2006) as above
10. Riach, P A and Rich, J (2002) 'Field Experiments of Discrimination in the Market Place', *Economic Journal,* November 2002. Summary at http://www.res.org.uk/society/mediabriefings/pdfs/2002/November /riach_rich.pdf, accessed 2 February 2007
11. Curtis, P, 'Sex discrimination at work hits men too', *The Guardian,* 25 February 2006, http://www.guardian.co.uk/gender/story/0,,1717638,00 .html, accessed 1 October 2006
12. International Labour Office (2004) 'Breaking Through the Glass Ceiling;

Women in Management, Geneva,' at http://www.ilo.org/dyn/gender/docs/RES/292/F267981337/Breaking%20Glass%20PDF%20English.pdf, accessed 9 June 2006

13. United States General Accounting Office, 'Women's Earnings, Work Patterns Partially Explain Difference between Men's and Women's Earnings', Report to Congressional Requesters, October 2003, at http://www.gao.gov/new.items/d0435.pdf, accessed 24 March 2006, p 60

14. Bellamy, K, and Cameron, S (2006) 'Gender Equality in the 21st Century: modernising the legislation', Fawcett Society at http://www.fawcettsociety.org.uk/documents/exec_sum mery1.pdf, accessed 5 January 2007

15 Women and Work Commission (2006) 'Shaping a Fairer Future', at http://www.womenandequalityunit.gov.uk/publications/wwc_shaping_fairer_future06.pdf, accessed 2 June 2006

16. Carlson, B, Peace, J, Nair, S and Hanson, K (undated; early 2000s), *Middle School Youth Answer the Question: 'What Do You Want to be When You Grow Up'*, Gender Diversities & Technology Institute, at http://www2.edc.org/GDI/publications_SR/CareerSummFINAL.pdf, accessed 1 June 2007

17. Curtis, P (2006) 'Pound for Pound', *The Guardian*, 18 February 2006, at http://www.guardian.co.uk/gender/story/0,,1712162,00.html, accessed 1 September 2006

18. Prosser, M (2006) as above

19. Women at Work Commission (2006) as above

20. United States General Accounting Office (2003) as above, p 9–20

21. Institute for Women's Policy Research Fact Sheet (2006) 'The Economic Security of Older Women and Men in Michigan', at http://www.iwpr.org/pdf/Michigan_D467.pdf, accessed 1 June 2007

22. Jefferson, T (2003) *Women and retirement incomes in Australia; A Review*, Working Paper Series of the Women's Economic Policy Analysis Unit, at http://www.cbs.curtin.edu.au/files/WEPAU_WP-32_Nov_2003.pdf, accessed 1 June 2007

23. Burke, J B and Nelson, D L 'Advancing Women in management: progress and prospects', in Burke, J B and Nelson, D L (Eds) (2002) *Advancing Women's Careers*, Blackwell Publishers Limited, Oxford

24. International Labour Office (2004) as above

25. http://www.breaktheglassceiling.com/solutions.htm, accessed 2 June 2006

26. Grant, J (2006) Right time for a baby, interviewed for the BBC television programme *Panorama*, at http://news.bbc.co.uk/1/hi/programmes/panorama/5076872.stm, accessed 23 June 2006

27. Moorhead, J (2004) 'For decades we've been told Sweden is a great place to be a working parent. But we've been duped', 22 September 2004, *The Guardian*, at http://politics.guardian.co.uk/publicservices/story/0,11032,1309874,00.html, accessed 26 May 2006

28. Chinchilla, N and Leon, C (2005) *Female Ambition: How to reconcile work and family*, Palgrave Macmillan, New York, p 81

3. Unjust Governments

1. Lederer, E (2006) 'Record number of women in politics, but still only one in six', *The Guardian*, 1 March 2006, at http://www.guardian.co.uk/gender

/story/0,,1720577,00.html, accessed 5 January 2007

2. Women and Equality Unit (2006) 'Women's Representation in Politics', at http://www.womenandequalityunit.gov.uk/public_life/parliament.htm, accessed 17 March 2006

3. http://www.stuff.co.nz/stuff/0,2106,3588279a6160,00.html, accessed 17 March 2006

4. Report by the Centre for Advancement of Women in Politics, Queen's University, Belfast, http://www.qub.ac.uk/cawp/latest.html, accessed 7 April 2007

5. Equal Opportunities Commission (2001) 'Women in Parliament: A Comparative Analysis', at http://www.eoc.org uk/PDF/women_in_parlia ment_findings.pdf, accessed 17 March 2006

6. Wild, L (2005) 'Politics remains a man's world', Young Fabians, 1 July 2005, at http://www.ippr.org.uk/articles/?id=1555, accessed 17 March 2006

7. 'The Gender Gap and the 2004 Women's Vote, Setting the Record Straight' , Center for American Women and Politics Advisory note, 2004, at http://www.cawp.rutgers.edu/Facts/Elections/GenderGapAdvisory04.pdf, accessed 4 April 2007

8. 'Women's Votes Pivotal in Shifting Control of US Senate to Democrats' Press release, November 9, 2006, Center for American Women and Politics, at http://www.cawp.rutgers.edu/Facts/Elections/Post_elec tio06_exitpollanalysis.pdf, accessed 4 April 2007

9. This research, carried out on behalf of The Electoral Commission by academics at Birkbeck College, University of London, England, and Harvard University, US, also found that women now cast their vote as regularly or more often than men; the gender gap in turnout that existed before 1979 has now closed and may have even reversed. http://www.electoralcommission.gov.uk /media-centre/newsreleasereviews.cfm/news/305, accessed 17 March 2006

10. Davidson-Schmich, L K (2006) 'Gender and Political Ambition Revisited: What Questions Does American Politics Research Raise for Western Europeanists?', Fifteenth International Conference of the Council for European Studies, at http://www.europanet.org/pub/papers/Davidson.pdf, accessed 8 April 2007

11. Sherman, E (2001) 'Women in Political Leadership: Reflections on Larger Social Issues', at http://www.ksg.harvard.edu/leadership/compass/2001 /index.php?itemid=566, accessed 4 April 2007

12. Soanes, B with Moran, M and Lovenduski, J (2005) Women in Parliament: The new Suffragettes, Politico's Publishing, London

13. United Nations Economic and Social Commission for Asia and the Pacific, Australia – Report on the State of Women in Urban Local Government, at http://www.unescap.org/huset/women/reports/australia.pdf , accessed 14 March 2007

14. Culture page of Australianbeers.com, at http://www.australianbeers. com/culture/women.htm, accessed 8 April 2007

15. Follett, B (2000) 'View from Westminster', at http://www.barbara-follett .org.uk/columns_2002/0004.html, accessed 9 September 2006

16. Mellor, J (2002) 'EOC says it's time to call time on MPs working hours madness', Equal Opportunities Commission press release, at http://www .eoc.org.uk/Default.aspx?page=15066&lang=en, accessed 17 March 2006

17. 'Women and Politics in South Australia', Report on Women in Parliament, at **http://www.slsa.sa.gov.au/women_and_politics/parl4.htm,** accessed 4 April 2007

18. Summers, A (2007) 'Australia was the second country to give women the vote but lags behind much of the world in letting them lead. Why can't we have a female prime minister?', at **http://www.annesummers.com.au/arti cles.htm,** accessed 14 March 2007

19. Watt, N (2003) 'Women win half Welsh seats', *The Guardian*, 3 May 2003, at **http://politics.guardian.co.uk/wales/story/0,9061,948680,00.html,** accessed 17 March 2006

20. Chaney, P (2003), 'Women and Constitutional Change in Wales', *Occasional Paper No. 7 Centre for Advancement of Women in Politics*, School of Politics and International Studies, Queen's University Belfast, p 7 and footnotes

21. Castiglione, D, and Warren, M E (2005) 'Rethinking Representation: Seven Theoretical Issues', Midwest Political Science Association Annual Conference, Chicago, IL, April 6–10, 2005, quoting as sources: Mansbridge 1999, Williams 1998, Philips 1995, Young 2000, Dovi 2002, at **http://www. huss.ex.ac.uk/politics/research/readingroom/CastiglioneWarrenRepresen tation.doc,** accessed 17 March 2006

22. Sherman, E (2001) 'Women and Leadership; Women in Political Leadership: Reflections on Larger Social Issues' at **http://www.ksg.harvard.edu /leadership/compass/2001/index.php?itemid=566,** accessed 14 March 2007

23. AFL-CIO (2006) 'Ask a Working Woman Survey Report' at **http://www.afl cio.org/issues/politics/labor2006/upload/AWWsurvey.pdf,** accessed 9 September 2006

24. 'From Voices', reported in *Modernising Government News*, November 1999, at **http://archive.cabinetoffice.gov.uk/servicefirst/2000/mod ernising/issue3.pdf,** accessed 7 April 2006

25. Australian Government web pages: 'Moving into Work', at **http://www. movingintowork.gov.au/movingintowork/Overview/,** accessed 7 April 2007

26. Australian Chamber of Commerce and Industry, 'Workplace Reform – Working for Australian Women, Position' Paper, November 2005, at **http:// www.acci.asn.au/text_files/Discussion%20Papers/Aust%20Women%20& %20WR%20Reform%20Electronic%20Copy.pdf,** accessed 8 April 2007

27. Australian Chamber of Commerce and Industry (2005) as above

28. Soanes, B with Moran, M and Lovenduski, J (2005) as above, p 187

29. AFL-CIO (2006) as above, p 10

30. AFL-CIO (2006) as above

31. Heymann, J, Earle, A, Simmons, S, Breslow, S M and Kuehnhoff, A, (undated, post-2003) 'Where does the United States stand globally?', The Work, Family and Equity Index: The Project on Global Working Families, at **http://www.hsph.harvard.edu/globalworkingfamilies/images/report.pdf,** accessed 9 September 2006

32. Leira, A (1992) in Anttonen, A, 'The Welfare State and Social Citizenship', p 22, in Kauppinen, K and Gordon, T (Eds) (1997), *Unresolved Dilemmas; Women, work and the family in the United States, Europe and the former Soviet Union*, Ashgate Publishing, Aldershot

33. Siim, B (1993) as above, p 22

34. Siim, B (1993) as above, p 25

35. Roos, J (undated) 'The Consequences of the Crisis of 1990s to the Nordic

Welfare State: Finland and Sweden', at http://www.valt.helsinki.fi/staff
/jproos/Nordsocp.htm, accessed 21 April 2006

36. The Finnish Ministry of Social Affairs and Health (2002) 'The Finnish social
protection system – a Summary', at http://pre20031103.stm.fi/english/
tao/publicat/year2001/summary.htm, accessed 21 April 2006

37. Manninen, M (2004) 'Women's status in Finland', at http://virtual.finland
.fi/netcomm/news/showarticle.asp?intNWSAID=25736, accessed 15
December 2006

38. Grant, J (2006) 'Right time for a baby', interview for the BBC television programme Panorama, at http://news.bbc.co.uk/1/hi/programmes/panora
ma/5076872.stm, accessed 23 June 2006

39. Women and Work Commission Government Action Plan, 'Implementing
the Women and Work Commission recommendations', September 2006, at
http://www.womenandequalityunit.gov.uk/publications/wwc_govtaction
plan_sept06.pdf, accessed 15 September 2006

40. Chartered Institute of Personnel & Development (2004) 'Five years free
from work ageism', at http://news.bbc.co.uk/1/hi/business/3368497.stm,
accessed 23 June 2006

41. Clapperton, G (2006) 'Ageist bosses forced to wise up', The Guardian, 26
May 2006, at http://technology.guardian.co.uk/businesssense/story/
0,,1782885,00.html, accessed 23 June 2006

42. Carroll, P (2006) 'We need fewer babies in Britain, not more'; letters, at
http://observer.guardian.co.uk/letters/story/0,,1718138,00.html, accessed
26 February 2006

4. Unjust Perceptions of Mothers

1. United States General Accounting Office, 'Women's Earnings, Work
Patterns Partially Explain Difference between Men's and Women's
Earnings', Report to Congressional Requesters, October 2003, at http://
www.gao.gov/new.items/d0435.pdf, accessed 24 March 2006, p 9–20

2. Wolf, A (2006) in the Times Higher Education Supplement, 7 July 2006

3. Correll, S, in Deam, J (2006) 'Despite women's gains, mothers still face
hiring obstacles', The Denver Post, 16 February 2006, at http://www.
azcentral.com/families/articles/0216momswork0216.html, accessed 14
July 2006

4. Berthoud, R, in Campbell, D (2006) 'Mothers' job prospects are worst of
all', The Guardian, 19 March 2006, at http://money.guardian.co.uk
/work/story/0,,1734458,00.html, accessed 7 July 2006

5. http://www.manifest.co.uk/manifest_i/2005/0512December/05121
0ethicsbriefs.htm, accessed 7 July 2006, and http://www.rec.uk.com/
rec/research/industry-survey-summary.aspx, accessed 5 January 2007
and http://www. guardian.co.uk/gender/story/0,11812,1650372,00.html
accessed 1 June 2007

6. Campbell, D (2006), as above

7. CBS News, 7 October 2003, 'More Pregnancy Bias Complaints', at
http://www.cbsnews.com/stories/2003/10/07/national/main576938.shtml,
accessed 7 July 2006

8. Campbell, D (2006), as above

9. Murphy, E with Graff, E (2005) Getting Even: Why women don't get paid like

men – and what to do about it, Touchstone, New York, p 195

10. United States General Accounting Office, 'Women's Earnings, Work Patterns Partially Explain Difference between Men's and Women's Earnings', Report to Congressional Requesters, October 2003, at **http://www.gao.gov/new.items/d0435.pdf**, accessed 24 March 2006, p 61

11. Lewis, S (2002) in Burke, B and Nelson, D J (Eds) *Work and Family Issues: Old and New, in Advancing Women's Careers*, Blackwell Publishers Limited, Oxford

12. Chinchilla, N and Leon, C (2005) *Female Ambition: How to reconcile work and family*, Palgrave Macmillan, New York, pp 27–29

13. *CBS News*, 7 October 2003, 'More Pregnancy Bias Complaints', as above

14. Mooney, N (2006) 'Mother May I?' at **http://www.inc.com/resources/ women/articles/20060701/nmooney.html**, accessed 11 July 2006

15. Defago, N (2005) *Childfree and Loving It!*, Vision Paperbacks, London, p 118

16. Hoffman, L (undated) 'Mums returning to work', at **http://www.careerone .com.au/jobs/job-search/get-that-job/pid/543**, accessed 14 July 2006

17. Lusardi Connor, L (undated) 'Guide for Smart Working Moms', at **http:// lifestyle.msn.com/MindBodyandSoul/CareerandMoney/Articleiv2.aspx ?cp-documentid=299669**, accessed 14 July 2006

18. Author's telephone conversation, 11 July 2006

19. **http://www.motheratwork.co.uk/employers_of_choice/**, accessed 11 July 2006

20. **http://www.hno.harvard.edu/gazette/2004/09.23/04-workingmother.html**, accessed 14 July 2006

21. **http://nccic.org/ccpartnerships/home.htm**, accessed 11 July 2006

22. Mooney, N (2006) 'Mother May I?', as above

23. Williams, J C (undated) 'Hitting the Maternal Wall', *American Association of University Professors*, at **http://www.aaup.org/publications/Academe/ 2004/04nd/04ndwill.htm**, accessed 11 July 2006

24. Fazackerly, A (2006) 'Women are still 15% cheaper', *Times Higher Educational Supplement,* 1 September 2006

25. Baty, P (2006) Selection of Staff for Inclusion in RAE 2001, in 'Career breaks hit selection for RAE', *Times Higher Educational Supplement*, 18 August 2006

26. Curry, J (1999) 'Why Bench Science May Scare Off Potential Scientific Mothers-to-Be', at **http://sciencecareers.sciencemag.org/career_devel opment/previous_issues/articles/0140/why_bench_science_may_scare_ off_potential_scientific_mothers_to_be**, accessed 11 July 2006

27. Coltrane, S (2004) 'Family Man', in Sacks, N and Marrone, C (Eds) *Gender and Work in Today's World*, Westview Press, USA

28. Bell, D (2006) 'A new definition of fairness?', in The Calm Zone, **http://www.thecalmzone.net/tune_in/articles/default.aspx?id=55**, accessed 14 July 2006

29. Dermott, E (2006) *The Effect of Fatherhood on Men's Employment*, Economic and Social Research Council, Swindon

30. Houston, D (2006) University of Kent, in Hilpern, K, 'Wait 'til your Father Gets Home', *The Guardian*, 25 September 2006.

31. Campbell, D (2006) 'Mothers' job prospects are worst of all', *The Guardian*, 19 March 2006, at **http://money.guardian.co.uk/work/story/0,,1734458 ,00.html**, accessed 7 July 2006

32. Smith, C. (2004), 'Men Don't Do This Sort of Thing', in Sacks, N and Marrone, C, as above, p 387

33. United States General Accounting Office (2003) as above, p 63

34. Bellamy, K, and Cameron, S (2006) 'Gender Equality in the 21st Century: Modernising the legislation', Fawcett Society at **http://www.fawcettsoci ety.org.uk/documents/exec_summery1.pdf**, accessed 5 January 2007

5. WHAT MOTHERS HAVE TO OFFER

1. Kimura, D (2002) 'Sex Differences in the Brain', Scientific American.comat **http://www.sciam.com/article.cfm?articleID=00018E9D-879D-1D06-8E49809EC588EEDF&pageNumber=1&catID=9**, accessed 15 September 2006

2. Chinchilla, N and Leon, C (2005) *Female Ambition, How to reconcile work and family*, Palgrave Macmillan, New York, p 12

3. Examples of books include that by Simon Baron-Cohen below (which incidentally, looks further, at issues of autism); an advanced scholar internet search on Google will lead into the abstracts of many papers on the topic. Local libraries also carry books written for the general public – it's a huge area.

4. Baron-Cohen S (2003) *The essential difference. Men, women and the extreme male brain*, Allen Lane, London, p 256

5. Lawrence, P A (2006) 'Men, Women, and Ghosts in Science', PLoS Biol 4(1): e19, at **http://biology.plosjournals.org/perlserv?request=get-document &doi=10.1371/journal.pbio. 0040019**, accessed 15 September 2006

6. Burke, J B and Nelson, D L (Eds) (2002) *Advancing Women's Careers*, Blackwell Publishers Limited, Oxford, p 4

7. Hochschild, A (2004), 'Time Blind', in Sacks, N and Marrone, C (Eds)(2004) *Gender and Work in Today's World.*, Pub Westview Press, USA, p 322.

8. Coltrane, S. (2004) 'Family Man', in Sacks, N and Marrone, C, as above

9. Lewis, S, (2002) 'Work and Family Issues, old and new', in Burke and Nelson, as above, p 68

6. IS IT WORTH THE FIGHT?

1. Gordon, T and Kauppinen, K (1997) 'Dual Roles and Beyond', in Kauppinen, K and Gordon, T (Eds) *Unresolved Dilemmas: Women, work and the family in the United States, Europe and the former Soviet Union*, Ashgate Publishing, Aldershot, p 1

2. ESRC press release (2006) 'Most young women retain "traditional" view of life', at **http://www.esrcsocietytoday.ac.uk/ESRCInfoCentre/PO/releas es/2003/march/most.aspx?ComponentId=2093&SourcePageId=1404**, accessed 30 March 2006, reporting on research by Fenton, S, Bradley, H K, and West, J A from the Department of Sociology at the University of Bristol

3. Pearson, A (2003) *I Don't Know How She Does It*, Vintage, London

4. **http://www.amazon.co.uk/Dont-Know-How-She-Does/dp/0099469669**, accessed 8 December 2006

5. Such as Defago, N (2005) *Childfree and Loving It!*, Vision Paperbacks, London

6. Passey, J (2006) 'Yes, I think my mother would have been better off if she hadn't had children', at http://jacquelinepassey.blogs.com/blog/2006/06/yes_i_think_my_.html, accessed 21 July 2006

7. Passey, J (2006) as above

8. Sacks, N and Marrone, C (Eds)(2004) *Gender and Work in Today's World*. Westview Press, USA, p 373

9. Hoffman, L and Youngblade, L (2004) in Sacks, N and Marrone, C, as above, p 375–7; this paper inform s the data in this and preceding paragraph.

10. Noer, M (undated) 'Don't Marry Career Women', at http://www.forbes.com/home/2006/08/23/Marriage-Careers-Divorce_cx_mn_land.html, accessed 30 September 2006

11. Corcoran, E (undated) 'Don't Marry A Lazy Man', at http://www.forbes.com/home/2006/08/23/Marriage-Careers-Divorce_cx_mn_land.html, accessed 30 September 2006

12. Frostrup, M (2006) 'Dear Mariella', *The Observer Magazine*, 20 August 2006

13. Gibbens, N (2005) 'High price of bringing up child', from a survey by the Liverpool Victoria friendly society, November 2005 at http://www.999today.com/moneyandfinance/news/story/2360.html, accessed 6 October 2006

14. The Daycare Trust (2006) 'Childcare Costs Survey 2006', at http://www.daycaretrust.org.uk/mod.php?mod=userpage&menu=1003&page_id=165, accessed 6 October 2006

15. Matthews, P (2005) 'The Parent Premium', *Daily Mail*, 25 November 2005

16. MSN Money (2007) 'Raising your quarter-million dollar baby', at http://moneycentral.msn.com/content/CollegeandFamily/Raisekids/P37245.asp, accessed 1 June 2007

17. Unattributed, 'Disabled parents and children', at http://www.disabilitydebate.org/Docs/child_poverty.doc, accessed 3 June 2007

18. Shaw, A (2006) 'The true cost of bringing up a child', at http://www.moneyextra.com/features/feature-true-cost-023088.html, accessed 6 October 2006

19. Annual survey by BACS Payment Schemes Limited (BACS) , at http://www.bacs.co.uk/BPSL/corporate/presscentre/pressreleases/pressrelease.htm?abc=%7BCD51EA45-54D2-421A-B9C6-33A496FD7916%7D, accessed 6 October 2006

20. Office for National Statistics, at http://www.statistics.gov.uk/cci/nugget.asp?ID=951, accessed 5 January 2007

21. Grant, J (2006) 'Right time for a baby', interviewed for the BBC television programme *Panorama*, at http://news.bbc.co.uk/1/hi/programmes/panorama/5076872.stm accessed 23 June 2006

22. AuWerter, S and Eaker, J (2006) 'Moms Returning To Work', *CBS News*, 15 May 2006, at http://www.cbsnews.com/stories/2006/05/15/uttm/main1616655.shtml, accessed 6 October 2006

23. Frostrup, M (2006) 'Dear Mariella', *The Observer Magazine*, 20 August 2006

24. Carroll, L, *Alice in Wonderland*, first published 1865, available through Penguin and other publishers

25. Hirsh, W, Hayday, S, Yeates, J and Callender, C (1992) *Beyond the career break*, Brighton: Institute for Employment Studies, report no. 223

26. Lewis, S (2002) 'Work and Family Issues: Old and New', in Burke, J B and Nelson, D L (Eds), *Advancing Women's Careers*, Blackwell Publishers Limited, Oxford pp 71–72

27. Hertz, R (1997) in Lewis, as above

28. Lewis, S (2002) as above, p 72

29. Moorhead, J (2004) 'For decades we've been told Sweden is a great place to be a working parent. But we've been duped', 22 September 2004, *The Guardian*, at http://politics.guardian.co.uk/publicservices/story/0,11032 ,1309874,00.html, accessed 26 May 2006

30. *The Observer*, Sunday July 9, 2006

7. How to Balance your Life

1. Hirshman, L (2005) 'Homeward Bound: The American Prospect Online', at http://www.prospect.org/web/page.ww?section=root&name=ViewWeb &articleId=10659, accessed 7 March 2006

2. Dobson, R and Chittenden, M (2005) 'Clever devils get the bird', UK Times Online, 2 January 2005, at http://www.makinglovework4u.com/high_iq _vs_marriage, accessed 9 October 2006

3. Dobson, R and Chittenden, M (2005) as above

4. Dobson, R and Chittenden, M (2005) as above

5. Dobson, R and Chittenden, M (2005) as above

6. Van Rood, S (undated) 'Husband Finding Tips from The Date Doctor', at http://www.uktvstyle.co.uk/index.cfm/uktvstyle/standardItem.Index/aid/5 72973.shtml, accessed 9 October 2006

7. Hirshman, L (2005) 'Homeward Bound', as above

8. BBC online news, 16 February 2006, at http://news.bbc.co.uk/1/hi/educa tion/4719222.stm, accessed 10 October 2006

9. Camillieri, J (2007), *New University Online*, 'The Student Debt Yearbook aims to persuade lawmakers to lower interest rates for student loans', at http:/ /www.newuniversity.org/showArticle.php?id=5560, accessed 1 June 2007

10. Training and Development Agency for Schools (2006) 'Workforce Boredom Index', at http://www.tda.gov.uk/Recruit/whatsnew/monthlynews/previ ous/issue8/issue8art7.aspx, accessed 10 October 2006

11. Smith, L (2005) 'Want to enjoy your job? Be a crimper', *The Guardian*, at http://money.guardian.co.uk/news_/story/0,1456,1424777,00.html

12. University of the West of England/RIBA, 'Why do women leave architec-ture?' Press release, at http://info.uwe.ac.uk/news/UWENews/article .asp?item=371&year=2003, accessed 9 October 2006

13. Women into Science, Engineering and Construction, at http://www.wise campaign.org.uk/wise.nsf/About/$First?OpenDocument, accessed 9 October 2006

14. Ebner, S (2006) 'Why stop?, *The Guardian* newspaper, 4 February 2006, at http://www.guardian.co.uk/family/story/0,,1701474,00.html, accessed 9 October 2006

15. Horwell, Veronica (1999) 'Obituary of Quentin Crisp', *The Guardian* news-paper 22 November 1999, at http://www.guardian.co.uk/obituaries/story/ 0,,252094,00.html accessed, 9 October 2006

16. Stroud, C (2006) 'Is this what a feminist looks like now?', *Marie Claire*

magazine, November 2006, IPC Media

17. Hahn-Burkett, T (2006) 'Can Bring Home the Bacon OR Fry It Up in a Pan', at http://www.unchartedparent.com/index.php/2006/06/26/i-can-bring-home-the-bacon-or-fry-it-up-in-a-pan/, accessed 10 October 2006

18. Moore, J (2003) 'A better work-life balance? Homeworking is no panacea', ESRC, at http://www.esrc.ac.uk/ESRCInfoCentre/about/CI/CP/the_edge/issue12/betterworklifebalance.aspx?ComponentId=2539&SourcePageId=6468

19. Moore, D P (2002) 'Boundaryless Transitions: global entrepreneurial women challenge career concepts', in Burke, J B and Nelson, D L (Eds) *Advancing Women's Careers*, Blackwell Publishers Limited, Oxford, p 246

20. Hewitt, P in 'Female entrepreneurs – the facts at Startups.co.uk' at http://www.startups.co.uk/Female_entrepreneurs_the_facts.YQjetNw.html, accessed 9 October 2006

21. Figures for 2003 from the Labour Force Survey, at 'Female entrepreneurs – the facts at Startups.co.uk' as above

22. at 'Female entrepreneurs – the facts at Startups.co.uk' as above

23. Bank of Scotland survey (2002), at http://www.startups.co.uk/Female_entrepreneurs_the_facts.YQjetNw.html, accessed 9 October 2006

24. Moore, D P (2002) as above, p 246

25. International Labour Office in Geneva (2004) 'Breaking through the glass ceiling: women in management', at http://www.ilo.org/dyn/gender/docs/RES/292/F267981337/Breaking%20Glass%20PDF%20English.pdf, p 2, accessed 2 June 2006

26. Chinchilla, N and Leon, C (2005) Female Ambition: How to reconcile work and family, Palgrave Macmillan, New York, p 22

27. Chinchilla, N and Leon, C (2005), as above, pps 11–14, for an overview of male/female 'personal complementariness'

28. Pedants note that I know it won't exist but please bear with the argument

29. Levine, J (2006) Not Buying It: My year without shopping, Free Press, New York

30. Hahn-Burkett, T (2006) 'Can Bring Home the Bacon OR Fry It Up in a Pan', at http://www.unchartedparent.com/index.php/2006/06/26/i-can-bring-home-the-bacon-or-fry-it-up-in-a-pan/, accessed 10 October 2006

31. http://therealhot100.org/thenominees.html, accessed 2 June 2006

8. WHAT'S NEXT?

1. Neish, D (2006) 'Future Trends', Scottish Enterprise Glasgow, at http://www.glasgoweconomicfacts.com/documents/IS12_Future_Growth_Issues_Paper_Final.doc, accessed 11 October 2006

2. Lewis, S (2002) 'Work and Family Issues, Old and New', in Burke, J B and Nelson, D L (Eds) Advancing Women's Careers, Blackwell Publishers Limited, Oxford, p 70

3. The issues discussed over the next few pages fill libraries many times over; this is an over-brief and subjective summary taken by picking one of many views; a summary of Drucker's approach can be found on Wikipedia at http://en.wikipedia.org/wiki/Peter_Drucker and from there readers can continue to research other views.

4. Drucker, P (1999) Management Challenges for the 21st Century, Harper Business, New York

5. Drucker, P (2002) Managing in the Next Society, Truman Talley Books, New York

6. Leitschuh, C (2005) 'The Changing World of Work', at http://www.abanet.org/lpm/lpt/articles/mgt03056.html, accessed 11 October 2006

7. See for example the Q&A section of the Optimum Population Trust web pages, at http://www.optimumpopulation.org/opt.faqs1.html, accessed 6 July 2006

8. American Association for the Advancement of Science, at http://atlas.aaas.org/index.php?part=1&sec=trends, accessed 9 June 2006

9. American Association for the Advancement of Science (2006) as above

10. The Trinidad Guardian, 4 August 2005, at http://www.guardian.co.tt/archives/2005-08-04/bussguardian16.html, accessed 9 June 2006

11. Description of The Levy Economics Institute Gender Equality and Economy Program, at http://www.siyanda.org/forum/xviewthread.cfm?Thread=1200 40105020249&FullMsg=220060921040125, accessed 1 December 2006

12. United Nations, at http://www.un.org/millenniumgoals/ accessed, 1 December 2006

13. http://www.un.org/womenwatch/daw/beijing/platform/declar.htm, accessed 1 December 2006

14. McDonald, P and Kippen, R (2000) 'The implications of below replacement fertility for labour supply and international migration, 2000-2050',1 Demography Program, Australian National University http://demography.anu.edu.au/Publications/ConferencePapers/PAA2000/labourpaper.pdf, accessed 9 June 2006

15. Judy, R W and D'Amico, C (1997) 'Work and workers in the 21st century', Hudson Institute Indianapolis, Indiana Executive summary, p 5

16. Judy, R W and D'Amico, C (1997) 'Work and workers in the 21st century Hudson Institute Indianapolis', as above, p 3

17. McKinsey & Company (2005) 'The Coming Demographic Deficit', at http://www.mckinsey.com/mgi/publications/demographics/index.asp, accessed 13 October 2006

18. Microsoft Public Services and eGovernment Strategy: Discussion Paper Series (2006) 'The New World of Government Work Transforming the Business of Government with the Power of Information Technology' at http://download.microsoft.com/download/2/7/1/27129a0a-3c4e-4ca9-933b-d867d09c59cf/NewWorldGovtWorkWP.doc, accessed 9 June 2006

19. The Tomorrow Project, 'Globalisation: What might be the implications?', at http://www.tomorrowproject.net/pub/1__GLIMPSES/Globalisation/-169.html, accessed 9 June 2006

20. Microsoft Public Services and eGovernment Strategy: Discussion Paper Series (2006) as above

21. From Optimum Population Trust, at http://www.optimumpopulation.org/opt.faqs1.html, accessed 9 June 2006

22. The Leitch Review of Skills 2005, at http://www.hm-treasury.gov.uk/inde pendent_reviews/leitch_review/review_leitch_index.cfm, accessed 1 December 2006

23. Institute for Manufacturing (2004) 'A future without manufacturing?' at http://www.ifm.eng.cam.ac.uk/service/cmr/04cmrautumn/future.html, accessed 9 June 2006

24. Baumol, W (2002) 'The Free Market Innovation Machine', in Institute for Manufacturing: A future without manufacturing?, at **http://www.ifm.eng.cam.ac.uk/service/cmr/04cmrautumn/future.html**, accessed 13 October 2006

25. Institute for Manufacturing (2004) 'How Rolls-Royce cares for you', at **http://www.ifm.eng.cam.ac.uk/service/cmr/04cmrautumn/company.html**, accessed 13 October 2006

26. Drucker, P (1999) Management Challenges for the 21st Century, Harper Business, New York

27. 'Happy Workers, High Returns' poll by Gallup (1998) in Fortune magazine, 12 January, p 81

28. Taylor, R (2001) 'Labour flexibility in Europe', in The Edge, ESRC, at **http://www.esrc.ac.uk/ESRCInfoCentre/about/CI/CP/the_edge/issue6/labourflexibility_1.aspx?ComponentId=2359&SourcePageId=10773**, accessed 11 October 2006

29. Taylor, R (2001) 'Labour flexibility in Europe', as above

30. Neish, D (2006) as above

31. **http://www.tomorrowproject.net/pub/2__Website/The_Tomorrow_Project/-25.html**, accessed 11 October 2006

32. White, M, et al (2004), Managing to Change?, Palgrave, Basingstoke, pp 57-58, at The Tomorrow Project, **http://www.tomorrowproject.net/pub/1__GLIMPSES/Employment/-252.html**, accessed 11 October 2006

33. The Tomorrow Project; Employment, at **http://www.tomorrowproject.net/pub/1__GLIMPSES/Employment/-252.html**, accessed 12 October 2006, from Nolan, P, and Wood, S (2003) 'Mapping the Future of Work', British Journal of Industrial Relations, 41 (2), pp 168–169

34. Thomas and Ganster, 1995, 'Work and Family Issues, old and new' in Burke, J B and Nelson, D L (Eds)(2002) as above, page 68

35. Chinchilla, N and Leon, C (2005) Female Ambition: How to reconcile work and family, Palgrave Macmillan, New York, p 109

36. Taylor, R (undated) 'The Future of Work-Life Balance' p 7, at **http://www.leeds.ac.uk/esrcfutureofwork/downloads/fow_publication_2.pdf**, accessed 11 October 2006

37. Taylor, R (undated) 'The Future of Work-Life Balance', as above

38. Bloom, N, Kretschmer, T and Van Reenen, J (2006), 'Work-life balance: The links with management practices and productivity, CentrePiece/CEP, at **http://cep.lse.ac.uk/centrepiece/v11i1/bloom_kretschmer_vanreenen.pdf#search=%22work%20life%20balance%20better%20worker%22**, accessed 6 January 2006

39. White, M and Hill, S (undated) 'Future of Work Programme' in Taylor, R, The Future of Work-Life Balance, p 7, as above

40. Hurst, J, Baker, S, French, S and Daniels, G, (2006) '24-7 Survey', Work Life Balance Centre, at **http://www.tuc.org.uk/work_life/tuc-11567-f0.cfm**, accessed 9 October 2006

41. Slaughter, M (2006) 'The Economic Outlook', National Chamber Foundation at **http://www.whitehouse.gov/cea/econ-outlook20060105.pdf**, accessed 13 October 2006

42. Neish, D (2006) 'Future Trends', Scottish Enterprise Glasgow, p 5, as above

43. Lewis, S (2002) 'Work and family issues, old and new', in Burke and Nelson, p 70, as above

44. Summary at http://www.ned.co.uk/105, accessed 12 October 2006

45. Gordon, T and Kauppinen, K (1997) 'Dual Roles and Beyond', in Kauppinen, K and Gordon, T (Eds) Unresolved Dilemma: Women, work and the family in the United States, Europe and the former Soviet Union, Ashgate Publishing, Aldershot, p 2

46. Gordon, T and Kauppinen, K (1997) as above, p 3

47. Tremlett, G, 'Swedish men about the house leave Portuguese standing', The Guardian, 8 June 2006, at http://www.guardian.co.uk/gender/story /0,,1792694,00.html, accessed 12 October 2006

48. Klanchy, K (2004) 'Our parents were right after all', The Guardian, 22 April 2004, at http://www.guardian.co.uk/comment/story/0,3604,1200346,00.html

49. Department of Trade and Industry (DTI) (2004) 'Flexible working in the IT Industry: long-hours cultures and work-life balance at the margins', Report to the DTI and the Women in IT Forum by Flexecutive, at http://www.dti.gov.uk/files/file11416.pdf, accessed 3 November 2006

50. Smeaton, D (2006) 'Dads and their Babies: a household analysis', Policy Studies Institute, 2006, press release is at http://www.eoc.org.uk/Default .aspx?page=18874, accessed 3 November 2006

51 Hyman et al in 'The Future of Work-Life Balance', by Taylor, R, p 7 as above at http://www.leeds.ac.uk/esrcfutureofwork/downloads/fow_publi cation_2.pdf, accessed 11 October 2006 p 12

52. Moorhead, J (2004) 'Have we created a generation of joyless, selfish monsters?', in The Guardian, 21 April 2004

53. Shaw, R (2003) The Epidemic, Regan Books, New York

54. Neish, D (2006) 'Future Trends', Scottish Enterprise Glasgow, as above

55. Neish, D (2006) 'Future Trends', Scottish Enterprise Glasgow, as above

56. Neish, D (2006) 'Future Trends', Scottish Enterprise Glasgow, as above

57. Life Style Extra (2006) 'Modern Women "Happy To Be Housewives"', 3 August 2006, at http://www.lse.co.uk/ShowStory.asp?story=BZ227713T &news_headline=modern_women_happy_to_be_housewives, accessed 13 October 2006

58. (No author named), 'Mexico: Migrants, Politics, Remittances', Migration News, Vol. 11 No. 1, January 2004, at http://migration.ucdavis.edu/MN/more.php?id=2970_0_2_0, accessed 3 June 2007

59. As Scottish workers did to Poland in the 16th century: 'The ties between Scotland and Poland go back to the family of Bonnie Prince Charlie, whose mother was Polish', As debated in the UK Parliament 17 May 2006, at http://www.publications.parliament.uk/pa/cm200506/cmhansrd/cm06051 7/halltext/60517h0059.htm, accessed 15 September 2006

60. figures from AFLCIO, 'Ask a working woman survey', as above

61. from AFLCIO, 'Ask a working woman survey', as above

62. Neish, D (2006) 'Future Trends', Scottish Enterprise Glasgow, as above

63. Tomorrow Project website, at http://www.tomorrowproject.net/pub/1__ GLIMPSES/Employment/-285.html

9. CHANGING THE WORLD

1. Martin Hekker, T (2006) 'How I paid the price of being a stay-at-home mother',

The Times Online, at http://www.timesonline.co.uk/article/0,,7-20022 87_1,00.html, accessed 21 October 2006

2. Clinton, B (1996) 'Clinton/Gore 96', at http://www.movingimage.us/cg96 /GAK.pdf, accessed 20 October 2006

3. Blair, T (2004) 'Speech to the Daycare Trust', at http://www.number-10.gov .uk/output/Page6564.asp, accessed 20 October 2006

4. Iraq Analysis Group (2006) 'The Rising Costs of the Iraq War', at http:// www.iraqanalysis.org/local/481_costofwar1.pdf, accessed 20 October 2006

5. Network for European Women's Rights (2004) Update report on the burning issues concerning women's social entitlements, at http://www.newr .bham.ac.uk/pdfs/Social/Update%20report%20on%20soc%20ent.pdf, accessed 9 June 2006

6. Robeyns I (2000) The Political Economy of Non-Market Work, in Update report on the burning issues concerning women's social entitlements, Network for European Women's Rights (2004), at http://www.newr .bham.ac.uk/pdfs/Social/Update%20report%20on%20soc%20ent.pdf, accessed 9 June 2006

7. Hakim, C (2006) in Tischler, L (2006) The Best of Both Worlds, Pub Fast Company, at http://www.fastcompany.com/articles/2004/01/hakim.html

8. Interview, September 2006

9. Soanes, B. with Moran, M. and Lovenduski, J. (2005) Women in Parliament, The new Suffragettes. Pub Politico's Publishing, London p 92

10. Taylor, R (undated) The Future of Work-Life Balance, p 7 at http://www.leeds .ac.uk/esrcfutureofwork/downloads/fow_publication_2.pdf, accessed 11 October 2006

11. Taylor, R (undated) as above

12. Taylor, R (undated) as above

13. Wintour, N (2003) Recognize and Revalue Women's Work, Interviewed by Anne Renaut, International Confederation of Free Trade Unions at http://www.globalpolicy.org/socecon/inequal/labor/2003/0306psi.htm, accessed 7 March 2006

14. Frostrup, M (2006) 'Can you have a career and be a woman?' The Observer, 18 June 2006, at http://observer.guardian.co.uk/magazine/story/ 0,,1798038,00.html, accessed 3 June 2007

15. Soanes, B with Moran, M and Lovenduski, J (2005) as above, p 93

16. Almond, B (2006) The Fragmenting Family, Clarendon Press, Oxford, p 29

About the Author

Joanna Grigg's career collapsed when she relocated to a new part of the country with her young family and had to give up her sales management job and start again. Now the mother of three teenagers and a university administrator, she's worked as a writer, qualified as a teacher, worked with young people and adults in the community, worked for the Careers Service, set up and run a training organisation and engaged in many voluntary activities. This is her 12th book.